T0213663

Mobile Forensics – The File Format Handbook

Christian Hummert • Dirk Pawlaszczyk

Editors

Mobile Forensics – The File Format Handbook

Common File Formats and File Systems Used in Mobile Devices

 Springer

Editors
Christian Hummert
Agentur für Innovation in der Cybersicherheit
Halle (Saale), Germany

Dirk Pawlaszczyk
Fachgruppe Informatik
Hochschule Mittweida
Mittweida, Germany

ISBN 978-3-030-98469-4   ISBN 978-3-030-98467-0   (eBook)
https://doi.org/10.1007/978-3-030-98467-0

This Springer imprint is published by the registered company Springer Nature Switzerland AG
The registered company address is: Gewerbestrasse 11, 6330 Cham, Switzerland

Preface

One of the biggest challenges in digital forensics is to gain a deep understanding of file systems and file formats. This knowledge is needed to recover files from corrupt file systems or reveal artefacts of former states of a computer system. For most file systems, it is easy to find resources that describe file systems at a high level. But for the detailed knowledge on the Hex-code level that is needed for digital forensics there are only few sources.

Brian Carrier did a great job in his book: "File System Forensic Analysis" [10]. This book was definitely a model for this work. When I started digital forensics, I really devoured this book. Reading Carrier I understood in detail how files are stored on computers and how to recover deleted files. "File System Forensic Analysis" gives deep insights into FAT, NTFS, EXT2, EXT3 and UFS. However, there are more file systems to discover: In my further work, I learned about EXT4, HFS+ and APFS. Concentrating on mobile forensics, there are even more file systems to explain.

In addition, there is more than file systems. Especially in mobile forensics, there are new file formats to encounter, which have a broader and more universal scope. File Formats like the SQLite database format are used in nearly every mobile device by millions of different Apps.

In January 2018, I started to write the proposal for the EU project FORMOBILE[1]. I aimed to provide an end-to-end mobile forensic investigation chain. I succeeded to build an outstanding consortium with 19 partners from 11 countries. Together we created a work plan that delivers novel tools to support mobile forensics, builds a new standard for mobile forensics and offers novel training for the forensic experts in this area. Happily, the project was funded and started in May 2020.

At the beginning of the proposal creation phase, we agreed to write a File Format Handbook that summarizes knowledge about various file formats and file systems common in mobile devices. I am more than happy to provide this file format handbook as a deliverable to the European Commission and a broader audience of forensic experts.

---

[1] https://formobile-project.eu

However, this book is not only a toolbox for experienced investigators that have learned about digital investigations from real cases and using analysis tools. The other target audience is students. Moreover, the book is aimed at people who are new to digital forensics and are more interested in the general theory of file recovery and file systems. It has to be admitted that this work is not a tutorial on how to use a specific tool but has a broader idea.

Roadmap

This book is organized into two distinct parts (Fig. 1). Part I describes several different file systems that are commonly used in mobile devices. APFS is the file system that is used in all modern Apple devices. This includes the iPhones, iPads but also the Apple Computers like the MacBook Series. At the same time, Ext4 is very common in Android devices. Ext4 is the successor of the Ext2 and Ext3 file systems that were commonly used on Linux-based computers. The Flash-Friendly File System (F2FS) is a Linux system designed explicitly for NAND Flash memory. This type of memory is common in removable storage devices and mobile devices. Samsung Electronics developed the system in 2012. The QNX6 filesystem is present in Smartphones delivered by Blackberry (e.g. Devices that are using Blackberry 10) and modern vehicle infotainment systems that use QNX as their operating system.

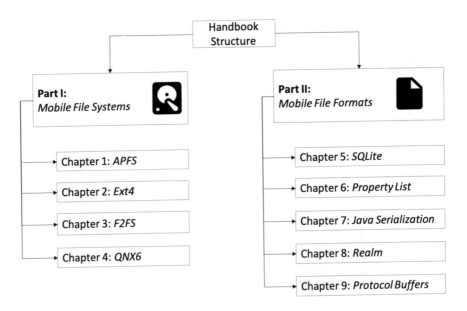

Fig. 1: Structure of the book

Part II describes five different file formats that are commonly used on mobile devices. SQLite is nearly omnipresent in mobile devices. The overwhelming majority of all mobile applications (Apps) store their data in such databases. Another important file format in the mobile world are Property Lists. They are especially frequent on Apple devices. Java Serialization is a popular technique for storing object states in the Java programming language. In the field of mobile forensics, we come across such artefacts. App developers very often resort to this technique to make their application state persistent. The Realm database format has emerged over recent years as a possible successor to the now ageing SQLite format and has a growing use on mobile devices. Protocol Buffers provide a format for taking compiled data and serializing it by turning it into bytes represented in decimal values. This technique is also often used in mobile devices.

Scope of the Book

After the Roadmap shows the forthcoming chapters' names, it is time to summarize what is not included in this book. The book summarizes four file systems and five commonly used file formats. Next to the fundamental description of the formats, there are hints about the forensic value of possible artefacts and tools that can decode the files or file systems.

This book is not a step-by-step guide to investigating mobile devices, reconstructing file systems, or decoding file formats. In addition, the book does not describe what files a specific OS or application creates. So you want to gather information about which files to examine if a specific app or OS is given.

The book is appropriate for forensic experts who need knowledge about a specific file system or file format or students who want to become forensic experts. This book requires some knowledge about computers, mobile devices, file systems and file formats, so this is not an absolute beginners guide.

Conventions Used in This Book

We cite numerous books, articles, and websites throughout the book. These citations appear in the text using square brackets [999]. All references can be found at the end of this book. The reader should further pay special attention to annotations that are marked with the following symbols from the text:

! Attention

Certain things should not be done to avoid mistakes. At one point or another, the reader will be warned of possible mistakes during a forensic investigation.

> **Important**

This hint field is used whenever we think something is significant.

Tips

If you find such a box in the text, we would like to give the reader an important hint. Taking these tips to heart can save much time in practice.

Acknowledgements

The project has received funding from the European Union's Horizon 2020 Research and Innovation Program under Grant Agreement No. 832800.

We would wish to thank everyone who has participated in any way and made this book possible. In particular, we would like to thank Georgina Humphries, without whose help the project would certainly not have gotten this far for their valuable comments and corrections, as well as Phil Cobley and Chris Currier, who have proofread the text.

Mittweida, Germany   *Christian Hummert*
December 2021   *Dirk Pawlaszczyk*

Contents

Part I
Mobile File System Formats

File system analysis examines one volume of a disk respective disk image. The data contained in the volume is interpreted as a file system. Typically an interpreted file system offers a listing of files organized in directories (at least this is true for the four described file systems in this book). One aim of file system analysis is usually recovering deleted files. In contrast to files that have been restored by a carving process and lack all formerly available metadata, files that have been undeleted via the file system may contain at least some metadata.

In this part of the book, the general design of four common file systems in mobile devices is described, and different analysis techniques are presented. This part abstractly approaches the topic and is not limited to how a specific tool analyzes a file system.

File systems are used by the operating system and provide mechanisms to store data in a hierarchy of files and directories. File systems organize metadata and user data such that the operating system can use this. Some operating systems rely on one specific file system, whereas others can handle many different file systems. The described file systems in this part are typically used in mobile devices.

Chapter 1
APFS

Rune Nordvik

Abstract The Apple File System (APFS) has been the standard FS for Apple devices since 2017. At that time, no digital forensic tools supported it, leaving tool dependent digital or mobile forensic investigators without the ability to investigate this file system properly. The APFS was first enabled on iOS, the operating system of iPhone, and later that same year on MacOS. APFS replaced the HFS+ FS. This chapter will document the important metadata structures of APFS, which is based on state of the art research, and we are focusing on the investigative meaning of the structures.

1.1 Introduction

Apple developed the APFS , and the main architect was Dominic Giampaolo [33]. Hansen and Toolan [33] started reverse engineering of the APFS for investigation purposes using pre-releases of the APFS as early as 2016, which were included for educational and development purposes in MacOS v 10.12 (Sierra) in September 2016. In March 2017, APFS was deployed on iPhone and iPad [33]. Recently, Apple has released developer documentation for APFS [4], and we use this accurate documentation. In order to develop offset tables that can be used when interpreting hex dumps, we scrutinize the C-structures from the APFS Developer documentation [4] and the type of the fields found in these structures.

We found research on how the APFS uses encryption on the user data partition of an iPhone and that users can not disable the encryption [17]. In this chapter, we have decided to use an image of an iPhone using iOS v 13.3 to see if there could be other partitions that are not encrypted.

Rune Nordvik
The Norwegian Police University College (Politihøgskolen), Slemdalsveien 5, 0369 Oslo, Norway, e-mail: rune.nordvik@phs.no

C. Hummert, D. Pawlaszczyk (eds.), *Mobile Forensics – The File Format Handbook*, https://doi.org/10.1007/978-3-030-98467-0_1

> **Important**

Other partitions can contain information that are relevant for the investigation. There could be logs that describe activated features, or information about when a device was rebooted, etc.

1.2 APFS - File system category

A new feature for APFS is how it structures volumes, and it does not use a typical partition table to divide the storage into partitions, each with its own FS volume. Instead, it uses storage or a partition to set up a container. This container will contain both container metadata, metadata for snapshots and volumes, and data blocks. This is illustrated in Fig. 1.1.

From an investigative perspective, this means it is not enough to document the partition systems like the Master Boot Record (MBR) and the Globally Unique Identifier (GUID) Partition Table (GPT). Now it is also a need to scrutinise the APFS container.

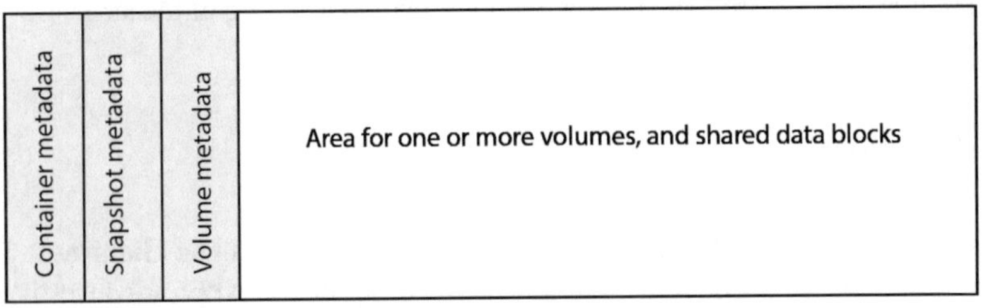

| Container metadata | Snapshot metadata | Volume metadata | Area for one or more volumes, and shared data blocks |

Fig. 1.1: APFS Container.

! Attention

Files located on one volume may share the identical data blocks with files located on another volume within the same APFS container.

1.2.1 Finding the APFS container

In order to find the APFS container, it is necessary to parse the GUID partition table (GPT) and a partition with the type 7C3457EF-0000-11AA-AA11-00306543ECAC (APFS_GPT_PARTITION_UUID) is an APFS container. How to read the GPT is described by Nikkel, 2009 [51]. The easiest way is to skip directly to the partition table starting on sector 2 of the disk. Each partition described in this table is 128 bytes (0x80), and it starts with the partition type (its first 16 bytes), followed by a globally unique identifier for this specific partition (also 16 bytes). From relative offset 32 (0x20), we find the start sector of the partition, and it is from that location we find the container.

We used an image from an iPhone 7 running iOS v 13.3, which should have one of the first implementations of the APFS. The first thing we noticed is that the default sector size is 4096 bytes, not the usual 512 bytes. In Fig. 1.2 we show with green background the GUID type of this partition as it is shown in a hex dump. We need to read this data in a special way in order to compare it to the APFS partition type GUID (7C3457EF-0000-11AA-AA11-00306543ECAC). The first four bytes need to be read as little-endian (LE), and therefore ef57347c is read from right to left (backwards) as 7c3457ef, which matches the first part of the APFS partition type. Then we continue with the next two bytes, and they are only zeros, meaning it does not change just because we read it backwards. The next two bytes are aa11, and must be read as 11aa. The next two bytes are not a multi-byte, and the endianness does not matter. They need to be read as single bytes, meaning aa11, then the final six bytes is also not a multi-byte, and must be read as they are, meaning 00306543ECAC. Now we have identified this partition as an APFS container.

```
00000000: ef57 347c 0000 aa11 aa11 0030 6543 ecac  .W4|.......0eC..
00000010: a487 6696 dac6 3543 8401 4f98 27f0 0790  ..f...5C..O.'...
00000020: 0800 0000 0000 0000 47d6 dc01 0000 0000  ........G.......
00000030: 0000 0000 0000 0000 4300 6f00 6e00 7400  ........C.o.n.t.
00000040: 6100 6900 6e00 6500 7200 0000 0000 0000  a.i.n.e.r.......
00000050: 0000 0000 0000 0000 0000 0000 0000 0000  ................
00000060: 0000 0000 0000 0000 0000 0000 0000 0000  ................
00000070: 0000 0000 0000 0000 0000 0000 0000 0000  ................
```

Fig. 1.2: APFS Container within GUID partition table.

The field with black background is the eight bytes describing the start sector of this APFS container, and since this is a multi-byte field, it must be read as LE, meaning 0x8 (8 in decimal). That is the sector we need to show in order to find the APFS Container. Highlighted with the yellow background, we can see the Unicode string "Container", which is the name of this partition.

1.2.2 Object header

Every object in APFS has an object header, shown in Fig. 1.3, which consists of the fields as described in Table 1.1.

```
00000000: 15fd 6ff8 2da1 de43 0100 0000 0000 0000  _..o.-..C........
00000010: 0e81 5800 0000 0000 0100 0080 0000 0000  _..X............
```

Fig. 1.3: Object Header.

Table 1.1: obj_phys_t

Offset	Size	Name	Description
0x0	0x8	o_cksum	Fletcher 64 bit checksum
0x8	0x8	o_oid	The object id
0x10	0x8	o_xid	The transaction id
0x18	0x4	o_type	The object type
0x1C	0x4	o_subtype	The object subtype

The object type field low 16 bits indicate a specific object type, while the high 16 bits are used for object type flags:

Object type, some examples

- OBJECT_TYPE_NX_SUPERBLOCK, 0x00000001
- OBJECT_TYPE_BTREE, 0x00000002
- OBJECT_TYPE_OMAP, 0x0000000b
- OBJECT_TYPE_FS, 0x0000000d
- OBJECT_TYPE_FSTREE 0x0000000e
- OBJECT_TYPE_INVALID, 0x00000000

Object type masks

- OBJECT_TYPE_MASK, 0x0000ffff
- OBJECT_TYPE_FLAGS_MASK, 0xffff0000

Object type flags

- OBJ_VIRTUAL, 0x00000000
- OBJ_EPHEMERAL, 0x80000000
- OBJ_PHYSICAL, 0x40000000
- OBJ_NOHEADER, 0x20000000
- OBJ_ENCRYPTED, 0x10000000
- OBJ_NONPERSISTENT, 0x08000000

In Fig. 1.3 we can see the object header, which is 32 bytes in size. The first eight bytes 0x43dea12df86ffd15 (LE) is the *Fletcher checksum* (highlighted in dark blue), the *object id* is 0x1 (highlighted in light green), and the *transaction id* is 0x58810e (highlighted in yellow). The object id and transaction id combined specify a specific state in time.

$$ObjectType = o\_type \ \& \ OBJECT\_TYPE\_MASK$$

$$ObjectTypeFlags = o\_type \ \& \ OBJECT\_TYPE\_FLAGS\_MASK$$

The object type is 80000001 (highlighted in red), and after computing the object type and flags, we found that the object type value is 0x00000001, and the object type flags is 0x80000000 (OBJ_EPHEMERAL). We can also see the subtype has the value 0x0000 (highlighted in purple), and here we can use the same approach computing the subtype and flags. However, when the o_subtype value is 0x0 it means no subtype. Based on our header interpretation, we can see that this superblock is an ephemeral object.

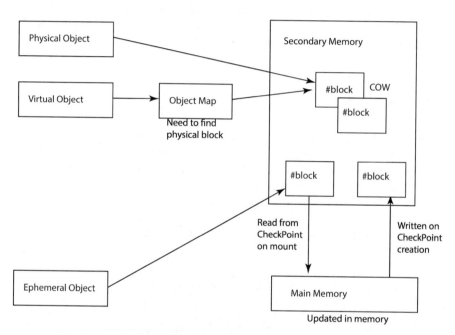

Fig. 1.4: APFS use of the ephemeral, physical, and virtual objects.

Ephemeral Objects

Objects that should be in memory (ephemeral) and are changed in memory when needed, and will be written to disk as a part of a checkpoint.

Physical Objects

Objects that are stored in a known block address, and change needs to be written to another location because of the Copy-On-Write (COW) feature. The *object id* is the same as the block address, and therefore any change means saving to a new block address, this also means a new object id.

Virtual Objects

Virtual objects stored at a block address that can be found by looking up in a *object map* (often a B-Tree). However, the object id is the same after updating a virtual object. When we look up a virtual object, we use its object id and the transaction id to specify the object at a specific time. This means that when a virtual object changes, it will be written to another physical block (COW), but the virtual object id is still the same in the object header o_oid field.

1.2.3 Superblocks

APFS uses different kinds of superblocks, and the first we find is the Container Superblock (CSB), a nx_superblock_t structure. Addresses that point to locations on the disk are in 64bits, meaning eight bytes. These addresses point to ephemeral, physical or virtual objects. The latter objects need an object map in order to find the physical address where the object is located. The difference between these object types is illustrated in Fig. 1.4. In Fig. 1.6 we show a simplified overview of how we plan to go through the File System Category for the APFS.

```
00000000: 15fd 6ff8 2da1 de43 0100 0000 0000 0000  ..o.-..C........
00000010: 0e81 5800 0000 0000 0100 0080 0000 0000  ..X.............
00000020: 4e58 5342 0010 0000 40d6 dc01 0000 0000  NXSB....@.......
00000030: 0000 0000 0000 0000 0000 0000 0000 0000  ................
00000040: 0200 0000 0000 0000 1a4b a4a7 6d9f 4803  .........K..m.H.
00000050: 9fa1 27a6 d9c6 56c1 e044 7b00 0000 0000  ..'...V..D{.....
00000060: 0f81 5800 0000 0000 1801 0000 186c 0000  ..X..........l..
00000070: 0100 0000 0000 0000 1901 0000 0000 0000  ................
00000080: 5d00 0000 db51 0000 0000 0000 0000 0000  ]....Q..........
00000090: 0000 0000 0000 0000 0004 0000 0000 0000  ................
000000a0: 2563 d501 0000 0000 0104 0000 0000 0000  %c..............
000000b0: 0000 0000 6400 0000 0204 0000 0000 0000  ....d...........
000000c0: 93d0 5600 0000 0000 6116 0400 0000 0000  ..V.....a.......
000000d0: 427e 7a00 0000 0000 b57e 7a00 0000 0000  B~z......~z.....
```

Fig. 1.5: APFS first superblock in block 0 of the partition.

In Fig. 1.5 we find the magic key NXSB (0x4e585342), which identifies this as a superblock. The next field (4 bytes) with blue background is the block size used, here 0x1000 (4096) bytes[1]. With black background, we have an 8-byte field describing

---

[1] The minimum block size is 4096 (default), and the maximum is 65536

how many blocks this container contains, here 0x1dcd640 (31249984). We can multiply this with the block size if we want the size in bytes. We want the size in GiB[2], and use this computation.

$$GiB = \frac{31249984 * 4096}{1024^3} = 119.2$$

In light green background we can see the GUID, which uniquely identifies this container. It has the value A7A44B1A-9F6D-0348-9FA1-27A6D9C656C1.

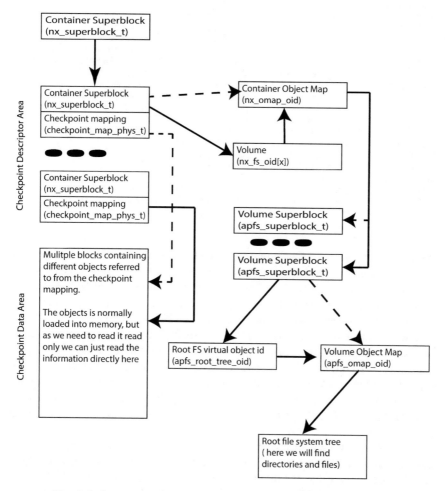

Fig. 1.6: Overview of how to manually read an APFS file system.

---

[2] The smallest supported container size is 1 MiB

Table 1.2: nx_superblock

Offset	Size	Name	Description
0x20	0x4	magic	Container Magic
0x24	0x4	nx_block_size	Block Size in bytes
0x28	0x8	nx_block_count	Block count
0x30	0x8	nx_features	Features
0x38	0x8	nx_read_only_compatible_features	Read only compatible features
0x40	0x8	nx_incompatible_features	Incompatible features
0x48	0x10	nx_uuid	Container UUID
0x58	0x8	nx_next_oid	Next Object ID (OID)
0x60	0x8	nx_next_xid	Next Transaction ID (XID)
0x68	0x4	nx_xp_desc_blocks	Blocks used by the Checkpoint Descriptor Area
0x6C	0x4	nx_xp_data_blocks	Blocks used by Checkpoint Data Area
0x70	0x8	nx_xp_desc_base	Base address of Checkpoint Descriptor Area or Physical OID
0x78	0x8	nx_xp_data_base	Base address of Checkpoint Data Area or Physical OID
0x80	0x4	nx_xp_desc_next	Next index for Checkpoint Descriptor Area
0x84	0x4	nx_xp_data_next	Next index for Checkpoint Data Area
0x88	0x4	nx_xp_desc_index	Index for first item in Checkpoint Descriptor Area
0x8C	0x4	nx_xp_desc_len	Number of blocks used in Checkpoint Descriptor Area
0x90	0x4	nx_xp_data_index	Index for first item in Checkpoint Data Area
0x94	0x4	nx_xp_data_len	Number of blocks used in Checkpoint Data Area
0x98	0x8	nx_spaceman_oid	Space Manager Object ID (OID)
0xA0	0x8	nx_omap_oid	Container Object Map Object ID (OID)
0xA8	0x8	nx_reaper_oid	Reaper Object ID (OID)
0xB0	0x4	nx_test_type	Reserved for testing
0xB4	0x4	nx_max_file_systems	Maximum number of volumes in this container
0xB8	0x8	nx_fs_oid[0]	Start of array of OIDs for volumes in this container

We need to find the latest checkpoint superblock, an eight-byte address starting from offset 0x70 (the nx_xp_desc_base field), here in yellow background. Here we can see that this points to block 1, relative to the start of this container. At that location, we will either find a new superblock object, or a B-tree map in case this checkpoint superblock is not contiguous. This may or may not be the latest checkpoint.

The documentation from Apple [4] describes that we need to parse through all the blocks in the *Checkpoint Descriptor Area*, and find the block with the highest transaction id (XID) with the same object id (OID). If this block includes the magic key and the *Fletcher checksum* can be verified, then this block is the latest checkpoint.

In our example, the nx_xp_desc_blocks field highlighted in light brown at offset 0x68 has the value 0x118 (280). This means the checkpoint descriptor area consists of 280 blocks.

When going through each of these 280 blocks, we noticed that the magic key was only present in every second block, and this is correct since each additional superblock had the value 0x2 in the field nx_xp_desc_len at offset 0x8C. This field describes the number of blocks this checkpoint used in the Checkpoint Descriptor Area. We found that the superblock with the highest value in XID was, in our example, located at block 19 relative to the start of the container.

Fig. 1.7 is similar to the superblock we found in the first sector (sector 0) of the container. However, it has the highest transaction number of all the checkpoint

```
00000000: 0a2d e3f6 ac07 6b45 0100 0000 0000 0000  .-....kE........
00000010: 4b81 5800 0000 0000 0100 0080 0000 0000  K.X.............
00000020: 4e58 5342 0010 0000 40d6 dc01 0000 0000  NXSB....@.......
00000030: 0000 0000 0000 0000 0000 0000 0000 0000  ................
00000040: 0200 0000 0000 0000 1a4b a4a7 6d9f 4803  .........K..m.H.
00000050: 9fa1 27a6 d9c6 56c1 2745 7b00 0000 0000  ..'...V.'E{.....
00000060: 4c81 5800 0000 0000 1801 0000 186c 0000  L.X..........l..
00000070: 0100 0000 0000 0000 1901 0000 0000 0000  ................
00000080: d700 0000 4553 0000 d500 0000 0200 0000  ....ES..........
00000090: 4053 0000 0500 0000 0004 0000 0000 0000  @S..............
000000a0: 9868 d501 0000 0000 0104 0000 0000 0000  .h..............
000000b0: 0000 0000 6400 0000 0204 0000 0000 0000  ....d...........
000000c0: 93d0 5600 0000 0000 6116 0400 0000 0000  ..V.....a.......
000000d0: 427e 7a00 0000 0000 b57e 7a00 0000 0000  B~z......~z.....
```

Fig. 1.7: Latest checkpoint Superblock in the Checkpoint Descriptor Area.

superblocks, and is, therefore, the current (latest) checkpoint. Two other requirements must be fulfilled:

- The NXSB magic must be found.
- The checksum must verify, or else there is something wrong with the checkpoint superblock.

> **Important**

Finding the latest checkpoint is important since this is the last state for this file system. However, the other previous checkpoints may be interesting in order to recover files that are deleted in the latest checkpoint.

1.2.4 Checkpoint mapping

We need to scrutinise the second block in this checkpoint descriptor. This block starts in the block after the superblock, as seen in Fig. 1.8.

There could be multiple checkpoint mapping blocks in a checkpoint, but in our example case it was just one superblock and one checkpoint mapping block for each checkpoint.

The 0x20 (32) bytes highlighted in yellow is the usual object header, but here the field is called cpm_o, and cpm is an abbreviation for checkpoint mapping. If we interpret the o_type, we can see that the object type is 0x0000000C (OBJECT_TYPE_CHECKPOINT_MAP), and this object type flag is 0x40000000 (OBJ_PHYSICAL). The last mapping block is always marked as the last, using the cpm_flags field, highlighted in blue. In this case, it is 0x01, since we only have one such mapping block. In our mapping, we have 0x5 records in an array (highlighted in

```
00000000: e70b 0047 c524 a1f8 d800 0000 0000 0000  ...G.$..........
00000010: 4c81 5800 0000 0000 0c00 0040 0000 0000  L.X........@....
00000020: 0100 0000 0500 0000 0500 0080 0000 0000  ................
00000030: 0010 0000 0000 0000 0000 0000 0000 0000  ................
00000040: 0004 0000 0000 0000 5e54 0000 0000 0000  ........^T......
00000050: 0200 0080 0900 0000 0010 0000 0000 0000  ................
00000060: 0000 0000 0000 0000 0304 0000 0000 0000  ................
00000070: 5f54 0000 0000 0000 0200 0080 0900 0000  _T..............
00000080: 0010 0000 0000 0000 0000 0000 0000 0000  ................
00000090: 0504 0000 0000 0000 6054 0000 0000 0000  ........`T......
000000a0: 1100 0080 0000 0000 0010 0000 0000 0000  ................
000000b0: 0000 0000 0000 0000 0104 0000 0000 0000  ................
000000c0: 6154 0000 0000 0000 1200 0080 0000 0000  aT..............
000000d0: 0010 0000 0000 0000 0000 0000 0000 0000  ................
000000e0: f346 0400 0000 0000 6254 0000 0000 0000  .F......bT......
```

Fig. 1.8: Checkpoint mapping block in the Checkpoint Descriptor Area.

Table 1.3: checkpoint_map_phys_t

Offset	Size	Name	Description
0x0	0x20	cpm_o	Object header
0x20	0x4	cpm_flags	Checkpoint flags
0x24	0x4	cpm_count	Records in this mapping
0x28	var	cpm_map[cpm_count]	Array of Checkpoint mappings

green). The records are 0x28 bytes long, and we have only highlighted the important fields of the first record. Then we highlight the next records with either grey or white background. This shows we have a total of five records.

Table 1.4: checkpoint_mapping_t

Offset	Size	Name	Description
0x0	0x4	cpm_type	Low 16 bits for object type, and high 16 bits for object type flags
0x4	0x4	cpm_subtype	The object's subtype
0x8	0x4	cpm_size	The object size in bytes
0xC	0x4	cpm_pad	Not in use, padding
0x10	0x8	cpm_fs_oid	Virtual FS OID that this object is associated with
0x18	0x8	cpm_oid	Ephemeral object id
0x20	0x8	cpm_paddr	The address in the checkpoint data area where this object is stored

The first record cmp_type highlighted in black colour is after mapping 0x00000005 (OBJECT_TYPE_SPACEMAN), and the object type flag is 0x80000000(OBJ_EPHEMERAL). The size of the object is described by the cpm_size (highlighted in orange) is 0x1000 (4096), or the same as the size of a block. The virtual object id of the fs volume that this object is associated with is defined in the field cpm_fs_oid, and has the value 0x0 (highlighted in red). In the fields cpm_oid, we will find the ephemeral object id, 0x400 (highlighted in purple). Finally, we find the field cpm_paddr, which contains the value 0x545e (21598), the address to the checkpoint data area where this object is stored (highlighted in dark blue).

Table 1.5: Actual checkpoint mapping

Record	Type	Subtype	Ephemeral OID	Phys Address
1	SPACEMAN	Not used	0x400	0x545e (21598)
2	BTREE	SPACEMAN_FREE_QUEUE	0x403	0x545f (21599)
3	BTREE	SPACEMAN_FREE_QUEUE	0x405	0x5460 (21600)
4	NX_REAPER	Not used	0x401	0x5461 (21601)
5	NX_REAP_LIST	Not used	0x0	0x446f3 (280307)

All the records describe an object with the size 4096, and they all use the FS virtual object 0x0. The other values for these five records are listed in Table 1.5. We can follow the address of the first record to get statistics about the container and its internal pool bitmap. The bitmap describes which blocks are allocated (used) or unallocated (free). Table 1.6 can be used to interpret the space manager.

Table 1.6: spaceman_phys_t

Offset	Size	Name	Description
0x0	0x20	sm_o	Object header
0x20	0x4	sm_block_size	Block size
0x24	0x4	sm_blocks_per_chunk	Blocks per chunk
0x28	0x4	sm_chunks_per_cib	Chunks per cib
0x2C	0x4	sm_cibs_per_cab	Cibs per cab
0x30	0x60	spacdev[2]	Special structure
0x90	0x4	sm_flags	Flags
0x94	0x4	sm_ip_bm_tx_multiplier	Bitmap multiplier
0x98	0x8	sm_ip_block_count	Block count
0xA0	0x4	sm_ip_bm_size_in_blocks	Bitmap size in Blocks
0xA4	0x4	sm_ip_bm_block_count	Bitmap block count
0xA8	0x8	sm_ip_bm_base	Address to Bitmap base
0xB0	0x8	sm_ip_base	Address to ip base
0xB8	0x8	sm_fs_reserve_block_count	FS reserved block count
0xC0	0x8	sm_fs_reserve_alloc_count	FS reserved allocation count
0xC8	0x78	spacemanfreequeue[3]	Free queues
0x140	0x2	sm_ip_bm_free_head	bitmap free head
0x142	0x2	sm_ip_bm_free_tail	bitmap free tail
0x144	0x4	sm_ip_bm_xid_offset	Transaction id offset
0x148	0x4	sm_ip_bitmap_offset	bitmap offset
0x14C	0x4	sm_ip_bm_free_next_offset	Next bitmap free offset
0x150	0x4	sm_version	Spacemanager version

```
00000000: fa45 8765 b8d5 cff5 0004 0000 0000 0000  .E.e...........
00000010: 4c81 5800 0000 0000 0500 0080 0000 0000  L.X.............
00000020: 0010 0000 0080 0000 7e00 0000 fb01 0000  ........~.......
00000030: 40d6 dc01 0000 0000 ba03 0000 0000 0000  @...............
00000040: 0800 0000 0000 0000 4024 4901 0000 0000  ........@$I.....
00000050: 080a 0000 0000 0000 0000 0000 0000 0000  ................
00000060: 0000 0000 0000 0000 0000 0000 0000 0000  ................
00000070: 0000 0000 0000 0000 0000 0000 0000 0000  ................
00000080: 480a 0000 0000 0000 0000 0000 0000 0000  H...............
00000090: 0100 0000 1000 0000 460b 0000 0000 0000  ........F.......
000000a0: 0100 0000 1000 0000 316d 0000 0000 0000  ........1m......
000000b0: 416d 0000 0000 0000 f509 0000 0000 0000  Am..............
000000c0: 8500 0000 0000 0000 1000 0000 0000 0000  ................
000000d0: 0304 0000 0000 0000 4a81 5800 0000 0000  ........J.X.....
000000e0: 0300 0000 0000 0000 0000 0000 0000 0000  ................
000000f0: 2d00 0000 0000 0000 0504 0000 0000 0000  -...............
00000100: 4a81 5800 0000 0000 0002 0000 0000 0000  J.X.............
00000110: 0000 0000 0000 0000 0000 0000 0000 0000  ................
00000120: 0000 0000 0000 0000 0000 0000 0000 0000  ................
00000130: 0000 0000 0000 0000 0000 0000 0000 0000  ................
00000140: 0c00 0a00 d809 0000 e009 0000 e809 0000  ................
00000150: 0100 0000 d809 0000 0000 c700 0000 0000  ................
```

Fig. 1.9: SPACEMAN block, for finding the internal pool bitmap.

We use Table 1.6 to interpret the Fig. 1.9. The easiest way to identify the block where the current bitmap starts is to add the fields sm_ip_bm_base (0x6D31), which is pointed to by the first spaceman device in the field sm_addr_offset at 0x50 (0xa08, relative to the start of the block), and the sm_ip_bitmap_offset (0x9E0) and then subtract with sm_ip_bm_size_in_blocks (0x1). This gives the block 0x7710. The fields mentioned above depend on the number of spaceman devices, each occupying 0x30 bytes (in our case, there were two spaceman devices).

```
00000000: 00fe 1ffe e1ff 0100 0000 e001 001e 0000  ................
00000010: 1ee0 e101 1e00 e001 e001 fe1f feff ffff  ................
00000020: ffff ffff ffff ff3f 0000 0000 0000 0000  .......?........
00000030: 0000 00c0 ffff ffff ffff 1f00 0000 e0ff  ................
00000040: ffff ffff ffff ffff ffff ffff ffff ffff  ................
00000050: ffff ffff ffff ffff ffff ffff ffff ffff  ................
00000060: ffff ffff ffff ffff ffff ffff ffff ffff  ................
00000070: ffff ffff ffff ffff ffff ffff ffff ffff  ................
00000080: ffff ffff ffff ffff ffff ffff ffff ffff  ................
00000090: ffff ffff ffff ffff ffff ffff ffff ffff  ................
000000a0: ffff ffff 0700 0000 0000 0000 0000 0000  ................
000000b0: 0000 ffff ffff ffff ffff ffff ffff ffff  ................
000000c0: ffff ffff ffff ffff ffff ffff ffff ffff  ................
000000d0: ffff ffff ffff ffff ff07 0000 0000 fcff  ................
```

Fig. 1.10: Internal pool bitmap, if bit is 1 then the block is allocated, or if it is 0 then the block is free.

In Fig. 1.10 we see the start of the bitmap. Every byte must be converted to binary, and each bit represents the allocation status of one block (1=allocated, 0=unallocated). The first byte is 0x0, meaning the block 0-7 is defined as not allocated. The following byte is 0xFE (binary: 1111 1110). We start reading from the least significant bit. Moreover, since this is the second byte, the first bit represents block 8 (not allocated) but blocks 9-15 is allocated.

> **❗ Attention**
>
> The SPACEMAN is poorly documented in the APFS developer documentation, which means there could be more accurate methods to identify the bitmap.

1.2.5 Volumes

The maximum number of possible volumes are defined in field nx_max_file_systems found in the checkpoint superblock, and in this case, the number is 0x64 (100)[3]. However, not all of them are in use. From offset 0xB8 we find an array of fs volume virtual object ids, of which the first has the value 0x402. Only a few of them have a value different from zero. Each of these are virtual object ids that eventually will lead us to a file system tree. In order to identify the location of the volume boot record (VBR) for a file system, we need to map the virtual object id with the one found in the Container Object Map, where we can find the block, which is the address to the VBR. The Container Object Map object id can be found in the checkpoint superblock at byte offset 0xA0 (nx_omap_oid) and is a 64-bit value, here 0x1D56898 (30763160). However, this block consists of a B-Tree that needs to be parsed. Before we do the actual mapping, we need to learn the structure of the B-Tree.

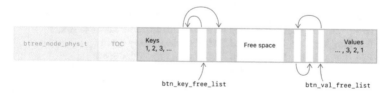

Fig. 1.11: The structure of a B-Tree node block (source: Apple File System Reference)

We can see from Fig. 1.11 that the first part of the block contains the btree_node_phys_t structure, which we also have described in Table 1.7, and both include the object header (0x20 in size) and the node header (0x18 in size). The data area is everything after the headers. This data area contains the table of content (TOC), keys, free space and the values.

---

[3] The maximum number of volumes is defined as 100

```
00000000: 518d eb7c eea0 3022 9868 d501 0000 0000  Q..|..0".h......
00000010: c382 5800 0000 0000 0200 0040 0b00 0000  ..X........@....
00000020: 0700 0000 0500 0000 0000 c001 6000 200d  ............`. .
00000030: 3000 1000 4000 1000 2000 3000 0000 1000  0...@... .0.....
00000040: 5000 6000 4000 5000 1000 2000 1000 2000  P.`.@.P... ... .
00000050: 0000 0000 0000 0000 0000 0000 0000 0000  ................
...
000001f0: 0000 0000 0000 0000 6116 0400 0000 0000  ........a.......
00000200: 1281 5800 0000 0000 b57e 7a00 0000 0000  ..X......~z.....
00000210: 0981 5800 0000 0000 0204 0000 0000 0000  ..X.............
00000220: 0e81 5800 0000 0000 ffff 1000 0000 0000  ..X.............
00000230: c282 5800 0000 0000 427e 7a00 0000 0000  ..X.....B~z.....
00000240: 2481 5800 0000 0000 93d0 5600 0000 0000  $.X.......V.....
00000250: c382 5800 0000 0000 0000 0000 0000 0000  ..X.............
00000260: 0000 0000 0000 0000 0000 0000 0000 0000  ................
...
00000f60: 0000 0000 0000 0000 0000 0000 0000 0000  ................
00000f70: 0000 0000 0000 0000 0000 0000 0010 0000  ................
00000f80: 6068 d501 0000 0000 0000 0000 0010 0000  `h..............
00000f90: 7b72 d501 0000 0000 ffff 1000 0010 0000  {r..............
00000fa0: 9866 d501 0000 0000 0000 0000 0010 0000  .f..............
00000fb0: f262 d501 0000 0000 0000 0000 0010 0000  .b..............
00000fc0: 4165 d501 0000 0000 0000 0000 0010 0000  Ae..............
00000fd0: f178 d501 0000 0000 1200 0000 0010 0000  .x..............
00000fe0: 1000 0000 1000 0000 1000 0000 1000 0000  ................
00000ff0: 0500 0000 0000 0000 0100 0000 0000 0000  ................
```

Fig. 1.12: Container FS Volume Object Map.

Table 1.7: btree_node_phys_t

Offset	Size	Name	Description
0x0	0x20	btn_o	Object header of the B-Tree block
0x20	0x2	btn_flags	Flags for this B-Tree
0x22	0x2	btn_level	Number of child levels under this node
0x24	0x4	btn_nkeys	Number of keys stored in this node
0x28	0x4	btn_table_space	Location(16 bits offset, 16 bits length) of Table of Content(TOC)
0x2C	0x4	btn_free_space	Location for shared free space for keys and values
0x30	0x4	btn_key_free_list	A linked list that tracks free key space
0x34	0x4	btn_val_free_list	A linked list that tracks free value space
0x38	0x8	btn_data[var]	The nodes storage area (toc, keys, free space, and values)

From the B-tree object header in Figure 1.12 we can see that the o_type describe a physical (0x40000000) B-tree (0x2). The o_subtype is a object map (0xb). Then we

interpret the B-tree node header:

- btn_flags: 0x7,
    BTNODE_ROOT, BTNODE_LEAF, BTNODE_FIXED_KV_SIZE

Table 1.8: B-Tree Node Flags

Define Name	Define Value	Description
BTNODE_ROOT	0x0001	The root node
BTNODE_LEAF	0x0002	A leaf node
BTNODE_FIXED_KV_SIZE	0x0004	Only use the offset for keys-value pairs
BTNODE_HASHED	0x0008	Contains child hashes
BTNODE_NOHEADER	0x00010	Object header consist of zeros
BTNODE_CHECK_KOFF_INVAL	0x8000	Will never appear on disk

- btn_level: 0x0, There is no level under this one.
- btn_nkeys: 0x05, there are 5 records.
- btn_table_space: 0x00 offset, 0x1c0, meaning TOC starts after the node header at 0x38, and is 0x1c0 in length. This also means the key are starts at 0x1f8, directly after the TOC.
- The shared free space starts at 0x60 in the key area, meaning $0x1f8 + 0x60 = 0x258$, and it is 0xd20 in length, meaning it end at 0x258+0xd20=0xf78, where it meet the last part of the value area (the top of value area, where the free space ended).

From the TOC, we can find the key-value pairs. If BTNODE_FIXED_KV_SIZE flag is set, only offsets to keys and values are used. If not, both offset and length are used. All offsets for keys are relative to the start of the key area, and all offsets for values are relative from the end of the value area (the bottom of the value area). At the end of the Root node block, we have the btree_info_t structure, which can be interpreted using Table 1.9. Only Root nodes should have this additional structure. For instance, the value 0x1, 0x3, 0x7 are also Root nodes, which have a btree_info_t structure at the end.

Table 1.9: btree_info_t

Offset	Size	Name	Description
0xfd8	0x4	bt_flags	The B-tree's flags
0xfdc	0x4	bt_node_size	The B-tree's node size
0xfe0	0x4	bt_key_size	The B-tree's key size
0xfe4	0x4	bt_val_size	The B-tree's value size
0xfe8	0x4	bt_longest_key	The B-tree's longest key ever stored
0xfec	0x4	bt_longest_val	The B-tree's longest value ever stored
0xff0	0x8	bt_key_count	Number of keys in the B-tree
0xff8	0x8	bt_node_count	Number of nodes in the B-tree

It is important to interpret the key-value offsets in the TOC in a special way. Since the offsets, in this case, have a static length (the BTNODE_FIXED_KV_SIZE flag was set), the key and value are represented as 16-bit offsets. If the key value is not fixed, the key and the value both use 32 bits (the first 16 bits is the offset, and the following 16 bits is the length). The key-value offsets occur in the TOC directly after the headers, but this can be deviated by the btn_table_space field.

When we read the offset for the key, we need to consider that the offset is relative to the start of the key area. However, when we read the offset for the value, it is relative from the end of the value area and backwards in the direction of the free space area. This is also why the key area in the illustration in Fig. 1.11 show Keys 1,2,3,..., while the Values are listed as ..., 3,2,1.

The last structure of the B-tree Root node is the btree_info_t, which we can use the Table 1.9 to interpret. The bt_flags are 0x12, which consist of 0x10 (BTREE_PHYSICAL) and 0x2 (BTREE_SEQUENTIAL_INSERT) which means avoiding splitting nodes in half during sequential inserts, avoiding a lot of half-full nodes [4, p. 130]. The bt_node_size (node size) is 0x1000 (4096) bytes. The bt_key_size (key size), bt_value_size (value size), bt_longest_key (longest key size), and the bt_longest_val (longest value size) are all 0x10 (16) bytes. Both the key and value sizes are necessary to know when using fixed sizes for keys and values. The bt_key_count (keys in this B-tree) is 0x5, and bt_node_count (nodes in this B-tree) is 0x1. The value 1 for node count means that this node is both the root and the leaf node.

Finding the Volume

In Fig. 1.13 we have the object header in light yellow, followed by the node header in grey background, interpreted in the previous section.

The first record key-pair is highlighted in blue from offset 0x38, the first 16 bits key value 0x20 points to the key, while the second 16 bits value 0x30 points to the value. We know the key area starts at offset 0x1f8, and the value area starts before the btree_info_t structure, and if we count 0x30 backwards we find the start of the value that is in this case 0x10 bytes long, also highlighted in blue. The key can be found counting 0x20 from the start of the key area, and it is also in this case 0x10 in size. The key is also highlighted in blue. It is important to read the keys and values as 0x10 (16 bytes) each, as described in the btree_info_t structure.

In this case the key OID (the first 8 bytes) is 0x402 (LE), and the key XID (the next 8 bytes) is 0x58810e (LE), and its corresponding value physical OID address (the last 8 bytes in the value) is 0x1d562f2 (LE). The same can be done for all the other volumes in this node, highlighted using different highlight colours. We have finished this mapping in Table 1.10.

Showing the Volume (APSB)

A volume in APFS uses the magic key APSB, which is a superblock that describes one volume. This is similar to a VBR in traditional file systems. It contains an FS,

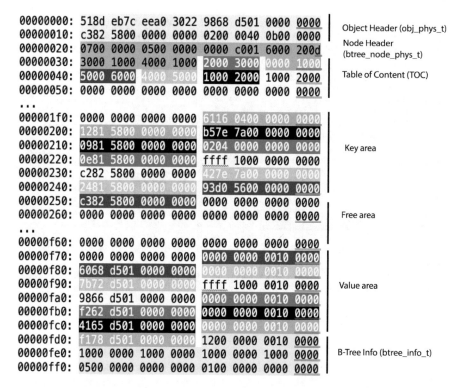

```
00000000: 518d eb7c eea0 3022 9868 d501 0000 0000    Object Header (obj_phys_t)
00000010: c382 5800 0000 0000 0200 0040 0b00 0000
00000020: 0700 0000 0500 0000 0000 c001 6000 200d    Node Header
00000030: 3000 1000 4000 1000 2000 3000 0000 1000    (btree_node_phys_t)
00000040: 5000 6000 4000 5000 1000 2000 1000 2000    Table of Content (TOC)
00000050: 0000 0000 0000 0000 0000 0000 0000 0000
...
000001f0: 0000 0000 0000 0000 6116 0400 0000 0000
00000200: 1281 5800 0000 0000 b57e 7a00 0000 0000
00000210: 0981 5800 0000 0000 0204 0000 0000 0000    Key area
00000220: 0e81 5800 0000 0000 ffff 1000 0000 0000
00000230: c282 5800 0000 0000 427e 7a00 0000 0000
00000240: 2481 5800 0000 0000 93d0 5600 0000 0000
00000250: c382 5800 0000 0000 0000 0000 0000 0000
00000260: 0000 0000 0000 0000 0000 0000 0000 0000    Free area
...
00000f60: 0000 0000 0000 0000 0000 0000 0000 0000
00000f70: 0000 0000 0000 0000 0000 0000 0010 0000
00000f80: 6068 d501 0000 0000 0000 0000 0010 0000
00000f90: 7b72 d501 0000 0000 ffff 1000 0010 0000    Value area
00000fa0: 9866 d501 0000 0000 0000 0000 0010 0000
00000fb0: f262 d501 0000 0000 0000 0000 0010 0000
00000fc0: 4165 d501 0000 0000 0000 0000 0010 0000
00000fd0: f178 d501 0000 0000 1200 0000 0010 0000
00000fe0: 1000 0000 1000 0000 1000 0000 1000 0000    B-Tree Info (btree_info_t)
00000ff0: 0500 0000 0000 0000 0100 0000 0000 0000
```

Fig. 1.13: Mapping of FS Volumes, from virtual to physical block.

Table 1.10: FS Volume mapping

Virtual OID	XID	Physical Address
0x402	0x58810e	0x1d562f2
0x41661	0x588112	0x1d578f1
0x56d093	0x5882c3	0x1d56860
0x7a7e42	0x588124	0x1d5727b
0x7a7eb5	0x588109	0x1d56541

files, metadata, and object map. In this section, we will be using the file system example for the virtual object id 0x402, physical address 0x1d562f2.

We can use Table 1.11 to interpret the values of the APFS volume superblock (APSB) shown in Fig. 1.14. We have not included all fields in this structure, only fields that we assume are important. Please refer to the complete apfs_superblock_t structure as found in the Apple developer documentation [4].

The magic of this apfs volume superblock has the signature APSB is ASCII values, found int the apfs_magic field. This value can be used when searching for APFS volumes in a corrupted file system. In the checkpoint superblock in Fig. 1.7

```
00000000: c1e4 a178 de20 3929 0204 0000 0000 0000  ....x. 9)........
00000010: 0e81 5800 0000 0000 0d00 0000 0000 0000  ..X.............
00000020: 4150 5342 0000 0000 0200 0000 0000 0000  APSB............
00000030: 0000 0000 0000 0000 0000 0000 0000 0000  ................
00000040: f4fe ca02 cfd1 7b16 0000 0000 0000 0000  ......{.........
00000050: 0000 0000 0000 0000 81e8 1300 0000 0000  ................
00000060: 0500 0000 0000 0000 0600 0000 5900 460e  ............Y.F.
00000070: 0100 0000 0200 0000 0200 0040 0200 0040  ...........@...@
00000080: 8f65 d501 0000 0000 8b87 7a00 0000 0000  .e........z.....
00000090: 0765 d501 0000 0000 7065 d501 0000 0000  .e......pe......
000000a0: 0000 0000 0000 0000 0000 0000 0000 0000  ................
000000b0: 0ed8 0b00 0100 0000 e645 0200 0000 0000  .........E......
000000c0: f90e 0100 0000 0000 ac06 0000 0000 0000  ................
000000d0: 0000 0000 0000 0000 0100 0000 0000 0000  ................
000000e0: 6b5d a200 0000 0000 9f97 8f00 0000 0000  k].............
000000f0: 939b 63ec 6dc4 3946 8910 5e68 39bf 0530  ..c.m.9F..^h9..0
00000100: 2dda 75c9 94c9 e315 0100 0000 0000 0000  -.u.............
00000110: 6866 735f 636f 6e76 6572 7420 2861 7066  hfs_convert (apf
00000120: 732d 3234 392e 3630 2e32 3029 0000 0000  s-249.60.20)....
...
000002c0: 436f 7272 7931 3443 3932 2e44 3130 4431  Corry14C92.D10D1
000002d0: 3031 4f53 0000 0000 0000 0000 0000 0000  01OS............
```

Fig. 1.14: The APFS Superblock for the volume.

we had an array of file system object identifiers, and we can decide which of these file systems this volume belongs to by reading the apfs_index value, here it is 0, meaning the first file system.

One very important field is the apfs_unmount_time, which must be interpreted as nanoseconds since January 1, 1970 at 0:00 UTC, not including leap seconds. In this case is the unmount time, 0x167bd1cf02cafef4, or Tuesday, 4 May 2021 09:06:18. We converted to decimal and divided with 10^9 to get the value as seconds. Then we used a UNIX epoch converter to translate it to a human-readable time format.

! Attention

The apfs_unmount_time is updated whenever unmounted, and this will normally mean at the reboot of the device, especially for the system volume. This also mean if an investigator reboots the device, then this value is modified.

There is also another timestamp in the APFS volume superblock, in the field 0x100 (apfs_last_mod_time) we find the 64 bit value 0x0x15E3C994B2AF9600, or Thursday, 26 December 2019 02:05:35. This is when the volume was last modified, and as it seems, modifying the metadata does not update this timestamp. One hypothesis is that only modifying file content or metadata related to files will update this timestamp.

Table 1.11: apfs_superblock_t

Offset	Size	Name	Description
0x0	0x20	apfs_o	The object header
0x20	0x4	apfs_magic	The magic signature for an APSB
0x24	0x4	apfs_index	The FS index in the container list of file systems
0x40	0x8	apfs_unmount_time	Last time this FS was unmounted (last reboot?)
0x58	0x8	apfs_alloc_count	Blocks allocated to this FS
0x60	0x14	apfs_meta_crypto	Information about encryption
0x74	0x4	apfs_root_tree_type	Root tree type
0x78	0x4	apfs_extentref_tree_type	Type of the extent-reference tree
0x7C	0x4	apfs_snap_meta_tree_type	Type of the snapshot metadata tree
0x80	0x8	apfs_omap_oid	Object id of the object map
0x88	0x8	apfs_root_tree_oid	Virtual Object id of the root file system tree
0x90	0x8	apfs_extentref_tree_oid	Object id of the extent-reference tree
0xB8	0x8	apfs_num_files	Number of regular files in the volume
0xC0	0x8	apfs_num_directories	Number of directories in the volume
0xD8	0x8	apfs_num_snapshots	Number of snapshots in the volume
0xE0	0x8	apfs_tot_blocks_alloced	Total number of blocks that have been allocated by this volume
0xF0	0x10	apfs_vol_uuid	Universal Unique identifier for the volume
0x100	0x8	apfs_last_mod_time	The time when this volume was last modified
0x108	0x8	apfs_fs_flags	Volume flags
0x110	0x8	apfs_formatted_by	Software created this volume
0x2c0	0x100	apfs_volumename	Name of the volume
0x3c0	0x4	apfs_next_doc_id	Todo
0x3c4	0x2	apfs_role	Role
0x3c6	0x2	reserved	Reserved

! Attention

The apfs_last_mod_time is updated when the volume is modified. If what is relevant for the investigation is after this time, it may not be worth analysing this volume.

The apfs_alloc_count field yields the currently allocated blocks for this file system, 0x13e881 blocks, or 4.98 GiB of the storage is used. Later, another field describes the total number of blocks ever allocated, which increase for every new block allocated but do not decrease when a block is freed. This field is named apfs_tot_blocks_alloced. Do not use this field when computing the currently used size of a volume.

Then there is some information about encryption in the field apfs_meta_crypto, which is for encryption purposes. We need to check in the apfs_fs_flags to see if the fs utilise encryption. The field apfs_root_tree_type describes the type of tree. Here it is a B-tree. This is followed by the field apfs_extentref_tree_type, which is described as a physical B-tree. The next field is the apfs_snap_meta_tree_type, and it is also described as a physical B-Tree.

We need an object map because we need to map virtual object ids to physical object ids. We can find the object map object identifier in the apfs_omap_oid, and we depend on this field and the next field (apfs_root_tree_oid) to find objects for files and directories. The virtual object id for the root tree can be found in the field apfs_root_tree_oid, and since this is a virtual object id, we need to map it to the physical object id using the apfs_omap_oid, see sect. 1.2.5.

The apfs_num_files describes the number of files in the volume, here 0x245e6 (148966) files. We can find the number of directories in the field apfs_num_directories, here 0x10ef9 (69369) directories. This volume contains 1 snapshot, described in the field apfs_num_snapshots. The apfs_vol_uuid is a unique identifier for this volume, in this case it is EC639B93-C4D6-4639-8910-5E6839BF0530. At offset 0x108, we find the volume Flags (apfs_fs_flags), and here it is 0x01, meaning this volume is not encrypted.

> **Important**

Not all volumes on an iOS are encrypted.

The first entry starting from offset 0x110 is the name of the software that formatted this APFS volume, and it can be seen that it has been converted from HFS (hfs_convert(apfs-249.60.20)). Finally, we have included the name of this volume, with grey background starting at offset 0x2c0. Here it is Corry14C92.D10D101OS.

Volume Object mapping

The object mapping block (apfs_omap_oid) is shown in Fig. 1.15, and can be interpreted using the Table 1.12.

```
00000000: 46a0 4771 8aaf 87c8 8f65 d501 0000 0000  F.Gq.....e......
00000010: 0d81 5800 0000 0000 0b00 0040 0000 0000  ..X........@....
00000020: 0000 0000 0100 0000 0200 0040 0200 0040  ...........@...@
00000030: a365 d501 0000 0000 ea62 d501 0000 0000  .e.......b......
00000040: f500 5800 0000 0000 0000 0000 0000 0000  ..X.............
00000050: 0000 0000 0000 0000 0000 0000 0000 0000  ................
```

Fig. 1.15: Physical mapping of FS B-trees.

As usual, we can find the object header in the first 0x20 (32) bytes, which describes this as a physical object map. There are no flags used (om_flags), and there is one snapshot in this object map (om_snap_count). The root object tree is a physical B-tree (om_tree_type), and the same is the snapshot tree. We will focus on the current object map B-tree (om_tree_oid), where we find its physical object id, here 0x1d565a3. In this case, we want to map the virtual object id for the FS root B-tree, which is 8b87 7a00 0000 0000 (0x7a878b), to its physical object id.

At block 0x1d565a3 we find the top of the object map B-tree. However, in order to find the virtual object id we are searching for, we need to parse the B-tree, and in

Table 1.12: omap_phys_t

Offset	Size	Name	Description
0x0	0x20	om_o	The object header
0x20	0x4	om_flags	Flags used by omap
0x24	0x4	om_snap_count	Number of snapshots within omap
0x28	0x4	om_tree_type	Type of B-tree
0x2C	0x4	om_snapshot_tree_type	Type of snapshot B-tree
0x30	0x8	om_tree_oid	Object id of current B-tree
0x38	0x8	om_snapshot_tree_oid	Object id of snapshot tree
0x40	0x8	om_most_recent_snap	Transaction id of most recent snapshot
0x48	0x8	om_pending_revert_min	Smallest transaction id for a in-progress revert
0x50	0x8	om_pending_revert_max	Largest transaction id for a in-progress revert

our case, by using the 7th record number, we found the block that will contain the virtual object we are searching for, and now it is time to ask: Why did we select this record?

In Fig. 1.16 we show the hex dump of the object map root B-tree. The 7th key, and its value is highlighted in dark blue. The 8th key and value is highlighted in red. The 7th key is 0x6b9a81 (OID part), and the 8th key is 0x7ab7d6 (OID part). The key we are searching for (0x7a878b) is between these two keys. Therefore the virtual object id (key) we are searching for can be found by focusing on the former key (7th). This 7th value is found in the value area 0x18 bytes before the end of the value area, and it has the physical object id address 0x1d7309f. This is the physical OID address of the child node that should contain the virtual object id (0x7a878b) in one of the node's key or a key of a sub-node that we are searching for. Before we continue to this object, we need to check the object node header of the current object. Its node header is interpreted below.

- btn_flags: 0x5, BTNODE_ROOT, BTNODE_FIXED_KV_SIZE
- btn_level: 0x2, There are two levels of child nodes under this one.
- btn_nkeys: 0x0a, there are 0xa (10) records.
- btn_table_space: 0x00 offset, 0x240, meaning TOC starts after the node header at 0x38, and is 0x240 in length. This also means the key are starts at 0x278, directly after the TOC.
- The shared free space starts at 0x120 in the key area, meaning $0x278 + 0x120 = 0x398$, and it is 0xbb0 in length, meaning it end at 0x398+0xbb0=0xf48, where it meet the last part of the value area.

This means we are located on the top of the tree, the Root node, and we can expect two levels of child nodes under this root level. We continue to the physical location 0x1d7309f, as previously mapped, here we find the next level in this B-tree, shown in Fig. 1.17. This object node header is interpreted below.

- btn_flags: 0x4, BTNODE_FIXED_KV_SIZE, must be an index node.
- btn_level: 0x1, There is one level of child nodes under this one.

```
00000000: 4242 7b31 71cc 7f5c a365 d501 0000 0000  BB{1q..\.e......
00000010: 0d81 5800 0000 0000 0200 0040 0b00 0000  ..X........@....
00000020: 0500 0200 0a00 0000 0000 4002 2001 b00b  ..........@. ...
00000030: 3000 8000 2000 4000 0000 0800 7000 4000  0... .@.....p.@.
00000040: 5000 3000 6000 3800 b000 6000 8000 4800  P.0.`.8...`...H.
00000050: 2000 1800 f000 8000 a000 5800 d000 7000   .........X...p.
00000060: d000 7000 d000 7000 d000 7000 d000 7000  ..p...p...p...p.
00000070: d000 7000 d000 7000 d000 7000 d000 7000  ..p...p...p...p.
00000080: 0000 0000 0000 0000 0000 0000 0000 0000  ................
...
00000270: 0000 0000 0000 0000 5304 0000 0000 0000  .........S......
00000280: 6fd2 1900 0000 0000 4000 1000 0000 0000  o.......@.......
00000290: 409b 5700 0000 0000 819a 6b00 0000 0000  @.W.......k.....
000002a0: 830d 3c00 0000 0000 1001 1000 0000 0000  ..<.............
000002b0: e900 5800 0000 0000 9000 1000 0000 0000  ..X.............
000002c0: 174a 2100 0000 0000 8851 4700 0000 0000  .J!......QG.....
000002d0: a95e 0800 0000 0000 07f6 5600 0000 0000  .^........V.....
000002e0: 6fd2 1900 0000 0000 cf02 0200 0000 0000  o...............
000002f0: 8b61 3500 0000 0000 54b0 6100 0000 0000  .a5.....T.a.....
00000300: 38fe 2b00 0000 0000 ffff 1000 0000 0000  8.+.............
00000310: f300 5800 0000 0000 b6bf 7a00 0000 0000  ..X.......z.....
00000320: e900 5800 0000 0000 6f3c 5b00 0000 0000  ..X.....o<[.....
00000330: 2d4a 2100 0000 0000 1000 1000 0000 0000  -J!.............
00000340: f300 5800 0000 0000 d6fd 7a00 0000 0000  ..X.......z.....
00000350: e900 5800 0000 0000 0001 1000 0000 0000  ..X.............
00000360: 4c9b 5700 0000 0000 d6b7 7a00 0000 0000  L.W.......z.....
00000370: e900 5800 0000 0000 c000 1000 0000 0000  ..X.............
00000380: 459b 5700 0000 0000 e000 1000 0000 0000  E.W.............
00000390: 4c9b 5700 0000 0000 0000 0000 0000 0000  L.W.............
000003a0: 0000 0000 0000 0000 0000 0000 0000 0000  ................
...
00000f40: 0000 0000 0000 0000 7800 0800 0000 0000  ........x......
00000f50: 6800 0800 0000 0000 d627 d701 0000 0000  h........'......
00000f60: 8800 0800 0000 0000 f618 d701 0000 0000  ................
00000f70: 1000 0800 0000 0000 ea2f d701 0000 0000  ........./......
00000f80: d527 d701 0000 0000 ffff 0800 0000 0000  .'..............
00000f90: 4830 d701 0000 0000 792e d701 0000 0000  H0......y.......
00000fa0: 7c2f d701 0000 0000 2b2f d701 0000 0000  |/......+/......
00000fb0: 5000 0800 0000 0000 9000 0800 0000 0000  P...............
00000fc0: 9f30 d701 0000 0000 2800 0800 0000 0000  .0......(.......
00000fd0: 267b d501 0000 0000 1200 0000 0010 0000  &{..............
00000fe0: 1000 0000 1000 0000 1000 0000 1000 0000  ................
00000ff0: 0e1e 0100 0000 0000 8b03 0000 0000 0000  ................
```

Fig. 1.16: The root of the object map B-Tree.

- btn_nkeys: 0x8e, there are 0x8e (142) records.
- btn_table_space: 0x00 offset, 0x240, meaning TOC starts after the node header at 0x38, and is 0x240 in length. This also means the key area starts at 0x278, directly after the TOC.
- The shared free space starts at 0x900 in the key area, meaning $0x278 + 0x900 = 0xB78$, and it is 0x8 in length, meaning it end at 0xB78+0x8=0xB80, where it meet the last part of the value area. The value area is not shown completely in Fig. 1.17.

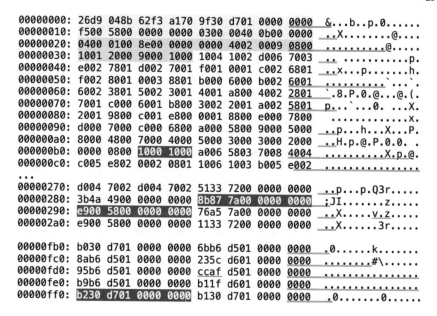

```
00000000: 26d9 048b 62f3 a170 9f30 d701 0000 0000   &...b..p.0......
00000010: f500 5800 0000 0000 0300 0040 0b00 0000   ..X........@....
00000020: 0400 0100 8e00 0000 0000 4002 0009 0800   ..........@.....
00000030: 1001 2000 9000 1000 1004 1002 d006 7003   .. ...........p.
00000040: e002 7801 d002 7001 f001 0001 c002 6801   ..x...p.......h.
00000050: f002 8001 0003 8801 b000 6000 b002 6001   ..........`...`.
00000060: 6002 3801 5002 3001 4001 a800 4002 2801   `.8.P.0.@...@.(.
00000070: 7001 c000 6001 b800 3002 2001 a002 5801   p...`...0. ...X.
00000080: 2001 9800 c001 e800 0001 8800 e000 7800    .............x.
00000090: d000 7000 c000 6800 a000 5800 9000 5000   ..p...h...X...P.
000000a0: 8000 4800 7000 4000 5000 3000 3000 2000   ..H.p.@.P.0.0. .
000000b0: 0000 0800 1000 1000 a006 5803 7008 4004   ..........X.p.@.
000000c0: c005 e802 0002 0801 1006 1003 b005 e002   ................
...
00000270: d004 7002 d004 7002 5133 7200 0000 0000   ..p...p.Q3r.....
00000280: 3b4a 4900 0000 0000 8b87 7a00 0000 0000   ;JI.......z.....
00000290: e900 5800 0000 0000 76a5 7a00 0000 0000   ..X.....v.z.....
000002a0: e900 5800 0000 0000 1133 7200 0000 0000   ..X......3r.....

00000fb0: b030 d701 0000 0000 6bb6 d501 0000 0000   .0......k.....
00000fc0: 8ab6 d501 0000 0000 235c d601 0000 0000   ........#\.....
00000fd0: 95b6 d501 0000 0000 ccaf d501 0000 0000   ..............
00000fe0: b9b6 d501 0000 0000 b11f d601 0000 0000   ..............
00000ff0: b230 d701 0000 0000 b130 d701 0000 0000   .0........0......
```

Fig. 1.17: An index node in the object map B-Tree containing the virtual object id searched for.

The object map index node can be seen in Fig. 1.17, where the 32nd key show offset 0x10 for key and 0x10 for value. In the key area, which starts at offset 0x278, we find this key 0x10 bytes further down. Here we find the virtual object id we are looking for (0x7a878b) and its transaction id 0x5800e9. However, since this is the only key with this OID value in the node, we know we have the latest one. The physical object id to which it is connected can be found 0x10 bytes from the end of this node, and where the value is 0x1d730b2. This is the physical address to the leaf node in this omap B-tree. Reading this object id (0x1d730b2), we can see in Fig. 1.18 the object map leaf node. As usual, we need to interpret the object node header.

- btn_flags: 0x6, BTNODE_LEAF, BTNODE_FIXED_KV_SIZE.
- btn_level: 0x0, There are no levels of child nodes under this one.
- btn_nkeys: 0x47, there are 0x47 (71) records.
- btn_table_space: 0x00 offset, 0x1c0, meaning TOC starts after the node header at 0x38, and is 0x1c0 in length. This also means the key are starts at 0x1F8, directly after the TOC.
- The shared free space starts at 0x700 in the key area, meaning $0x1F8 + 0x700 = 0x8F8$, and it is 0x8 in length, meaning it end at 0x8F8+0x8=0x900, where it meet the last part of the value area. The value area is not shown completely in Fig. 1.18.

The first record points to the root virtual object id 0x7a878b, which can be found at physical object id 0x1d66e7f (last 8 byte of value).

```
00000000: 8dad a1cc 04e2 545b b230 d701 0000 0000  .......T[.0......
00000010: f500 5800 0000 0000 0300 0040 0b00 0000  ..X........@....
00000020: 0600 0000 4700 0000 0000 c001 0007 0800  ....G...........
00000030: 8001 9002 9001 9002 7005 8005 b002 c002  .........p......
00000040: d004 e004 7001 8001 5006 6006 8004 9004  ....p...P.`.....
00000050: a002 b002 d005 e005 3000 4000 8003 9003  ........0.@.....
...
00000760: b300 5800 0000 0000 8b87 7a00 0000 0000  ..X.......z.....
00000770: e900 5800 0000 0000 af87 7a00 0000 0000  ..X.......z.....
00000780: e900 5800 0000 0000 1003 1000 0000 0000  ..X.............
...
00000a80: 0000 0000 0010 0000 7f6e d601 0000 0000  .........n......
00000a90: f002 1000 0010 0000 1669 d501 0000 0000  .........i......
...
00000fe0: 0000 0000 0010 0000 8d63 d501 0000 0000  .........c......
00000ff0: 0000 0000 0010 0000 7d63 d501 0000 0000  ........}c......
```

Fig. 1.18: Omap Leaf Node where we found the virtual object we searched for, which can be mapped to physical address 0x1d66e7f.

The physical address 0x1d66e7f, found in Fig. 1.18 is the physical address to the apfs_root_tree_oid (the file system B-Tree) with virtual object id 0x7a878b. We discuss this B-Tree more in sect. 1.3.

1.3 APFS - Metadata Category

We have already found the FS Root B-tree, and now we will start explaining structures that are related to files and directories.

In Fig. 1.19 we show the content of the physical object id block 0x1d66e7f, and this block has the virtual object id 0x7a878b, found in byte 8 in the object header. This is typical for a virtual object id when we read it from its physical address. The virtual object id will still be stored from byte 8 in the object header. When we read the object node header, we find the following information.

- btn_flags: 0x1, BTNODE_ROOT,
- btn_level: 0x3, There are three levels of child nodes under this one.
- btn_nkeys: 0x4, there are 4 records.
- btn_table_space: 0x00 offset, 0x40, meaning TOC starts after the node header at 0x38, and is 0x40 in length. This also means the key area starts at 0x78, directly after the TOC.
- The shared free space starts at 0x5b in the key area, meaning $0x78 + 0x5b = 0xD3$, and it is 0xee5 in length, meaning it end at 0xd3+0xee5=0xfb8, where it meet the last part of the value area.

We have listed all the four entries in this block using different background colors.

- OBJ_ID_MASK (0x0fffffffffffffff)

```
00000000: a2dc b144 c152 e64a 8b87 7a00 0000 0000   ...D.R.J..z.....
00000010: e900 5800 0000 0000 0200 0000 0e00 0000   ..X.............
00000020: 0100 0300 0400 0000 0000 4000 5b00 e50e   ..........@.[...
00000030: ffff 0000 ffff 0000 0000 1600 0800 0800   ................
00000040: 1600 2100 1000 0800 3700 1c00 1800 0800   ..!.....7.......
00000050: 5300 0800 2000 0800 0000 0000 0000 0000   S... ...........
00000060: 0000 0000 0000 0000 0000 0000 0000 0000   ................
00000070: 0000 0000 0000 0000 0100 0000 0000 0090   ................
00000080: 0c00 7072 6976 6174 652d 6469 7200 d4f1   ..private-dir...
00000090: 0900 0100 0040 1700 636f 6d2e 6170 706c   .....@..com.appl
000000a0: 652e 5265 736f 7572 6365 466f 726b 00c2   e.ResourceFork..
000000b0: f20a 0001 0000 4012 0063 6f6d 2e61 7070   ......@..com.app
000000c0: 6c65 2e64 6563 6d70 6673 0021 8f0b 0001   le.decmpfs.!....
000000d0: 0000 3000 0000 0000 0000 0000 0000 0000   ..0.............
...
00000fa0: 0000 0000 0000 0000 0000 0000 0000 0000   ................
00000fb0: 0000 0000 0000 0000 1efc 7a00 0000 0000   ..........z.....
00000fc0: b9d8 7a00 0000 0000 e5b2 7a00 0000 0000   ..z.......z.....
00000fd0: e6b2 7a00 0000 0000 4200 0000 0010 0000   ..z.....B.......
00000fe0: 0000 0000 0000 0000 7600 0000 de0e 0000   ........v.......
00000ff0: 0d1f 0a00 0000 0000 d183 0000 0000 0000   ................
```

Fig. 1.19: File System Root B-Tree.

- OBJ_TYPE_MASK (0xf000000000000000)
- OBJ_TYPE_SHIFT (60)

$$ObjectId = obj\_id\_and\_type \ \& \ OBJ\_ID\_MASK$$
$$ObjectType = obj\_id\_and\_type \ \& \ OBJ\_TYPE\_MASK >> OBJ\_TYPE\_SHIFT$$

The first 8 bytes of the first record key is 0x9000000000000001, and when computing the object id we get 0x1. When computing the object type we get 0x9, which is a APFS_TYPE_DIR_REC (found in Table 1.13). This means this record is a directory record.

> **⚠ Attention**
>
> One FS object may have several records describing the object, and therefore there could be multiple records with the same object id.

It seems like the value field of these four records only contains virtual object ids. For the first record, this is file id 0x7ab2e6. This means we need to look up in the apfs_omap_id (0x1d565a3) again to map this virtual address to the physical address. The two highlighted keys in Fig. 1.16, show that the virtual object id we are searching for is between them, and therefore we select the first record, and we continue down the B-Tree until we find the correct physical address, which was 0x1d6558f.

Table 1.13: j_obj_types

Enum Name	Enum Value
APFS_TYPE_ANY	0
APFS_TYPE_SNAP_METADATA	1
APFS_TYPE_EXTENT	2
APFS_TYPE_INODE	3
APFS_TYPE_XATTR	4
APFS_TYPE_SIBLING_LINK	5
APFS_TYPE_DSTREAM_ID	6
APFS_TYPE_CRYPTO_STATE	7
APFS_TYPE_FILE_EXTENT	8
APFS_TYPE_DIR_REC	9
APFS_TYPE_DIR_STATS	10
APFS_TYPE_SNAP_NAME	11
APFS_TYPE_SIBLING_MAP	12
APFS_TYPE_FILE_INFO	13
APFS_TYPE_MAX_VALID	13
APFS_TYPE_MAX	15
APFS_TYPE_INVALID	15

Table 1.14: j_drec_key_t

Offset	Size	Name	Description
0x0	0x8	hdr (objid and type)	The header of this record (type: j_key_t)
0x8	0x2	name_len	The length of the directory
0xA	name[name_len]	The name of this directory	

Table 1.15: j_drec_val_t

Offset	Size	Name	Description
0x0	0x8	file_id	The node identifier
0x8	0x8	date_added	Timestamp describing when directory was moved/created here
0x10	0x2	flags	Flag describing inode file type (masked with DREC_TYPE_MASK)
0x12	var	xfields[]	Extended fields

Figure 1.20 shows that the directory with file name *private-dir* object id 0x1, and from its value field we need to go to virtual address 0x7a87e8, so again we need to look up in the volume object map to find the physical address, which was 0x1d563bc. Fig. 1.21 shows the same record for the filename *private-dir*, still object id 1, and we are now in the second index node, and we have 1 level of child nodes under this one, and we want to see the child node for this record, which can be found at virtual object id 0x7a878d. We look up in the volume object map, and we find that the physical address is 0x1d5632b.

```
00000000: a5e8 68e5 2eef 14d3 e6b2 7a00 0000 0000  ...h.......z.....
00000010: e900 5800 0000 0000 0300 0000 0e00 0000  ...X............
00000020: 0000 0200 6600 0000 0000 4003 9c08 bc00  ....f.....@.....
00000030: ffff 0000 ffff 0000 0000 1600 0800 0800  ................
00000040: 1600 1800 1000 0800 2e00 2000 1800 0800  .......... .....
...
00000370: 0000 0000 0000 0000 0100 0000 0000 0090  ................
00000380: 0c00 7072 6976 6174 652d 6469 7200 6402  ...private-dir.d.
00000390: 0000 0000 0090 0e00 436f 6465 5265 736f  ........CodeReso
000003a0: 7572 6365 7300 3609 0000 0000 0090 1600  urces.6.........
000003b0: 4163 6365 7373 6962 696c 6974 792e 7374  Accessibility.st
000003c0: 7269 6e67 7300 be17 0000 0000 0040 1200  rings........@..
000003d0: 636f 6d2e 6170 706c 652e 6465 636d 7066  com.apple.decmpf
000003e0: 7300 7c25 0000 0000 0090 1600 4163 6365  s.|%........Acce
000003f0: 7373 6962 696c 6974 792e 7374 7269 6e67  ssibility.string
00000400: 7300 d731 0000 0000 0090 1300 4761 6d65  s..1.......Game
00000410: 4365 6e74 6572 2e73 7472 696e 6773 00c7  Center.strings..
00000420: 3e00 0000 0000 4012 0063 6f6d 2e61 7070  >.....@..com.app
...
00000f70: 908e 7a00 0000 0000 2c8e 7a00 0000 0000  ..z.....,.z.....
00000f80: b98d 7a00 0000 0000 548d 7a00 0000 0000  ..z.....T.z.....
00000f90: ef8c 7a00 0000 0000 7b8c 7a00 0000 0000  ..z.....{.z.....
00000fa0: 078c 7a00 0000 0000 a88b 7a00 0000 0000  ..z.......z.....
00000fb0: 4b8b 7a00 0000 0000 f48a 7a00 0000 0000  K.z.......z.....
00000fc0: 898a 7a00 0000 0000 2a8a 7a00 0000 0000  ..z.....*.z.....
00000fd0: b689 7a00 0000 0000 4789 7a00 0000 0000  ..z.....G.z.....
00000fe0: d188 7a00 0000 0000 5c88 7a00 0000 0000  ..z.....\.z.....
00000ff0: e787 7a00 0000 0000 e887 7a00 0000 0000  ..z.......z.....
```

Fig. 1.20: File System B-Tree Index (level 1).

```
00000000: 687b bcf9 d5fe 63b5 e887 7a00 0000 0000  h{....c...z.....
00000010: e900 5800 0000 0000 0300 0000 0e00 0000  ..X............
00000020: 0000 0100 5a00 0000 0000 0003 7c09 7c00  ....Z.......|.|.
00000030: ffff 0000 ffff 0000 0000 1600 0800 0800  ................
00000040: 1600 1d00 1000 0800 3300 2300 1800 0800  ........3.#.....
...
00000330: 0000 0000 0000 0000 0100 0000 0000 0090  ................
00000340: 0c00 7072 6976 6174 652d 6469 7200 1600  ...private-dir...
00000350: 0000 0000 0090 1300 4d65 6469 6153 7472  ........MediaStr
00000360: 6561 6d50 6c75 6769 6e73 0017 0000 0000  eamPlugins......
00000370: 0000 9019 0041 6363 6573 736f 7279 4175  .....AccessoryAu
00000380: 6469 6f2e 6672 616d 6577 6f72 6b00 1700  dio.framework...
00000390: 0000 0000 0090 2000 4170 706c 6542 6173  ...... .AppleBas
...
0000fc0: 9387 7a00 0000 0000 9287 7a00 0000 0000  ..z.......z.....
00000fd0: 9187 7a00 0000 0000 9087 7a00 0000 0000  ..z.......z.....
00000fe0: 8f87 7a00 0000 0000 8e87 7a00 0000 0000  ..z.......z.....
00000ff0: 8c87 7a00 0000 0000 8d87 7a00 0000 0000  ..z.......z.....
```

Fig. 1.21: File System B-Tree Index (level 2).

Fig. 1.22 shows files from the root directory, where also the *private-dir* is located, highlighted in dark blue. When we interpret a directory key, we use the Table 1.14. In the 8 bytes before the file name, we find the object id 0x1 and object type (0x9,

```
00000000:  27a0 4940 acb8 9de1 8d87 7a00 0000 0000    '.I@......z.....
00000010:  e900 5800 0000 0000 0300 0000 0e00 0000    ..X............
00000020:  0200 0000 4d00 0000 0000 8002 4006 2e00    ....M.......@...
00000030:  ffff 0000 ffff 0000 0000 1600 1200 1200    ................
00000040:  1600 0f00 2400 1200 2500 0800 9000 6c00    ....$...%.....l.
00000050:  2d00 1300 a200 1200 4000 0e00 b400 1200    -.......@.......
...
000002b0:  0000 0000 0000 0000 0100 0000 0000 0090    ................
000002c0:  0c00 7072 6976 6174 652d 6469 7200 0100    ..private-dir...
000002d0:  0000 0000 0090 0500 726f 6f74 0002 0000    ........root....
000002e0:  0000 0000 3002 0000 0000 0000 9009 002e    ....0...........
000002f0:  5472 6173 6865 7300 0200 0000 0000 0090    Trashes.........
00000300:  0400 2e62 6100 0200 0000 0000 0090 0600    ...ba...........
00000310:  2e66 696c 6500 0200 0000 0000 0090 0400    .file...........
00000320:  2e6d 6200 0200 0000 0000 0090 0d00 4170    .mb...........Ap
00000330:  706c 6963 6174 696f 6e73 0002 0000 0000    plications......
00000340:  0000 900a 0044 6576 656c 6f70 6572 0002    .....Developer..
00000350:  0000 0000 0000 9008 004c 6962 7261 7279    .........Library
00000360:  0002 0000 0000 0000 9007 0053 7973 7465    ...........Syste
00000370:  6d00 0200 0000 0000 0090 0400 6269 6e00    m...........bin.
00000380:  0200 0000 0000 0090 0600 636f 7265 7300    ..........cores.
00000390:  0200 0000 0000 0090 0400 6465 7600 0200    ..........dev...
000003a0:  0000 0000 0090 0400 6574 6300 0200 0000    ........etc.....
000003b0:  0000 0090 0800 7072 6976 6174 6500 0200    ......private...
000003c0:  0000 0000 0090 0500 7362 696e 0002 0000    ........sbin....
000003d0:  0000 0000 9004 0074 6d70 0002 0000 0000    .......tmp......
000003e0:  0000 9004 0075 7372 0002 0000 0000 0000    .....usr........
000003f0:  9004 0076 6172 0003 0000 0000 0000 3015    ...var........0.
00000400:  0000 0000 0000 3015 0000 0000 0000 9008    ......0.........
00000410:  004c 6962 7261 7279 0016 0000 0000 0000    .Library........
...
00000f60:  0400 0100 0000 12f5 ec46 ec09 4415 0800    .........F..D...
00000f70:  0100 0000 0000 0000 0200 0000 0000 0000    ................
00000f80:  00e4 9c33 c697 8d14 59ca c360 8ced 5715    ...3....Y..`..W.
00000f90:  59ca c360 8ced 5715 00ac 12ac 7d98 8d14    Y..`..W.....}...
00000fa0:  0080 0000 0000 0000 1100 0000 0000 0000    ................
00000fb0:  2400 0000 0000 0000 0000 0000 5000 0000    $.........P...
00000fc0:  fd43 0000 0000 0000 0000 0000 0100 0800    .C..............
00000fd0:  0402 0500 726f 6f74 0000 0000 0200 0000    ....root........
00000fe0:  0000 0000 28ca b448 9673 c914 0400 0300    ....(..H.s......
00000ff0:  0000 0000 0000 b0dd b448 9673 c914 0400    .........H.s....
```

Fig. 1.22: File System B-Tree Leaf, shows the files in the root directory.

APFS_TYPE_DIR_REC). The next two bytes 0xc (12) describe the directory name's
size. The next 12 bytes are the directory name *private-dir* + null terminator byte.

Then we interpret the value of this directory record, found from offset 0xfee and
0x12 (18) bytes, highlighted in dark blue. We use Table 1.15 to interpret the value.
The node id (file_id) is 0x3, and the directory was added at 0x14c9739648b4ddb0
(Monday, 19 June 2017 06:57:20 UTC). The flags field yield the inode file type, here
0x0004. We use flags & DREC_TYPE_MASK (0x000f), and we get file data type 4
(DT_DIR). This means that this directory entry is describing a directory. This type
can be found in Table 1.16.

Table 1.16: File Type Flags

Define Name	Define Value	Description
DT_UNKNOWN	0	An unknown directory entry
DT_FIFO	1	A named pipe
DT_CHR	2	A character-special file
DT_DIR	4	A directory
DT_BLK	6	A block-special file
DT_REG	8	A regular file
DT_LINK	10	A symbolic link
DT_SOCK	12	A socket
DT_WHT	14	A whiteout

We continue with the third record, from Fig. 1.22, highlighted in black. The key content is only 8 bytes, 0x3000000000000002, object id 2, and object type 3 (APFS_TYPE_INODE). Then we interpret the record value. The parent id is 0x01, private id is 0x2 (unique for this data stream, previously found to be describing the root filename (red highlight)). Then at 0xf80 we have four 8 byte fields that all describe timestamps; create_time: 0x148D97C6339CE400 (Tuesday, 6 December 2016 06:45:30), mod_time: 0x1557ED8C60C3CA59 (Wednesday, 26 September 2018 10:49:44), change_time: 0x1557ED8C60C3CA59 (Wednesday, 26 September 2018 10:49:44), access_time: 0x148D987DAC12AC00 (Tuesday, 6 December 2016 06:58:38). From offset 0xf0 we find the 8-byte internal flags 0x8000 INODE_NO_RSRC_FORK, which means this inode does not have a resource fork. We find the number of directory entries in this directory in offset 0xfa8, and the value is 0x11 (17). This means we have 17 files or directories in the root directory. The owner of this file is owner id 0, and group id 0x50 (80). From offset 0xfd4 we find the name of this inode, which is root.

Table 1.17: j_inode_val_t

Offset	Size	Name	Description
0x0	0x8	parent_id	The parent node id
0x8	0x8	private_id	This node id
0x10	0x8	create_time	Creation time
0x18	0x8	mod_time	Modification time
0x20	0x8	change_time	Change time
0x28	0x8	access_time	Access time
0x30	0x8	internal_flags	Internal flags
0x38	0x4	nchildren	Directory entries in this directory, or number sym links for a file
0x3C	0x4	default_protection_class	Default protection class [4]
0x40	0x4	write_generation_counter	A counter which increase when node is modified
0x44	0x4	bsd_flags	Inode's BSD flags
0x48	0x4	owner	The user id
0x4c	0x4	group	Group id

1.4 APFS - File Name category

We refer to the APFS metadata category, since the file names are part of the parsing of the FS B-tree. The part of the key that contain the file names are related to this category. Make sure to notice that in the Fig. 1.22 we can see typically directory

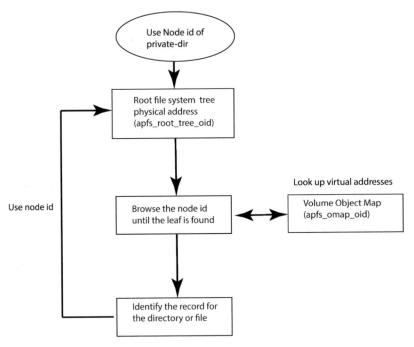

Fig. 1.23: How to browse for a file or directory in the File System Root B-Tree.

names found in the root directory; Trashes Applications, Developer, Library, System, bin, cores, dev, etc, private, sbin, tmp, usr, var.

One of the files we found was the *sbin* directory. However, we do not see the directory entries (files or directories) of this directory. We need to recognise the node identifier of the *sbin* directory (here 0x18c60), and then look it up using the File System Root B-Tree, and again we would need to use the volume object map. An overview of how to browse the File System Root B-Tree (physical address of apfs_root_tree_oid) is shown in Fig. 1.23. In order to find the files in the root directory we already parsed the private-dir using the File System Root B-tree, and the resulting leaf node was shown in Fig. 1.22, which also includes the *sbin* directory we now want to focus on. In Fig. 1.24 we show the same leaf node, but have highlighted the *sbin* record. The key was found at offset 0x3be and is 0xf (15) bytes in size. The object id is 0x2 (meaning it belongs to the parent id 2(root)), and the type is 0x9 (APFS_TYPE_DIR_REC). The size of the name is 0x5, and the name is sbin

```
00000000: 27a0 4940 acb8 9de1 8d87 7a00 0000 0000    '.I@......z.....
00000010: e900 5800 0000 0000 0300 0000 0e00 0000    ..X............
00000020: 0200 0000 4d00 0000 0000 8002 4006 2e00    ....M.......@...
00000030: ffff 0000 ffff 0000 0000 1600 1200 1200    ...............
00000040: 1600 0f00 2400 1200 2500 0800 9000 6c00    ....$...%.....l.
00000050: 2d00 1300 a200 1200 4000 0e00 b400 1200    -.......@......
00000060: 4e00 1000 c600 1200 5e00 0e00 d800 1200    N.......^......
00000070: 6c00 1700 ea00 1200 8300 1400 fc00 1200    l..............
00000080: 9700 1200 0e01 1200 a900 1100 2001 1200    ............ ...
00000090: ba00 0e00 3201 1200 c800 1000 4401 1200    ....2.......D...
000000a0: d800 0e00 5601 1200 e600 0e00 6801 1200    ....V.......h...
000000b0: f400 1200 7a01 1200 0601 0f00 8c01 1200    ....z..........
000000c0: 1501 0e00 9e01 1200 2301 0e00 b001 1200    ........#......

...
000002b0: 0000 0000 0000 0000 0100 0000 0000 0090    ................
000002c0: 0c00 7072 6976 6174 652d 6469 7200 0100    ..private-dir...
000002d0: 0000 0000 0090 0500 726f 6f74 0002 0000    ........root....
000002e0: 0000 0000 3002 0000 0000 0000 9009 002e    ....0...........
000002f0: 5472 6173 6865 7300 0200 0000 0000 0090    Trashes.........
00000300: 0400 2e62 6100 0200 0000 0000 0090 0600    ...ba..........
00000310: 2e66 696c 6500 0200 0000 0000 0090 0400    .file..........
00000320: 2e6d 6200 0200 0000 0000 0090 0d00 4170    .mb..........Ap
00000330: 706c 6963 6174 696f 6e73 0002 0000 0000    plications......
00000340: 0000 900a 0044 6576 656c 6f70 6572 0002    .....Developer..
00000350: 0000 0000 0000 9008 004c 6962 7261 7279    .........Library
00000360: 0002 0000 0000 0000 9007 0053 7973 7465    ...........Syste
00000370: 6d00 0200 0000 0000 0090 0400 6269 6e00    m...........bin.
00000380: 0200 0000 0000 0090 0600 636f 7265 7300    ..........cores.
00000390: 0200 0000 0000 0090 0400 6465 7600 0200    ..........dev...
000003a0: 0000 0000 0090 0400 6574 6300 0200 0000    ........etc.....
000003b0: 0000 0090 0800 7072 6976 6174 6500 0200    ......private...
000003c0: 0000 0000 0090 0500 7362 696e 0002 0000    ........sbin....
000003d0: 0000 0000 9004 0074 6d70 0002 0000 0000    .......tmp......
...
00000e70: 4415 0a00 608c 0100 0000 0000 00b6 3cc0    D...`.........<.
00000e80: 4998 8d14 0400 a34d 0000 0000 0000 00ba    I......M........
```

Fig. 1.24: File System Root B-Tree, with the sbin record.

+ null terminator. The key value was found at offset 0xe74 and is 0x12 (18) bytes in size. The node id is 0x18c60, the data added is 0x148d9849c03cb600 (Tuesday, 6 December 2016 06:54:55), and the flag is 0x4 (DT_DIR). In order to identify the node id 0x18c60 for the *sbin* directory, we need to parse the Root File System B-Tree. After parsing the File System B-Tree and using the node id 0x18c60 that corresponds to the sbin directory, we found its physical address in 0x1d5ef8f, as shown in Fig. 1.25. Since we already have explained how to parse the FS B-Tree and the volume object map, we do not repeat this here.

```
00000000: 4b83 7bce f992 8f1c 8399 7a00 0000 0000  K.{.......z.....
00000010: e900 5800 0000 0000 0300 0000 0e00 0000  ...X............
00000020: 0200 0000 2d00 0000 0000 8001 9603 1500  ....-...........
00000030: ffff 0000 ffff 0000 0000 2800 1200 1200  ..........(.....
...
000000e0: d101 0800 9d08 6c00 d901 0f00 af08 1200  ......l.........
000000f0: e801 1400 c108 1200 fc01 1500 d308 1200  ................
00000100: 1102 1300 e508 1200 2402 1500 f708 1200  ........$.......
...
00000380: 6d73 646f 732e 6673 0060 8c01 0000 0000  msdos.fs.`......
00000390: 3060 8c01 0000 0000 9005 0066 7363 6b00  0`.........fsck.
000003a0: 608c 0100 0000 0090 0a00 6673 636b 5f61  `.........fsck_a
000003b0: 7066 7300 608c 0100 0000 0090 0b00 6673  pfs.`.........fs
000003c0: 636b 5f65 7866 6174 0060 8c01 0000 0000  ck_exfat.`......
000003d0: 9009 0066 7363 6b5f 6866 7300 608c 0100  ...fsck_hfs.`...
000003e0: 0000 0090 0b00 6673 636b 5f6d 7364 6f73  ......fsck_msdos
000003f0: 0060 8c01 0000 0000 9008 006c 6175 6e63  .`.........launc
00000400: 6864 0060 8c01 0000 0000 9006 006d 6f75  hd.`.........mou
00000410: 6e74 0060 8c01 0000 0000 900b 006d 6f75  nt.`.........mou
00000420: 6e74 5f61 7066 7300 608c 0100 0000 0090  nt_apfs.`.......
00000430: 0a00 6d6f 756e 745f 6866 7300 608c 0100  ..mount_hfs.`...
00000440: 0000 0090 0a00 6d6f 756e 745f 6e66 7300  ......mount_nfs.
...
00000710: 0000 0000 0000 0000 000a 001e 1702 0000  ................
00000720: 0000 0000 0000 0000 0000 000a 00c6 1602  ................
00000730: 0000 0000 0000 0000 0000 000a 00c6       ................
00000740: 4902 0001 0000 00f8 51d3 b6ca 73c9 140a  I.......Q...s...
00000750: 0088 c309 0001 0000 00f0 beb9 73b5 b3e2  ............s...
00000760: 1508 0002 0000 0000 0000 0060 8c01 0000  ...........`....
00000770: 0000 0000 1efa 4bde d681 14ba 915e ab0a  ......K......^..
00000780: b4e2 15ba 915e ab0a b4e2 1500 76ad e77d  .....^......v..}
00000790: 988d 1400 8000 0000 0000 000e 0000 0000  ................
000007a0: 0000 0092 0000 0000 0000 0000 0000 0000  ................
000007b0: 0000 00ed 4100 0000 0000 0000 0000 0001  ....A...........
000007c0: 0008 0004 0205 0073 6269 6e00 0000 0015  .......sbin.....|
```

Fig. 1.25: File System Root B-Tree, showing some of the content of the sbin directory.

1.5 APFS - Content Category

Directory entries found in the FS B-Tree have many different types, and we have already scrutinised directories and inodes. However, a file needs somewhere to store its content. APFS uses extents for this. The data stream type j_phys_ext_key_t and j_phys_ext_val_t is normally used for this purpose. The private id (node id) from a file record found in the FS B-tree (apfs_root_tree_oid) is used as an identifier in the field owning_obj_id found in the structure j_phys_ext_val_t. If the file is fragmented, we need to browse the Extents B-Tree (apfs_extentref_tree_oid) in order to identify all the extents for the node id we are searching for.

There are also structures like j_file_extent_key_t and j_file_extent_val_t which describe an extent for a file, including the length (measured in bytes) of the extent and its physical block start address. However, sometimes a file can be compressed (especially system files that are part of the iOS system partition). These files utilise compression using extended attributes describing the resource fork and the compression algorithm used. If compression is used, then the files will have an empty data fork [90]. Files created in the user data partition normally do not use compression, but it is possible. In our example iOS image, the volume was converted from HFS+, and contained compressed files. Some tools do not support reading these compressed files.

We will focus on the entry highlighted in red from Fig. 1.25. From the key, we can see that the object id is 0x18c60, which means its parent directory is the *sbin* directory. We can also see that it is a Directory Entry (0x9 - APFS_TYPE_DIR_REC), which means it is a directory entry. The name of this directory entry is *fsck*. Moving to the corresponding value we can see that the node id (file_id) is 0x10009c388, then we have the date added value 0x15e2b3b573b9bef0 (Sunday, 22 December 2019 13:13:31 UTC+0). Then we have the last two bytes in the value describing the file type, which is 0x8 (DT_REG). DT_REG is a regular file. We used Table 1.16 to interpret the file type flags. Now we know this directory entry is a regular file.

> **Important**

Even if the key describes that it is a directory entry, this does not mean it is a directory. It is the last two bytes in the corresponding value field that yields the file type (0xA=symbolic link, 0x4=Directory, 0x8=Regular file). File types can be interpreted using Table 1.16.

We did not find more entries for this file in this node. Therefore, we should assume that we will find additional directory entries for the *fsck* by browsing through the FS B-tree for the specific object/node id. We used the FS B-tree (apfs_root_tree_oid) and the Volume Object map to find the start block of the *fsck* file with node id (file_id) 0x10009c388. We use this as an object id when browsing through the FS B-tree. This node id is less than the start of the second entry in the FS B-tree root. This means we will find it selecting the first entry.

Table 1.18: Addresses B-tree parsing

What	Virtual Address	Physical Address	Description
Volume OMAP		0x1d565a3	Using APFS superblock
FS B-Tree Root (L0)	0x7a878b	0x1d66e7f	Using APFS superblock and Volume OMAP
Index Node (L1)	0x7ab2e6	0x1d6558f	Using Volume OMAP
Index Node (L2)	0x7aafd3	0x01d64365	Using Volume OMAP
Leaf Node (L3)	0x7ab04c	0x1d645fb	Using Volume OMAP

Table 1.18 shows virtual addresses and the physical addresses that were found by browsing the Volume OMAP each time we had a virtual address.

```
00000000: 2406 5f14 e90a 9ad9 4cb0 7a00 0000 0000    $._.....L.z.....
00000010: e900 5800 0000 0000 0300 0000 0e00 0000    ..X.............
00000020: 0200 0000 3100 0000 0000 c001 6803 5400    ....1.......h.T.
00000030: ffff 0000 ffff 0000 0000 0800 7400 7400    ............t.t.
...
000001a0: 1303 0800 ec09 6c00 1b03 2100 200a 3400    ......l...!. .4.
000001b0: 3c03 1c00 340a 1400 5803 1000 4c0a 1800    <...4...X...L...
...
00000500: 0000 8000 0000 0000 0000      88 c309 0001    ................
00000510: 0000 3088 c309 0001 0000 4017 0063 6f6d    ..0.......@..com
00000520: 2e61 7070 6c65 2e52 6573 6f75 7263 6546    .apple.ResourceF
00000530: 6f72 6b00 88c3 0900 0100 0040 1200 636f    ork........@..co
00000540: 6d2e 6170 706c 652e 6465 636d 7066 7300    m.apple.decmpfs.
00000550: 89c3 0900 0100 0080 0000 0000 0000 0000    ................
00000560: 0000 0000 0000 0000 0000 0000 0000 0000    ................
00000570: 0000 0000 0000 0000 0000 0000 0000 0000    ................
00000580: 0000 0000 0000 0000 0000 0000 0000 0000    ................
00000590: 0000 0000 0000 0000 0000 0000 0000 0000    ................
000005a0: 0000 0000 0000 0000 0000 0000 0000 0000    ................
000005b0: 0000 0000 0030 0000 0000 0000 d7c7 8701    .....0..........
000005c0: 0000 0000 0000 0000 0000 0000 0200 1000    ................
000005d0: 6670 6d63 0400 0000 10d2 0000 0000 0000    fpmc............
000005e0: 0100 3000 89c3 0900 0100 0000 d924 0000    ..0..........$..
000005f0: 0000 0000 0030 0000 0000 0000 0000 0000    .....0..........
00000600: 0000 0000 d924 0000 0000 0000 0000 0000    .....$..........
00000610: 0000 0000 608c 0100 0000 0000 88c3 0900    ....`...........
00000620: 0100 0000 0056 c832 c1d4 8114 0056 c832    .....V.2.....V.2
00000630: c1d4 8114 3940 ea74 b5b3 e215 0008 e578    ....9@.t.......x
00000640: 0275 8b14 0840 0400 0000 0000 0100 0000    .u...@..........
00000650: 0400 0000 0200 0000 2000 0000 0000 0000    ........ .......
00000660: 0000 0000 6d81 0000 10d2 0000 0000 0000    ....m...........
00000670: 0100 0800 0402 0500 6673 636b 0000 0000    ........fsck....
```

Fig. 1.26: File System Root B-Tree, showing entries for the fsck file found in the sbin directory.

Fig. 1.26 shows more directory entries for the file *fsck*, for its inode and for extended attributes. In order to identify what is relvant of data content we first need to read the inode, highlighted in red. We can see from the key that it is for the inode 0x10009c388, and it is of the object type 3 (inode). The value field is described in Table 1.19, where we have included the first fields.

One of the most important inode fields for file content is the internal flags. In this case, it describes that this inode has a resource fork (INODE_HAS_RSRC_FORK), which means we should find directory entries describing extended attributes.

From Fig. 1.26 at offset 0x513 highlighted in dark blue, we find the first directory entry for the extended attribute (APFS_TYPE_XATTR) for the fsck file, and it has the name com.apple.ResourceFork. The corresponding value can be seen highlighted in dark blue at offset 0x5e0.

From Table 1.20 we can see that the resource fork data stream points to another inode (file_id), here 0x10009c389, which consists of 0x3000 bytes (3 blocks) and its real size is 0x24d9. We need to find the directory entry and use its extent in order to find the data belonging to this resource fork. At offset 0x534 highlighted in purple,

Table 1.19: Inode of fsck

Offset	Length	Field	Value description
0x0	0x8	parent_id	0x18c60 (sbin)
0x8	0x8	private_id	0x10009c388 (fsck)
0x10	0x8	create_time	0x1481d4c132c85600 (Friday, 28 October 2016 23:07:59)
0x18	0x8	mod_time	0x1481d4c132c85600 (Friday, 28 October 2016 23:07:59)
0x20	0x8	change_time	0x15E2B3B574EA4039 (Sunday, 22 December 2019 13:13:31)
0x28	0x8	access_time	0x148B750278E50800 (Tuesday, 29 November 2016 07:45:56)
0x30	0x8	internal_flags	0x44008 (Uncompressed size, **resource fork**, explicit protection class)
0x38	0x4	nlink	0x1 (number of hardlinks)

Table 1.20: xattr_val_t

Offset	Length	Field	Value description
0x0	0x2	flags	0x1 (XATTR_DATA_STREAM)
0x2	0x2	xdata_len	0x30
0x4	8	xdata	**0x10009c389** (first 8 bytes)
0xC	8	xdata	0x24d9 (size)
0x14	8	xdata	0x3000 (allocated size)
0x1C	8	xdata	0x0 (crypto id)
0x24	8	xdata	0x24d9 (total bytes written)
0x24	8	xdata	0x0 (total bytes read)

we have the second extended attribute (APFS_TYPE_XATTR) for the fsck file, with the name com.apple.decmpfs. This has to do with data compression.

From the corresponding value, we can see flags are 2 (XATTR_DATA_ EM-BEDDED), which means the data is embedded into this value field. The data length is 0x10 (16) bytes. The data starts with the fpmc name (cmpf when read as LE), which is the 4-byte magic signature (compression_magic). The next 4 bytes is the compression type used, here 0x4 (unknown, type 1 is uncompressed). Then the next 8 bytes are the uncompressed size, here 0xd210 (53776) bytes. There is no extra data, and we assume that this means that the resource fork data stream 0x10009c389 is compressed.

At offset 0x550 highlighted in yellow, we have a directory entry for a file extent for the inode id 0x10009c389, and this extent starts at logical address 0 (the start of the file). Please note that this is the node number after the one assigned to fsck, and is the same as the one identified as the data stream of the resource fork belonging to fsck. We assume it is compressed.

The corresponding value starts at offset 0x5b4, and is highlighted in yellow. The first 8 bytes is the field len_and_flags, and we can see the length is 0x3000 (number of bytes in the assigned blocks, here 3 blocks), and flags are not in use. The next 8 bytes are the physical block number this extent starts, here 0x187c7d7. The last 8 bytes are the encryption key or tweak used for the extent. Here it is 0x0 which means encryption is not used.

Extracting the file content is just extracting the three blocks starting from physical address 0x187c7d7. Then we will have an extracted file that is recognized as an Apple HFS/HFS+ resource fork. Since we extract a compressed resource fork, we will need to extract and decompress its data. However, to decompress the resource fork data content, we need to extract the compressed data from the resource fork and then decompress the data using the appropriate algorithm.

In most cases, we will be extracting non-compressed extents, and therefore it is out of scope to describe the resource fork format in this chapter.

1.6 APFS - Application Category

The APFS does not use a journal, instead it uses a feature called Atomic Safe-Save (ASS) to ensure that an FS operation is either completed, or it does not happen. This is implemented by using Copy on Write (COW), and the use of checkpoints.

1.7 Comparing our results with a commercial tool

We selected EnCase 8 as the commercial tool to compare our results with, and also to verify the accuracy and reliability of EnCase APFS support.

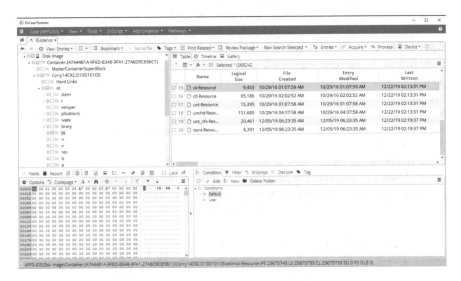

Fig. 1.27: EnCase v8.08.00.140

In Fig. 1.27 we can see that the directories and the file names are missing the first two characters in the *ot* folder, which we assume should be the *root* directory, and the *stem* directory should be the *System*, etc. EnCase used the correct volume name, but the GUID for the Container is not exactly correct. The third section shows B348, but should be 0348. Other than that the GUID from the superblock is correct.

The file we extracted in the content section had the name *fsck* and was in the sbin directory. EnCase had this file in the *in* directory (should be *sbin*, but misses the first two characters). Our file was 0x24d9 (9433) bytes in size, and it corresponds to the Logical Size in the selected file in the right table view in the Fig. 1.27. EnCase uses the selected timezone when showing the timestamps. File Creation (create_time), the Entry Modified (mod_time), Last Written (change_time), and Last Access (access_time) are identical to our results when taking the used timezone (UTC+1) into consideration.

EnCase shows the file with a filename *ck-Resource*, and the first two characters are missing. The "-Resource" is something EnCase have added to the file, which is not a part of the real file name. It may be their approach to show that this is a resource fork.

We can not validate this version of EnCase when it comes to APFS support, especially because it does not show the accurate directory and file names. This can be fixed in an updated version.

Chapter 2
Ext4

Rune Nordvik

Abstract The Ext4 file system is often used by Android cell phones and by Linux distributions. As a mobile forensic expert, it is necessary to understand the structures of this file system to recover data, verify tool results, and detect anti-forensics techniques that may be present in the file system. In this chapter, we will have a deep dive into topics important for an investigation. Many digital forensic tools do not recover much from the Ext4 file system [52], and therefore we show some of the most useful Ext4 recovery techniques proposed by current research.

The Ext4 file system is often used by Android[1] operating systems, and also by Linux desktop distributions [14], and this file system is open source. The Ext4 file system replaces the Ext2 and Ext3, but it is mostly backwards compatible. Carrier described Ext2 and Ext3 in his File System forensic analysis book [10], which includes information also relevant for Ext4. Fairbanks describes the Ext4 file system at a low level and from a Digital Forensics perspective. This chapter will describe file system information important for mobile forensic investigators and other digital forensic experts.

2.1 Introduction

This chapter will give in-depth knowledge about the Ext4 file system. We assume the readers know how to use a hex editor and how to interpret multi-byte fields in a structure. This includes how to read raw data based on the used endianness.

Even an open-source file system needs explanation because the source code is not necessarily easy to understand and does not highlight what is important for

---

Rune Nordvik

The Norwegian Police University College (Politihøgskolen), Slemdalsveien 5, 0369 Oslo, Norway, e-mail: rune.nordvik@phs.no

[1] Android is an operating system developed by Google, which is based on the Linux operating system

© The Author(s) 2022

C. Hummert, D. Pawlaszczyk (eds.), *Mobile Forensics – The File Format Handbook*, https://doi.org/10.1007/978-3-030-98467-0_2

investigations. We will show how important structures look on disk and explain how these structures should be interpreted. This chapter scrutinises the Ext4 file system of a Samsung S8 and focuses on the system partition. Detailed information about the Samsung S8 can be found at GSMArena [31]. The Samsung S8 system partition contains an Ext4 file system and should not contain user data. The phone was reset using the phone menus before acquisition to avoid including any personal data. However, using the phone's reset system is no guarantee for a complete wipe of previous data. Therefore, the data set will not be shared to ensure the anonymity of the device owner and that there is no possibility to identify any personal data from any partition. We will see that the system partition has not been reformatted during the reset. We do not know if this is also true for the user data partition because it is encrypted. The use of encrypted user data partition is often mandatory [1], and on the Samsung S8, it was enabled as default.

> ### ❗ Attention
>
> It is difficult to verify if a device is fully wiped without full access to the file system. If the phones own reset process is very fast, you should assume the data is not wiped. Even if the data was encrypted before resetting the device, it may be decrypted by existing or future methods.

2.2 Ext4 - File system category

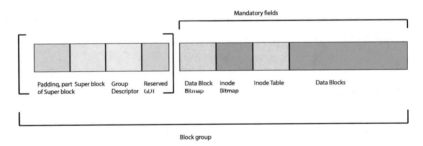

Fig. 2.1: Illustration of the elements of a block group.

The Ext4 contains multiple block groups, which have the same structure as shown in Figure 2.1. The first part of the block group is 1024 bytes reserved that can be used for boot code and form part of the first superblock [10, p. 402]. It is not a requirement that each block group has a superblock . The feature flag *sparse_super* is set by default [10, p. 400], and it will store superblocks and group descriptors in block group 0, and then in block group 3^x, 5^x, and 7^x. Another feature flag that organises superblocks is the feature flag *sparse_super2*. If set, the file system will only contain two superblock backups. If none of the *sparse_super* flags is set, the superblock and group descriptor can be found in each block group.

> **! Tip: File system feature flags**
>
> Document the supported features of the file system under investigation. Do not assume all Digital Forensic tools support all features.

Since the superblock describes the overall file system; any superblock can be used to recover the file system. After the superblock we can find the group descriptor, which describes the block group. It has location addresses, statistics, and checksums about other mandatory elements in the block group. These other elements are the data block bitmap (allocation status of data blocks in the block group), the inode bitmap (allocation status of inodes in the inode table), the inode table, and finally, the data blocks. Data blocks can be assigned to file or directory content. A file can have any content, and a directory has directory entries. In order to include all metadata related to a file, it is necessary to connect the directory entry describing the file and its inode.

2.3 Superblock

The file system uses superblocks in order to describe important structures of the file system. This includes information such as the number of total inodes and blocks, how many inodes and blocks that are free, the size of inodes and blocks, information about file system checks, which OS the file system was created on, features the file system supports, a unique UUID (Universally Unique Identifier) for the file system volume, etc.

2.3.1 Temporary data about the File system

The superblock contains its temporary information, such as when it was created, or last mounted, or last written to. In the superblock, we can also find the first time an error found place and even the time of the last error. All timestamps found in the superblock are described as seconds since 1970 (Unix Epoch) and are defined as 32-bit fields that must be interpreted as little-endian.

From a mobile forensic expert view, it will be important to know when the file system was created since we can expect to find user allocated files created between the file system creation time and before the file system last written time. If we find

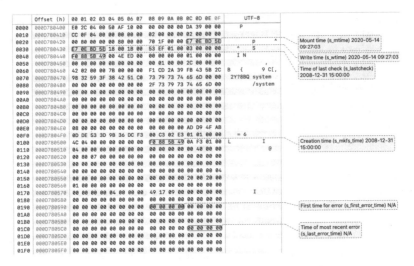

Fig. 2.2: Timestamps found in the Ext4 superblock.

allocated files outside this time range, then this can be explained by one or more theories (hypotheses):

- Files that are part of the OS system installation process may keep one or more of their original timestamps.
- Apps may keep the timestamps when extracting container files, depending on how they extract the files.
- The cell-phone has lost its date/time due to power failure.
- The user could have reset the cell-phone date/time manually.
- Someone has manipulated the timestamps using a tool.

It is also possible to find previous files from before the file system was created, unallocated, from a previous file system. All these different theories about the reasoning for why we can find timestamps out of range is not complete and which theory (hypothesis) is the most likely should be tested.

Tip: Use Experiments

Scientifically testing theories (hypotheses) is part of Digital Forensics. When it comes to file systems this can be done by performing experiments [35]. Do not base your investigation on assumptions!

When we reset the Samsung S8 device using the menus available, the system partition file system was not re-formatted. Since the partition was encrypted, we could not be certain if the user data partition file system was re-formatted. Figure 2.2 demonstrates the creation date is from 2008. This is 9 years before this device was available on the market [31].

2.3.2 Supported features

The superblock defines the features supported in three different 32 bit fields;

- 0x5C s_feature_compat
- 0x60 s_feature_incompat
- 0x64 s_feature_ro_compat

All the features found in these fields are supported by the file system driver version that created the file system. How the file system will be mounted depends on these three different fields. If the feature that is unrecognisable is found in the s_feature_compat, then the file system can be mounted with reading and writing support. If the feature not recognised is found in the s_feature_incompat, then it should not mount the file system. If the feature not recognised is found in the s_feature_ro_compat, then the file system can be mounted as read-only.

	Offset (h)	00 01 02 03 04 05 06 07	08 09 0A 0B 0C 0D 0E 0F	UTF-8
0000	000D780400	E0 2C 04 00 50 AF 10 00	00 00 00 00 DA 39 00 00	P
0010	000D780410	CC 0F 04 00 00 00 00 00	02 00 00 00 02 00 00 00	
0020	000D780420	00 80 00 00 00 80 00 00	70 1F 00 00 E7 0E BD 5E	p ^
0030	000D780430	E7 0E BD 5E 18 00 1B 00	53 EF 01 00 03 00 00 00	^ S
0040	000D780440	F0 88 5B 49 00 4E ED 00	00 00 00 00 01 00 00 00	I N
0050	000D780450	00 00 00 00 0B 00 00 00	00 01 00 00 2C 00 00 00	,
0060	000D780460	42 02 00 00 7B 00 00 00	F1 CD 2A 39 FB 43 5B 2C	B { 9 C[,
0070	000D780470	98 32 59 3F 38 42 51 C0	73 79 73 74 65 6D 00 00	2Y?8BQ system
0080	000D780480	00 00 00 00 00 00 00 00	2F 73 79 73 74 65 6D 00	/system
0090	000D780490	00 00 00 00 00 00 00 00	00 00 00 00 00 00 00 00	
00A0	000D7804A0	00 00 00 00 00 00 00 00	00 00 00 00 00 00 00 00	
00B0	000D7804B0	00 00 00 00 00 00 00 00	00 00 00 00 00 00 00 00	
00C0	000D7804C0	00 00 00 00 00 00 00 00	00 00 00 00 00 00 00 00	
00D0	000D7804D0	00 00 00 00 00 00 00 00	00 00 00 00 00 00 00 00	
00E0	000D7804E0	08 00 00 00 00 00 00 00	00 00 00 00 AD D9 4F AB	
00F0	000D7804F0	0D DE 53 3D 9B 36 DC F3	00 C3 02 E3 01 01 00 00	= 6
0100	000D780500	4C 04 00 00 00 00 00 00	F0 88 5B 49 0A F3 01 00	L I
0110	000D780510	04 00 00 00 00 00 00 00	00 00 00 00 48 00 00 00	@
0120	000D780520	00 80 07 00 00 00 00 00	00 00 00 00 00 00 00 00	
0130	000D780530	00 00 00 00 00 00 00 00	00 00 00 00 00 00 00 00	
0140	000D780540	00 00 00 00 00 00 00 00	00 00 00 00 00 00 00 04	

Compatible features (s_feature_compat):
0x2C= 0x20 Indexed directories, 0x8 Support extended attributes, 0x4 Journal

Incompatible features (s_feature_incompat) 242 = 0x200 Flexible block groups, 0x40 Files uses extents, 0x2 Directory entries record file type.

Read only compatible features (s_feature_ro_compatible) 7B = 0x40 Large inodes, 0x20 Ext3 32000 subdirectory limit no longer applies, 0x10 Group descriptors have checksums, 0x8 Files space usage is stored in units of inode block sizes (huge files), 0x2 Allow storing files larger then 2 GiB (large files), 0x1 sparse superblocks.

Fig. 2.3: Feature flags in the Ext4 superblock.

Tip: Features have an impact

The features described in the superblock impacts how the inodes and directory entries should be interpreted.

Compatible features

Even if the kernel does not understand one of the flags in this 32 bit field, it will mount the file system with read and write support. Table 2.1 can be used to interpret this field, and Figure 2.3 demonstrates an example of interpretation.

Table 2.1: Compatible features

Value	Description
0x1	Directory preallocation (COMPAT_DIR_PREALLOC)
0x2	Could mean the fs supports AFS magic directories. (COMPAT_IMAGIC_INODES)
0x4	Has a journal (COMPAT_HAS_JOURNAL)
0x8	Supports extended attributes (COMPAT_EXT_ATTR)
0x10	Has reserved GDT blocks for filesystem expansion (COMPAT_RESIZE_INODE)
0x20	Has directory indexes (COMPAT_DIR_INDEX)
0x40	"Lazy BG". Not in Linux kernel (COMPAT_LAZY_BG)
0x80	"Exclude inode". Not used. (COMPAT_EXCLUDE_INODE)
0x100	"Exclude bitmap". Not used (COMPAT_EXCLUDE_BITMAP)
0x200	Sparse Super Block, v2 (COMPAT_SPARSE_SUPER2)

From an investigator's perspective, not every compatible feature is relevant, however, the flag COMPAT_SPARSE_SUPER2 is especially important when locating the backup superblocks, in case the main one is partly corrupted or manipulated. If the COMPAT_SPARSE_SUPER2 flag is set, the super block field *s_backup_bgs*, found from superblock byte offset 0x24C, points to the two block groups that contain backup superblocks. It may seem strange that one field can point to two blocks, but this is because the field is an array of two 32 bits elements. In our example in Figure 2.3 the flag was not set. Another important flag is the COMPAT_HAS_JOURNAL. If this flag is set, recovery of data from the journal should be possible. Also note that when the journal is full, it will start writing transactions from the beginning of the journal file, effectively overwriting previous transactions [14]. More details about the Ext4 journal can be found in the sect. 2.7 at page 68. The feature COMPAT_EXT_ATTR is important since it allows extended attributes to be saved within the inode. This allows the user or programs to add extra information to individual files.

The flag COMPAT_RESIZE_INODE does not have a descriptive name, since it describes the number of blocks reserved for the extra Group Descriptor Table (GDT). These blocks are reserved for future file system expansion. These are important because the mandatory fields in the block group will be found after the blocks reserved GDT as illustrated in Figure 2.1, and this knowledge can be used for manual recovery of the file system.

Some of the flags are supported by Linux, but not necessarily used. For instance the COMPAT_DIR_PREALLOC which allows for pre-allocating a specific number of blocks to directories, defined in field *s_prealloc_dir_blocks* at superblock byte offset 0xCD. The field is currently not used by the Linux kernel [41].

Incompatible features

If the kernel does not understand one of the flags in this 32 bit field, it should not mount or repair the file system. Table 2.2 can be used to interpret this field, and Figure 2.3 demonstrates an example of interpretation.

Table 2.2: Incompatible features

Value	Description
0x1	Compression. Not implemented. (INCOMPAT_COMPRESSION)
0x2	Directory entries record the file type (INCOMPAT_FILETYPE)
0x4	Filesystem needs journal recovery. (INCOMPAT_RECOVER)
0x8	Filesystem has a separate journal device. (INCOMPAT_JOURNAL_DEV)
0x10	Meta block groups. See the earlier discussion of this feature. (INCOMPAT_META_BG)
0x40	Files in this filesystem use extents. (INCOMPAT_EXTENTS)
0x80	Enable a filesystem size over 2^{32} blocks. (INCOMPAT_64BIT)
0x100	Multiple mount protection. Prevent multiple hosts from mounting the filesystem concurrently (INCOMPAT_MMP)
0x200	Flexible block groups (INCOMPAT_FLEX_BG)
0x400	Inodes can be used to store large extended attribute values (INCOMPAT_EA_INODE)
0x1000	Data in directory entry. Feature still in development (INCOMPAT_DIRDATA)
0x2000	Metadata checksum seed is stored in the superblock (INCOMPAT_CSUM_SEED)
0x4000	Large directory >2GB or 3-level htree (INCOMPAT_LARGEDIR)
0x8000	Data in inode. Small files or directories are stored directly in the inode i_blocks and/or xattr space. (INCOMPAT_INLINE_DATA)
0x10000	Encrypted inodes are present on the filesystem (INCOMPAT_ENCRYPT)

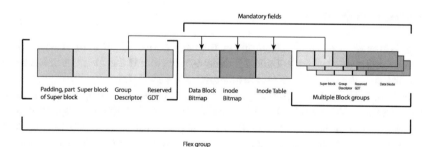

Fig. 2.4: Illustration of the elements of a flex group.

Flexible block groups are a unique way of organizing block groups into a set of flex groups. The first block of a flex group will include the bitmaps and the inode table for all groups within all the flex groups, and the other groups may contain super blocks and group descriptors depending on the sparse superblock feature, and will include data blocks, as shown in Figure 2.4. The group descriptor is used to define where the bitmaps and inode table should be located, which enables flex groups, meaning they all point to the same bitmaps and inode locations as the first group descriptor. This is important to understand, because it deviates from the standard organisation of a block group as shown in Figure 2.5.

Tip: Metadata location

The investigator should assume and test that the data block bitmap, inode bitmap, and inode table will exist in the first block group when flex groups are being used. In this case the metadata is near co-located in the beginning of the file system.

When flex groups are not used, it will be necessary to parse all superblocks and group descriptors in order to identify all bitmaps and the complete inode table.

Block groups

Flex Group 0 — 0	1		3		5		7		9				
Flex Group 1									25		27		
Flex Group 2													
Flex Group 3	49												

Fig. 2.5: Illustration of superblocks and group descriptors in flex groups or not flex groups when also the RO_COMPAT_SPARSE_SUPER is in use. Based on [5].

Read only compatible features

If the kernel does not understand one of the flags in this 32-bit field, it will mount the file system as read-only. Table 2.3 demonstrates that if the file system has large files, the superblock will use options like *RO_COMPAT_LARGE_FILE* (exist files larger than 2 GiB), *RO_COMPAT_BIGALLOC* (extents are using clusters instead of blocks) and *RO_COMPAT_HUGE_FILE* (file size is shown in logical blocks instead of sectors). Large files can be of investigative value since they may contain videos, file system containers, encrypted files, etc. It is important that these files are investigated.

Tip: Large Files

Use tools that flag large files, or sort a file listing by file size.

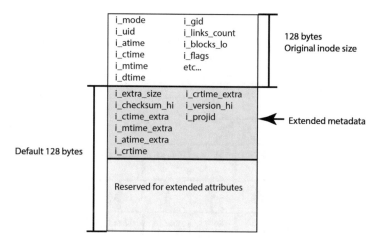

Fig. 2.6: Illustration of usage of extended metadata in inodes.

The default inode size was 128 bytes in Ext2 and Ext3, but in Ext4 it was typically 256 bytes. The option *RO_COMPAT_EXTRA_ISIZE* means that extended metadata is utilised, which will allow Ext4 features such as nano second parts of timestamps, the creation timestamp etc. The part after the extra inode size is still reserved for extended attributes. Figure 2.6 demonstrates that the extra metadata is found directly after the first 128 bytes of an inode, and that the extended attributes follow after the extended metadata. If extended metadata is not in use, then this area will be reserved for extended attributes. In our example Ext4 file system extended attributes was supported, see Figure 2.3 at page 45.

Using checksums of metadata is a measure to protect the metadata from being used if corrupted or manipulated. However, it does not protect metadata change if the checksum is updated and verifies the manipulated metadata.

Another important feature for the investigator is to check if the file system contains snapshots (a previous state of the file system). However, currently Ext4 in Linux/Android does not support snapshots.

The verity feature (*RO_COMPAT_VERITY*) may be interesting for the investigator, which means verity inodes may exist on the file system. These inodes have content that is read-only, and can be verified using a Merkle tree-based hash. A Merkle tree-based hash means that the file is divided into blocks that are hashed. Then these hashes are concatenated and represent larger blocks of data and re-hashed. This continues until there is one large block left, representing the complete file, which is hashed. It is this final hash the read-only file is verified against. The Figure 2.7 illustrates the Merkle tree hashes and is also explained by Merkle [50] who describes that in order to verify the public key, you only need the hashes of the first and second half of the public key and that you can compute half of the public key by knowing their quarters.

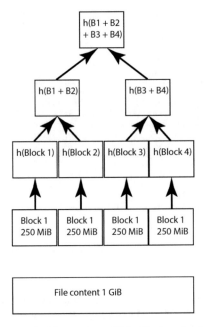

Fig. 2.7: Illustration of Merkle tree hash.

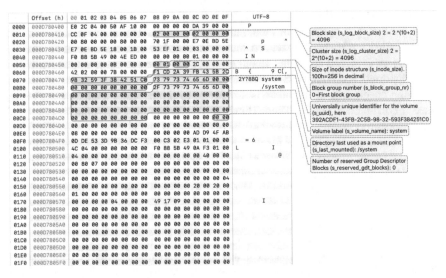

Fig. 2.8: Information about blocks in the Ext4 superblock.

The feature flag *RO_COMPAT_READONLY* means that this file system should only be mounted as read only. Most implementation of Ext4 file system drivers complies

Table 2.3: Read only compatible features

Value	Description
0x1	Sparse superblocks. See the earlier discussion of this feature (RO_COMPAT_SPARSE_SUPER)
0x2	This filesystem has been used to store a file greater than 2GiB (RO_COMPAT_LARGE_FILE)
0x4	Not used in kernel or e2fsprogs (RO_COMPAT_BTREE_DIR)
0x8	This filesystem has files whose sizes are represented in units of logical blocks, not 512-byte sectors (RO_COMPAT_HUGE_FILE)
0x10	Group descriptors have checksums (RO_COMPAT_GDT_CSUM)
0x20	Indicates that the old ext3 32,000 subdirectory limit no longer applies (RO_COMPAT_DIR_NLINK)
0x40	Indicates that large inodes exist on this filesystem (RO_COMPAT_EXTRA_ISIZE)
0x80	This filesystem has a snapshot (RO_COMPAT_HAS_SNAPSHOT)
0x100	Quota (RO_COMPAT_QUOTA)
0x200	This filesystem supports "bigalloc", extents are tracked in units of clusters (of blocks)(RO_COMPAT_BIGALLOC)
0x400	This filesystem supports metadata checksumming. (RO_COMPAT_METADATA_CSUM)
0x800	Filesystem supports replicas. This feature is neither in the kernel nor e2fsprogs (RO_COMPAT_REPLICA)
0x1000	Read-only filesystem image; the kernel will not mount this image read-write and most tools will refuse to write to the image (RO_COMPAT_READONLY)
0x2000	Filesystem tracks project quotas (RO_COMPAT_PROJECT)
0x8000	Verity inodes may be present on the filesystem (RO_COMPAT_VERITY)

with this setting, but there may exist driver implementations or tools who allow writing to the file system even if it is set to read only.

Tip: Test if a file system is read only

The investigator should perform experiments to test if it is possible to write to an identical copy of the read only file system using the same driver or tools found on the device under investigation.

2.3.3 The group descriptor

The group descriptor describes information about a particular group [14], for instance, the locations of the block bitmap, inode bitmap, and the inode table. In order to find the group descriptor, we need to know the block size, as shown in Figure 2.8. The value in this field is 2, and the formula we need to use is $10^{(10+s\_log\_block\_size)}$. We can find the group descriptor in the block following the superblock. In order to

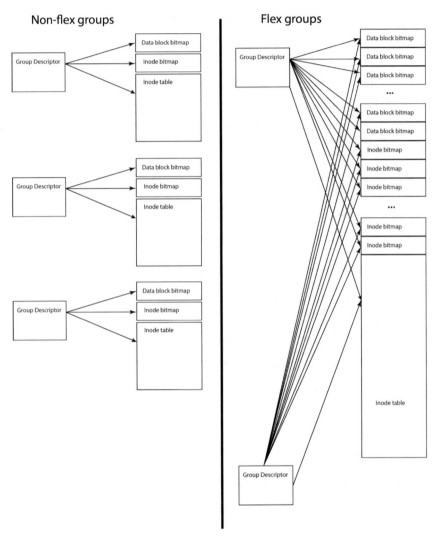

Fig. 2.9: Different designs for Group Descriptors

find the group descriptor, we, in this case, move 4096 bytes, one block, forward from the start of the superblock, from byte offset 0, not from 1024.

If the Ext4 has the 64-bit feature (INCOMPAT_64BIT) enabled, then the location of the bitmaps and the inodes table has two fields each. The first fields should describe the lower bits for the location, while the last describes the upper bits. These fields should describe the block location of the block bitmap. In our example, the 64-bit feature was not enabled, and therefore each group descriptor is only 32 bytes. The inode table can be found in the block defined in *bg_inode_table_lo* at group descriptor byte offset 0x08. The locations are relative to the start of the superblock.

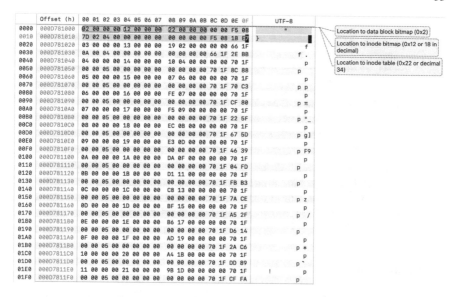

Fig. 2.10: Group descriptors in a flex group

The data block location is defined in field *bg_block_bitmap_lo* at offset 0x0, and the inode bitmap is defined in field *bg_inode_bitmap_lo* at offset 0x4. All these values are 32 bits and must be interpreted as little-endian, as shown in Figure 2.10. However, in Figure 2.10 we see that there are multiple 32-byte units, where each of them is a group descriptor, one for each block group in the flex group. A very similar copy of this group descriptor block is found in all other group descriptor blocks. However, *bg_flags* values may deviate. It is important to understand that not all block groups have superblocks or group descriptors if either the superblock RO_COMPAT_SPARSE_SUPER or the COMPAT_SPARE_SUPER2 feature flag is set. The field *bg_flags* can have any combination of these values :

- 0x1 Inode table and bitmap are not initialized
- 0x2 Block bitmap is not initialized
- 0x4 Inode table is zeroed (on initialisation)

In Figure 2.10 the flags value is 0x4 for block group 0, 1. While it is 0x5 for the rest of the block group descriptors in this descriptor block, which means that these block groups have not initialized their inode table or inode bitmaps. We could verify that there were only initialized inode tables in the first two locations (block 0x22 and 0x219).

Table 2.4: Group descriptor

Offset	Size	Name	Description
0x0	0x4	bg_block_bitmap_lo	Location to data block bitmap
0x4	0x4	bg_inode_bitmap_lo	Location to inode block bitmap
0x8	0x4	bg_inode_table_lo	Location to the inode table
0xC	0x2	bg_free_blocks_count_lo	Free blocks in block group
0xE	0x2	bg_free_inodes_count_lo	Free inodes in block group
0x10	0x2	bg_used_dirs_count_lo	Used directories in block group
0x12	0x2	bg_flags	Important for bitmaps and inode tables
0x14	0x4	bg_exclude_bitmap_lo	Location of snapshot exclusion bitmap
0x18	0x2	bg_block_bitmap_csum_lo	Data block bitmap checksum
0x1A	0x2	bg_inode_bitmap_csum_lo	Inode bitmap checksum
0x1C	0x2	bg_itable_unused_lo	Unused inodes in group

Universal Unique Identifier

In the superblock the field, *s_uuid*, assigns a unique identifier for the file system volume. This should be unique for every instance of a volume created, however, if we flash a partition, the target may be assigned the same UUID for its file system as the original source.

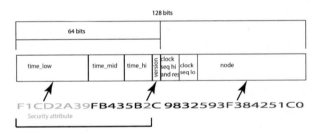

Fig. 2.11: Structure of the UUID v.2

The structures of the UUIDs are defined in RFC4122 [44], and the one used here is version 2 as shown in Figure 2.11. It uses a 60-bit timestamp (in which the four least significant bytes are overwritten with a security attribute) with an Epoch from 15th of October 1582, and a node identifier (MAC address) at the last 6 bytes. How is this important? Assuming the vendor is following the standard, it can approximate the file system creation and be connected to a MAC address. The MAC address in this example is globally unique and is a multicast address. However, the author is not convinced that the vendor follows the standard for the following reasons (1) the timestamp does not reflect the time of file system creation (2) the MAC address organisational part (OUI) is not recognised as a known organisation/vendor.

2.4 Ext4 - Metadata Category

Here we describe the inodes, inode bitmap, extended attributes.

2.4.1 The inode

The index node (inode) is defined in the structure *ext4_inode*, which defines most of the metadata related to a file, except its file name. Previous versions of Ext used a 128-byte size inode, while the Ext4 standard uses 256 bytes. However, the first 128 bytes are backwards compatible with previous versions of Ext. The information in this section is based on the Ext4 source code and the interpretation found at Kernel.org [41].

Table 2.5: Inode offset table

Offset	Size	Name	Description
0x00	0x2	i_mode	User privileges and type of file
0x02	0x2	i_uid	Lower 16 bits of the owner id
0x04	0x4	i_size_lo	Lower 32 bits of the file size
0x08	0x4	i_atime	Last access time
0x0C	0x4	i_ctime	Last inode change time
0x10	0x4	i_mtime	Last data modification time
0x14	0x4	i_dtime	Deletion time
0x18	0x2	i_gid	Lower 16 bits of group id
0x1A	0x2	i_links_count	Number of hard links pointing to this file
0x1C	0x4	i_blocks_lo	Lower 32 bits of 512 byte blocks this file uses
0x20	0x4	i_flags	Inode flags
0x24	0x4	i_osd1	For Linux this is the inode version
0x28	0x3C	i_block[]	Block map or Extent tree.
0x64	0x4	i_generation	File version for NFS
0x68	0x4	i_file_acl_lo	Lower 32 bit address of extended attribute block
0x6C	0x4	i_size_high	Higher 32 bit address of file size
0x70	0x4	i_obso_faddr	Obsolete fragment address
0x74	0xC	i_osd2	OS descriptor 2
0x80	0x2	i_extra_isize	Size of the used are of inode - 128
0x82	0x2	i_checksum_hi	Upper 16-bits of the inode checksum
0x84	0x4	i_ctime_extra	Extra change time bits
0x88	0x4	i_mtime_extra	Extra modification time bits
0x8C	0x4	i_atime_extra	Extra access time bits
0x90	0x4	i_crtime	File creation time, in seconds since the Unix Epoch
0x94	0x4	i_crtime_extra	Extra file creation time bits
0x98	0x4	i_version_hi	Upper 32-bits for version number
0x9C	0x4	i_projid	Project ID

2.4.2 User privileges and type of file

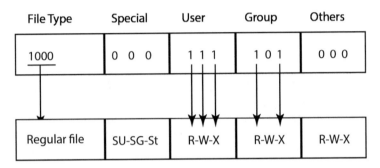

Fig. 2.12: File type and privileges.

As illustrated in Figure 2.12 the *i_mode* field name 12 least significant bits are used for user privileges. These privileges are important when investigating a file or directory since it explains ownership and user privileges. However, it is also important to understand that these privileges may be changed if the user has the privileges to do so. Let us assume they are 000111101000. The 3 least significant bits describe all others and are 000, which corresponds with r (read)-w(write)-x(execute). In this case, none of them are set, which means that users not defined as the owner of the file or not within the filegroup will not have privileges for this file. The second 3 least significant bits are 101, and they describe the group. In this case, read and execute is set, while the write is not. The third 3 least significant bits have the value 111, and they describe the owner. The 3 most significant bits are special privileges. Here they are 000, and it means the Set-UID, Set-GID, and the Sticky bit are not set. Set-UID makes sure an executable uses the owner as the user executing the file and not the actual user executing it.

Similarly, it is possible to force using the defined group id for this file as the executable group instead of the real user group assigned to the user executing the file. The least significant bit of the special bits is for the Sticky bit, which affects directories. If it is set, it means that all files within this directory can only be modified by the owner. The remainder 4 bits of the i_mode field are for describing the type of file. An inode can describe a regular file, a directory, a device (character-based or block-based), a symbolic link, a named pipe (FIFO) or a socket, as shown in Table 2.6. Knowing the type of the file tells the investigator what kind of inode is under investigation. This can give insight into if an inode describes a communication socket (two-ways communication) or FIFO (one-way communication), or if it is just a pointer (symbolic link) to another inode, or if the inode is used to access a storage device (for instance a sd_card). All kinds of devices can be accessed through an inode describing a device. There are two main types of devices: block and character. A block device stores data in predefined blocks that may be randomly accessed. A character device can be read from and written to and accessed as a sequential stream of bytes. A file system is a block device, and most devices could also be character devices. Hard disks could have interfaces for both block devices and character devices [55].

The difference between block device and character device is that the former is describe data in predefined blocks, and these blocks may be randomly accessed. A character device is accessed trough a stream of data in sequence, for instance a network card (REF).

Table 2.6: Inode file types

4 MSb	Meaning
0001	Special FIFO file (named pipe)
0010	Character device
0100	Directory
0110	Block device
1000	Regular file
1010	Symbolic link
1100	Socket

2.4.3 Temporary metadata describing inodes

Almost every inode has fields describing important timestamps. For backward compatibility, these are located from hex offset 0x08 from the start of the inode, and are 32-bit integers describing the number of seconds since 1970 (Unix Epoch). However, extra 32 bit fields in the inode use the least significant 2 bits to expand the timestamp to 34 bits. The remainder of the 30 bits is used for nanoseconds granularity.

We can only trust the timestamps if there is no malware installed on the device or any other tools to manipulate the inode metadata. The mobile device clock also needs to be accurate. The following section explains one method of manipulation.

When a file is created, the current time is set for all the timestamps in the inode. This means that if all the timestamps are the same, the file has not been changed after creation and it has not been accessed at a later time as long as the flags do not contain the flag 0x80 (bit 7 is set, counting from bit 0), which means the file system does not update the access date. If this flag is not set, the access date will update when a user or a program access the file. The investigator should always check if access times are close in time, indicating a program has accessed multiple files in the session. For instance, an anti-virus program may have opened each of the files without resetting the access time. A digital forensic logical extraction of selected files will update the accessed timestamp if the accessed timestamps are updated, assuming the tools requesting these files are using the operating system.

2.4.4 Temporary metadata manipulations

❗ Attention

It has been reported that it is possible to use the nano seconds part of a timestamp to hide information in Ext4 [18].

It is difficult to detect manipulations of the least significant parts of an Ext4 timestamp because most current listing tools do not show timestamps with the nanoseconds granularity, and even if they do, it is difficult to detect these manipulations by the user. The data hiding in the nanosecond part of a timestamp can easily get corrupted if all timestamps fields are used for hiding data. Timestamps such as *i_ctime* and *i_mtime* can be changed by user activity. However, the created timestamp (*i_crtime*) will not change since it defines the creation of a file, and a delete operation will not affect such a date [18]. Although, a deleted inode gets unallocated in the inode bitmap and can therefore be reallocated by new inodes. This reallocation will destroy parts of the hidden data, which requires error measures in order to recover hidden data [18]. To preserve secrecy, the user can utilize cryptography. [18] describe that they used symmetric string cyphers in their proof of concept tool. They also repaired the inode checksums for each manipulated inode. Therefore, the detection of manipulated inodes is difficult to detect.

Tip: Detect Manipulation

Document the Apps, tools, or malware installed on a mobile device. Try to identify their abilities from trusted sources. Investigate tools that have abilities to manipulate metadata.

Some tools may have timestamp manipulation or steganography abilities. This is one of the reasons why digital forensic experts should document the Apps, tools, or malware installed on a mobile device.

Fortunately, modern mobile devices have protection mechanisms to avoid installing software that is not approved by the device provider. Apple uses the App-Store, while Google uses the Google Play protect functionality. However, the latter can be easily disabled by the user. In addition, devices can be jailbroken on iOS or rooted on Android, allowing users to install anything.

❗ Attention

Malware needs to survive a reboot, and therefore it will try to stay hidden in the file system. Data hiding within file system metadata is a known approach [37].

2.4.5 Links count

The field *i_links_count* shows the number of directory entries referring to this inode. The directory entry has the inode number to which inode it points to. Multiple directory entries could be pointing to the same inode that indicate hard links. When the last directory entry pointing to an inode is deleted, this inode is marked as unallocated in the inode bitmap [10, p. 426]. This is not the same with soft links. Adding a soft link will not increase the links count of the inode it points to. Instead, it will create a symbolic inode. This symbolic inode points to a file path (directory entry), not to an inode [10, p. 426].

Blocks used by a file

The number of 512 byte blocks (sectors) used by a file is defined in the *i_blocks_lo* field. However, if the *inode i_flags* has the EXT4_HUGE_FILE_FL file option set and the the superblock has the huge file feature enabled then the field *i_blocks_hi* needs to be added using this formula.

$$(\text{i\_blocks\_lo} + \text{i\_blocks\_hi} \ll 32)$$

If the *i_flags* has the EXT4_HUGE_FILE_FL inode but file system does not have the huge file feature then field *i_blocks_hi* needs to be added using this formula.

$$\text{i\_blocks\_lo} + (\text{i\_blocks\_hi} \ll 32)$$

Inode flags

This field has several options describing special properties for the file. A few flags that could be important for the investigation:

- 0x10 File is immutable, which means the file can not be changed.
- 0x20 File can only be appended.
- 0x80 Does not update access time. This is important because we know this timestamp is no longer updated on access.
- 0x800 Encrypted inode, which means the file content is encrypted.
- 0x4000 File data must be written through the journal. This is important since the previous content from this file may be found in the journal as long as the journal has not been not overwritten with new transactions. This also depends on what is being recorded to the journal.
- 0x40000 This is a huge file, which has special meaning when computing the block size of a file.
- 0x80000 The file uses extents, which we explain in sect. 2.4.5. If this is not set it may use direct or indirect block pointers.

- 0x10000000 The inode contains inline data.
- 0x20000000 Create children with the same Project ID.

Block map, Extent tree or inline data

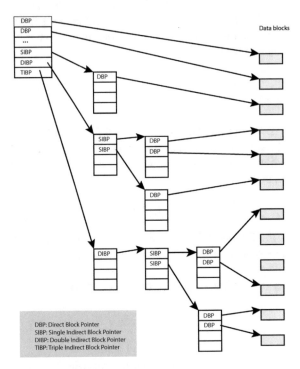

Fig. 2.13: Direct or indirect block pointers. Primarily used by previous Ext versions, but still supported in Ext4.

As illustrated in Figure 2.13, previous versions of Ext used block maps (direct or indirect blocks). However, Ext4 can still support it. Block maps are inefficient when a file uses many blocks since a maximum of 15 block pointers is available. The first 12 should be direct block pointers, while the last three could be single, double, or triple indirect block pointers [10].

For Ext4 it is more usual to find the use of extents, and they have their own structure. Table 2.7 demonstrates the extent header. Figure 2.14 illustrate how extents may be organised in an extent tree.

The 0xF30A (value interpreted as) can be used as a signature to find inodes, which can be used to recover files and metadata. However, using the extents magic to carve for inodes will not deviate between extent headers found within the inode at inode offset 0x28 or extent headers found in data blocks used by an extent tree.

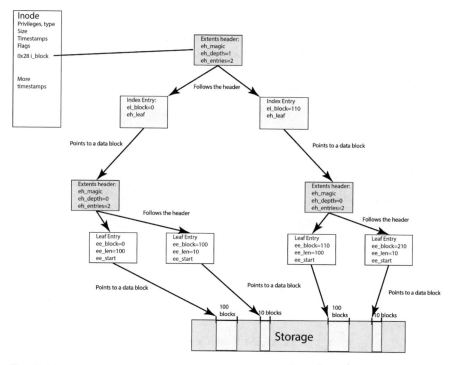

Fig. 2.14: Illustration of Extents in Ext4. Extent trees are not really needed with only 4 leaf extents, but more than 4 leaf extents will need a tree. We do not need two index entries, since the leafs could easily be included in one of the available 340 extents in one 4096 byte block. Each extent will describe one fragment. Ext4 tries to avoid fragments whenever possible, therefore, it is unusual to have many levels in the tree.

Table 2.7: Extent header

Offset	Size	Name	Description
0x0	0x2	eh_magic	Value 0xF30A
0x2	0x2	eh_entries	Number of extent entries
0x4	0x2	eh_max	Max number of entries
0x6	0x2	eh_depth	Depth of this extent node, 0= points to data.
0x08	0x4	eh_generation	Generation of the tree

This kind of recovery will not identify the file's name since the name is not included in the inode structure. However, some techniques can be used to connect the names found in directory entries and inodes found in the inode table [52].

After the header, the extent entries will follow. These are either extents pointing to new extent indexes or to the /data blocks containing the file content itself. If the extent header *eh_depth* is larger than zero, the extent index entries will point to blocks containing other extent entries. If the *eh_depth* is equal to zero, then the extent describes and points to the blocks containing the file content.

An Extent will define a contiguous number of blocks, and if the file is fragmented, it will contain multiple extents. An extent header entry (*ext4_extent_idx*) have the following structure, which is necessary to parse in order to find all blocks that a file is using eventually.

Table 2.8: Extent index entry

Offset	Size	Name	Description
0x0	0x4	ei_block	Covers file blocks from block forward
0x4	0x4	eh_leaf_lo	Lower 32 bits of the block containing next extent node in the tree
0x8	0x2	eh_leaf_hi	Higher 16 bits of the block containing next extent node in the tree
0xA	0x2	eh_unused	Not in use

If the extent header has the depth 0, it will contain the leaf extent node (*ext4_extent*), which describe the blocks used for file content.

Table 2.9: Extent leaf entry

Offset	Size	Name	Description
0x0	0x4	ee_block	First logical file block of this extent
0x4	0x2	ee_len	The length of the extent in blocks
0x6	0x2	ee_start_hi	Higher 16 bits of the extent physical start block
0x8	0x4	ee_start_lo	Lower 32 bits of the extent physical start block

The first block of a file will always start from logical block 0, but have a complete different physical disk location. The logical start block (*ee_block*) is defined to the extent, which is necessary in order to organize the fragments correctly. The start of the first physical block, where this extent starts can be found in *ee_start_hi* and *ee_start_lo*. The extent contains the blocks from this location and contains the number of contiguous blocks defined in the length field (*ee_len*).

After the last extent entry, there is a checksum named *eb_checksum* which is computed by using the file system uuid (from the superblock)+inum (from the directory entry)+igeneration (from the inode)+extent block (not including the checksum. This checksum is not necessary since the inode is already checksummed [41]. This checksum can be computed using the crc32c algorithm to identify manipulation attempts [41]. A crc32c library can be used to test this checksum [19].

The 60 byte i_block can also contain inline data, as long as the file system supports this and that the inode flag has defined that inline data is used. To create an Ext4 file system that supports inline data, it has to be formatted with the *mke2fs -O inline_data*. This area can also be used to store small extended attributes added by using the *xattr* tool. Large extended attributes will have a pointer to them (either direct or indirect block pointer, or an extent).

	Offset (h)	00 01 02 03 04 05 06 07	08 09 0A 0B 0C 0D 0E 0F	UTF-8
0000	000D7A2100	ED 41 00 00 00 10 00 00	F0 88 5B 49 DB 0E BD 5E	I ^
0010	000D7A2110	DB 0E BD 5E 00 00 00 00	00 00 1B 00 08 00 00 00	^
0020	000D7A2120	00 00 08 00 04 00 00 00	0A F3 01 00 04 00 00 00	
0030	000D7A2130	00 00 00 00 00 00 00 00	01 00 00 00 92 1F 00 00	
0040	000D7A2140	00 00 00 00 00 00 00 00	00 00 00 00 00 00 00 00	
0050	000D7A2150	00 00 00 00 00 00 00 00	00 00 00 00 00 00 00 00	
0060	000D7A2160	00 00 00 00 00 00 00 00	00 00 00 00 00 00 00 00	
0070	000D7A2170	00 00 00 00 00 00 00 00	00 00 00 00 00 00 00 00	
0080	000D7A2180	20 00 00 00 DC DB 26 B6	DC DB 26 B6 00 00 00 00	
0090	000D7A2190	F0 88 5B 49 00 00 00 00	00 00 00 00 00 00 00 00	I
00A0	000D7A21A0	00 00 00 02 EA 07 06 40 00	00 00 00 00 1A 00 00 00	@
00B0	000D7A21B0	00 00 00 00 73 65 6C 69	6E 75 78 00 00 00 00 00	selinux
00C0	000D7A21C0	00 00 00 00 00 00 00 00	00 00 00 00 00 00 00 00	
00D0	000D7A21D0	00 00 00 00 00 00 00 00	00 00 00 00 00 00 00 00	
00E0	000D7A21E0	00 00 00 00 75 3A 6F 62	6A 65 63 74 5F 72 3A 73	u:object_r:s
00F0	000D7A21F0	79 73 74 65 6D 5F 66 69	6C 65 3A 73 30 00 00 00	ystem_file:s0

Fig. 2.15: Example of a directory inode.

An example of an inode is shown in Figure 2.15. This inode is the second element in the inode table. This means we are looking at inode number 2 (the root directory) [10, p413]. If we look at the first two bytes of this inode, we can see the value 0x41ED (LE). The four most significant bits are 0100, which means it is a directory (see Table 2.6). The extent tree starts in inode byte offset 0x28, starting with a header. The header includes the 0xF30A magic for extents, it contains one extent, and this extent is a leaf node (depth is 0). The generation field is not in use. Directly after the extent header, we find the only extent. It starts from logical block 0, has a length of 1 block, the location of the block is 0x1F92 (we do not need to think of the higher 16 bits address in the ee_start_hi since it is 0). Since every block is 0x1000 (4096 bytes long), we know the block can be found at byte 0x1F92000 relative to the start of the Ext4 partition. This is demonstrated in 2.5.

File version

The *i_generation* is meant to be used for NFS (Network File System) and a random value will be created for every new file created. This is described in the function *__ext4_new_inode* found in the *ialloc.c* file. Note that the Ext2 and Ext3 file system uses another approach where the generation is set on mount, and then it is increased with 1 for every file created using the *ext2_new_inode* or *ext3_new_inode* function.

The value is not guaranteed to be unique, and the author observes that multiple inodes may contain a zero value. If the value is not zero, and the creation date of the two inodes are equal and found in the same file system, then they are both describing the same inode. This must be considered when comparing inodes found outside the inode table, for instance, in the journal. Correlating and interpreting different fields in this way can be used to find all previous instances of the same inode, assuming they are not overwritten. If we have found an inode that obviously is deleted in the inode table, finding previous versions of this inode can give us the previous extents

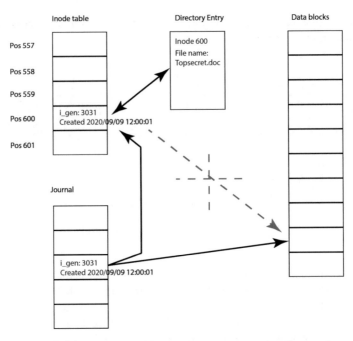

Fig. 2.16: Recovery of a file using a previous state of an inode.

in a non deleted state, allowing recovery of a previous state of this file. Knowing the position of the inode in the inode table allows us to search for the directory entry by parsing every directory. If the directory entry is found, it gives us the name and location in the file system directory tree, assuming that the directory entry is not overwritten. This recovery methodology for Ext4 is illustrated in Figure 2.16.

Operating System Descriptor 2

The osd_2 field has different content based on the OS used to create it, we describe this when Linux (Android) is used as the OS.

The operating system descriptors must be used together with similar fields described earlier in the inode. For instance, the higher value of the user id must be used together with the lower value of the user id, and so on. Most forensic tools show the owner or group of a file, but this can also be verified manually.

Project ID

The field *i_projid* is used for creating children with the same project id. This can be used to define size quotas for a group of files; for example, setting how much space

Table 2.10: Os Descriptor 2 (Linux)

Offset	Size	Name	Description
0x0	0x2	l_i_blocks_high	Upper 16-bits of the block count
0x2	0x2	l_i_file_acl_high	Upper 16-bits of the extended attribute block
0x4	0x2	l_i_uid_high	Upper 16-bits of the Owner UID
0x6	0x2	l_i_gid_high	Upper 16-bits of the GID
0x8	0x2	l_i_checksum_lo	Lower 16-bits of the inode checksum
0xA	0x2	l_i_reserved	Unused

a user can save in the user directory. This requires that the superblock supports this feature (RO_COMPAT_PROJECT).

2.5 Ext4 - File Name category

Directory entries are important since they include the name of a file or directory, and contain the inode number of the file or directory. It is easy to find the byte location in the inode table by multiplying the inode number with 256. This requires that the investigator knows where the inode table starts, which we have shown can be located by scrutinizing the first group descriptor. The directory entry depends on one of the incompatible features for recording file types in directory entries defined in the superblock . Figure 2.3 on page 45 demonstrated directory entries record file types. Therefore, we need to use the following structure as defined in Table 2.11.

Table 2.11: Directory Entry

Offset	Size	Name	Description
0x0	0x4	inode	The inode this entry points to
0x4	0x2	rec_len	Length of this entry
0x6	0x1	name_len	Length of name
0x7	0x1	file_type	The file type of this entry
0x8	Var	name[name_len]	ASCII name of file

If the superblock does not define the use of recording file names in directory entries, then we use an almost identical structure. The only difference is that the *name_len* and the *file_type* is merged into a 2 byte field that describes the *name_len*.

Figure 2.17 depicts all the directory entries found in the root directory. The location can be found by scrutinizing the second inode in the inode table. From this location, we can find every allocated file and directory in the file system, and the deleted files in their directory entries have, if not overwritten. This is why some

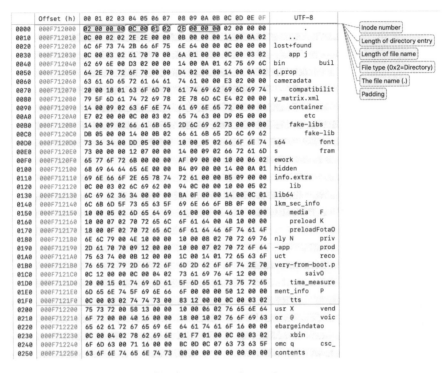

	Offset (h)	00 01 02 03 04 05 06 07	08 09 0A 0B 0C 0D 0E 0F	UTF-8
0000	000F712000	02 00 00 00 0C 00 01 02	2E 00 00 00 02 00 00 00	.
0010	000F712010	0C 00 02 02 2E 2E 00 00	0B 00 00 00 14 00 0A 02	..
0020	000F712020	6C 6F 73 74 2B 66 6F 75	6E 64 00 00 0C 00 00 00	lost+found
0030	000F712030	0C 00 03 02 61 70 70 00	6A 01 00 00 0C 00 03 02	app j
0040	000F712040	62 69 6E 00 D3 02 00 00	14 00 0A 01 62 75 69 6C	bin buil
0050	000F712050	64 2E 70 72 6F 70 00 00	D4 02 00 00 14 00 0A 02	d.prop
0060	000F712060	63 61 6D 65 72 61 64 61	74 61 00 00 E3 02 00 00	cameradata
0070	000F712070	20 00 18 01 63 6F 6D 70	61 74 69 62 69 6C 69 74	compatibilit
0080	000F712080	79 5F 6D 61 74 72 69 78	2E 78 6D 6C E4 02 00 00	y_matrix.xml
0090	000F712090	14 00 09 02 63 6F 6E 74	61 69 6E 65 72 00 00 00	container
00A0	000F7120A0	E7 02 00 00 0C 00 03 02	65 74 63 00 D9 05 00 00	etc
00B0	000F7120B0	14 00 09 02 66 61 6B 65	2D 6C 69 62 73 00 00 00	fake-libs
00C0	000F7120C0	DB 05 00 00 14 00 0B 02	66 61 6B 65 2D 6C 69 62	fake-lib
00D0	000F7120D0	73 36 34 00 DD 05 00 00	10 00 05 02 66 6F 6E 74	s64 font
00E0	000F7120E0	73 00 00 00 12 07 00 00	14 00 09 02 66 72 61 6D	s fram
00F0	000F7120F0	65 77 6F 72 6B 00 00 00	AF 09 00 00 10 00 06 02	ework
0100	000F712100	68 69 64 64 65 6E 00 00	B4 09 00 00 14 00 0A 01	hidden
0110	000F712110	69 6E 66 6F 2E 65 78 74	72 61 00 00 B5 09 00 00	info.extra
0120	000F712120	0C 00 03 02 6C 69 62 00	94 0C 00 00 10 00 05 02	lib
0130	000F712130	6C 69 62 36 34 00 00 00	BA 0F 00 00 14 00 0C 01	lib64
0140	000F712140	6C 6B 6D 5F 73 65 63 5F	69 6E 66 6F BB 0F 00 00	lkm_sec_info
0150	000F712150	10 00 05 02 6D 65 64 69	61 00 00 00 46 10 00 00	media F
0160	000F712160	10 00 07 02 70 72 65 6C	6F 61 64 00 4B 10 00 00	preload K
0170	000F712170	18 00 0F 02 70 72 65 6C	6F 61 64 46 6F 74 61 4F	preloadFotaO
0180	000F712180	6E 6C 79 00 4E 10 00 00	10 00 08 02 70 72 69 76	nly N priv
0190	000F712190	2D 61 70 70 09 12 00 00	10 00 07 02 70 72 6F 64	-app prod
01A0	000F7121A0	75 63 74 00 0B 12 00 00	1C 00 14 01 72 65 63 6F	uct reco
01B0	000F7121B0	76 65 72 79 2D 66 72 6F	6D 2D 62 6F 6F 74 2E 70	very-from-boot.p
01C0	000F7121C0	0C 12 00 00 0C 00 04 02	73 61 69 76 4F 12 00 00	saivO
01D0	000F7121D0	20 00 15 01 74 69 6D 61	5F 6D 65 61 73 75 72 65	tima_measure
01E0	000F7121E0	6D 65 6E 74 5F 69 6E 66	6F 00 00 00 50 12 00 00	ment_info P
01F0	000F7121F0	0C 00 03 02 74 74 73 00	83 12 00 00 0C 00 03 02	tts
0200	000F712200	75 73 72 00 58 13 00 00	10 00 06 02 76 65 6E 64	usr X vend
0210	000F712210	6F 72 00 00 40 16 00 00	18 00 10 02 76 6F 69 63	or @ voic
0220	000F712220	65 62 61 72 67 65 69 6E	64 61 74 61 6F 16 00 00	ebargeindatao
0230	000F712230	0C 00 04 02 78 62 69 6E	01 F7 01 00 0C 00 03 02	xbin
0240	000F712240	6F 6D 63 00 71 16 00 00	BC 0D 0C 07 63 73 63 5F	omc q csc_
0250	000F712250	63 6F 6E 74 65 6E 74 73	00 00 00 00 00 00 00 00	contents

Annotations (right side):
- Inode number
- Length of directory entry
- Length of file name
- File type (0x2=Directory)
- The file name (.)
- Padding

Fig. 2.17: Content of root directory.

digital forensic tools show that a specific file is deleted, but the content may be harder
to recover, discussed in sect. 2.6.

2.6 Ext4 - Content Category

The content of a file is pointed to by the inodes, as long as the file is allocated and
not deleted.

2.6.1 Recovery of files

When a file gets deleted, the file extents header zero out the number of extents and
depth of the tree. However, most of the extent entries may also be zeroed out. [14]
shows an extent index that is not zeroed out after deletion, and he shows that extent
leaves are zeroed out (except for the logical ei_block). This means that recovery of
an inode is most likely to succeed if the inode uses extent trees since it is possible

to parse down the tree to the leaf extent(s) that describes the block addresses used for data content [14]. The deleted timestamp is set to the time of deletion, and that many deleted files have been modified and changed equally to the deleted timestamp (Ext2, Ext3) [10, p. 420]. [14] also shows that on Ext4 the deleted inode's accessed, changed, and the modification time is set equal to the deletion time. On deletion, the file size, link count, and the number of blocks used by the file is zeroed out. However, it is possible to carve for file content only.

Inode Carving using extent magic signature

Since some of the extent information is wiped, recovery of deleted data in Ext4 is more difficult than previous versions of ExtX. However, it is possible by performing carving for previous inodes or other metadata structures. An inode does not have a special static signature, even though it is possible to search for the *eh_magic* if the inode uses extents [11]. [11] describe that the magic signature persist even for deleted files, and that they used the type field (*i_mode*) 4 most significant bits to identify false positives not corresponding to one of the 7 different file types, as seen in Table 2.6 at page 57. Dewald and Seufert (2017) [11] also describes that it is possible to combine further pattern testing; for instance, specific timestamp intervals, or a set of access rights, in order to filter out even more false positives. However, this will not identify inodes that do not use extents. This approach for inode metadata carving is very well suited to identify and recover Ext4 inodes from a re-formatted partition (for instance, an Ext4 file system re-formatted to NTFS). [11] did not manage to connect the file names to the carved inodes when using the inode carving method.

2.6.2 Generic metadata time carving

Another approach for metadata carving is thinking that the timestamps near co-located could act as a dynamic signature based on equality. File systems have structures describing their files' metadata, and they usually have temporal information near co-located. We can use equality to identify a set of timestamps based on their known granularity. The scientific paper selected this approach Generic Metadata Time Carving [52]. Using this technique, it is possible to find all inodes that match the equality pattern, not only inodes using extents.

2.6.3 Additional file content

Even though different file types are part of the content category, they are not filesystem-specific, and therefore not included in this chapter.

2.7 Ext4 - Application Category

The Ext4 journal is used for recovery purposes when the file system becomes out of sync. Modern file systems often use journals. Depending on the flags in the superblock it can be used, but it does not need to. The journal is described as an application-level feature [10, p. 437]

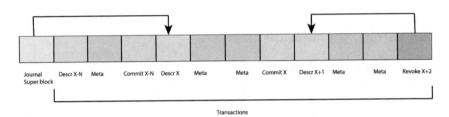

Fig. 2.18: Ext4 Journal transaction overview, based on an illustration from Carriers file system forensic analysis book [10, p. 438]

The first interesting part of the journal is the journal superblock, which contains a pointer to the first descriptor in the journal [14, 10]. The first descriptor may not be in the beginning of the journal because of the circular writing of transactions. When a transaction is stored at the end of the journal, the next transaction will be written at the start of the journal (overwriting previous transactions) [14, 10]. Every descriptor is followed by a set of metadata and/or data transactions and, finally, end with a commit block. If a file system crashes before the commit block is written, then the commit block is missing on the next mount of the file system, then a revoke block is created. This points to the previous descriptor, effectively undoing any of its transactions. Then the file system will be in a consistent state.

The journal is normally found in inode number 8, but can be placed in any other inode defined in the superblock. If the INCOMPAT_JOURNAL_DEV is set, the journal can be located on another device described by its UUID, defined in the superblock.

Chapter 3
The Flash-Friendly File System (F2FS)

Chris Currier

Abstract The Flash-Friendly File System (F2FS) is used not just by removable media but also by mobile devices and more. In this chapter, we look under the hood to better understand the structure of and recognize this file system. From a forensic perspective, we look for deleted files to see if we can retrieve them.

3.1 Introduction

The Flash-Friendly File System (F2FS) is a Linux system specifically designed for NAND Flash memory. This type of memory is common in removable storage devices and mobile devices. Samsung Electronics developed the system in 2012. One thing to mention is that the resources for F2FS are minimal. Many books and other resources, even regarding forensic examination, barely mention F2FS. Due to its increasing importance in the field of mobile forensics, we want to address file system information important to investigators.

3.1.1 NAND (Not And) Flash Memory

Universal Serial Bus (USB) flash drives (thumb drives), Solid State Drives (internal/external storage), SD Cards, and even mobile devices use NAND Flash memory. For a physical extraction, the chipset (flash memory) is what we are trying to get access to and obtain data from. This flash memory also contains a processor.

Depending on the internal geometry or flash memory management, aka Flash Translation Layer (FTL), NAND-based storage devices display different characteristics where parameters are added for configuring on-disk layout, allocation selection

Chris Currier
MSAB, Hornsbruksgatan 28 SE-117 34 Stockholm Sweden e-mail: chris.currier@msab.com

© The Author(s) 2022 69
C. Hummert, D. Pawlaszczyk (eds.), *Mobile Forensics – The File Format Handbook*,
https://doi.org/10.1007/978-3-030-98467-0_3

and algorithms for cleaning [42]. NAND is not an acronym. It stands for 'NOT AND'. It is a Boolean operator and logic gate. Both NAND and NOR gates are depicted in Fig. 3.1.

Fig. 3.1: NAND and NOR Gates

The NAND ($!(A \wedge B)$) logic yields FALSE when both input values (A and B) are True and yields TRUE if any input value is False. In contrast, the NOR ($!(A \vee B)$) operator yields TRUE if both input values (A and B) are False and yields FALSE if any input value is True (see Table 3.1 below).

Table 3.1: NAND and NOR Gate Logic

A	B	$!(A \wedge B)$	$!(A \vee B)$
T	T	F	F
T	F	T	F
F	T	T	F
F	F	T	T

We can further compare NAND and NOR flash memory [88]. The differences are as follows:

NAND flash memory

- contains an integrated circuit that uses NAND gates to store data in memory cells.
- devices write and erase data faster.
- devices store more data than NOR flash memory of the same physical size.

NOR flash memory

- uses NOR gates to store data in memory cells.
- devices write data slower.
- devices read data faster.
- data storage is less efficient.

Memory cells of flash memory can store more than one bit per cell across different voltages have a significantly limited lifetime of around 10000 write cycles. This necessitates an even distribution (wear-levelling) of the write operations over the entire flash memory. That is why flash mass storage is given an abstraction layer by its controller, the Flash Translation Layer (FTL).

3.1.2 Flash Translation Layer (FTL)

A flash translation layer is located in the controller of flash memory. It is responsible for the actual use of the memory. In doing so, it has to master a whole range of tasks:

"Unlike jffs2 and logfs, f2fs is not targeted at raw flash devices, but rather at specific hardware that is commonly available to consumers – SSDs, eMMC, SD cards, and other flash storage with FTL (flash translation layer) already built in." [8]

This includes relying on the FTLfor the wear levelling. Meaning that writing to the storage media is done evenly and not just to the first cells. Constant writing and rewrites to just the first cells of this flash memory would eventually corrupt the media. The FTL is a combination of hardware and software that can perform a number of central tasks for memory use through this interaction. It essentially ensures that writes are distributed evenly across the memory. This significantly increases the lifespan of an SD card. However, the FTL offers a conventional block device interface. It does not care about the erase-before-write property of a NAND flash device. Flash write-only can write zeros. And Flash erase can write the ones. Flash erase sets all bits to 1, so the flash write can leave the bit alone or switch it to 0. Because of this, in addition to FTL, special file systems developed for flash memory such as JFFS, Yaffs and Log FS are used further to increase the memory cells' lifetime and better address the erase-write problem.

3.2 Flash Filesystems

After taking a brief look at the hardware basics, we will now turn to the actual file system. File systems Log FS take the special properties of SD cards into account and operate as log-structured file systems. They write data sequentially to the flash memory, similar to a cyclic logbook, thus ensuring that all cells are used evenly. However, these file systems are exotic because they have an unfavourable side effect: Data and metadata end up sequentially in multiple versions on the storage medium. It is the task of an elaborate and relatively slow garbage collection to remove obsolete and deleted data from the log.

The F2FS file system addresses this problem. A compromise is made: It structures data for write operations like a log-structured file system in sequential series that are as long as possible but leaves it to the flash translation layer to eliminate the redundancies.

3.2.1 The Log-Structured File System (LSFS) or (LFS)

As already discussed, NAND flash devices can have different characteristics depending on their internal geometry, and the flash management scheme (FTL) used. In order to meet these, the new file system has several parameters with which it can be optimally adjusted to the respective memory.

F2FS is based on the Log-Structured File System (LSFS). This structure uses a block structure. The blocks are then written with data (files). The block/data is mapped using index nodes referred to as *inodes*. When data in a block is updated, the inode needs to be updated. Responsible for holding the location of the inodes is the imap. The imap will have a 4-byte entry(or pointer) for each inode. The imap will be written at the end. In the simplified example (see Fig. 3.2 below), we can see Block 0 and Block 1. The pointer for the files here is in INODE A. New Data is added to Block 2, and an INODE B is created to point to that data. The imap is updated and at the end to point to INODE A and B.

FREE SPACE

Fig. 3.2: Simple representation of the Blocks in a Log-Structured File System (LSFS)

If we have a single file split up into multiple sections spanning across different areas in a file system, this is fragmentation. Fragmentation causes issues with speed and more. We want the file to be complete in the same physical area. After data has been deleted, the Log-Structured File System takes the live data and brings them together in sections, updating the inode(s) and imap:

"A log structured file system writes all modifications to disk sequentially in a log-like structure, thereby speeding up both file writing and crash recovery. The log is the only structure on disk; it contains indexing information so that files can be read back from the log efficiently." [75]

3.2.2 Flash-Friendly File System (F2FS): Enter F2FS

The F2FS file system is a bit more complex than the basic diagram (Fig. 3.2) and information in sect. 3.2.1 with regards to the Log-Structured File System described above. Similarly to other filesystems, F2FS is comprised of blocks; each block is 4K in size. Although, "the code implicitly links the block size with the system page size." [8]

F2FS block addresses are 32 bits. [8] records that *"the total number of address-able bytes in the file system is at most $2^{(32+12)}$ bytes or 16 terabytes"*. The author acknowledges that this is unlikely to be a limitation for current flash hardware.

The name 'Flash-Friendly File System' derives from its design i.e., a filesystem that is designed for the NAND flash memory-based storage. [42] documents that a log structure file system approach was adopted while adapting to newer forms of storage. In addition, the filesystem was designed to fox some issues of the aging log-structured file system, such as the snowball effect of the wandering tree and the heavy cleaning workload.

3.2.3 Wandering Tree Problem

The Wandering Tree issue for the Log-Structured File System is that there are so many pieces when updating. When file data in LFS is updated and written to the end of log, there are several things to consider:

- its location has changed, and its direct pointer block must be updated.
- as a consequence of the change to the direct pointer block, its indirect pointer block must also be updated.
- upper index structures must recursively be updated (e.g. inode, inode map, and checkpoint block).

Bityutskiy cited in [3] describes this as the wandering tree problem and *"in order to enhance the performance, it should eliminate or relax the update propagation as much as possible"*.

3.3 On-Disk Layout of F2FS

A classic hard disk stores information through remanence (remaining magnetization), unlike flash memory. Rotating circular disks are used for storage. In order to locate a memory cell on such a medium, it is divided into different areas. The geometry of a hard disk is the division of the hard disk into tracks and sectors. It is essential first to introduce terms such as *sector* and *partition*. The former has to do with the geometry of a block device. The second term is aimed more at the logical management of a hard disk.

Sector

The term "Sector" refers to the physical sector or location on a physical disk. If you think back to the mechanical hard drives that had a platter it was divided into sectors or physical blocks (see Fig. 3.3). The starting position is Sector 0.

Track
Track Sector
Platter
Disk Sector
Head
Cluster
Actuator Arm

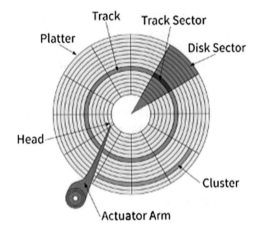

Fig. 3.3: A Breakdown Representation Inside a Hard Disk Drive (HDD) [53]

Partitions

When you format a hard disk drive or flash memory; you prepare it with a file system. In doing so you may have a single partition or create multiple partitions such as a system partition, recovery partition, and/or a user partition. You may also create additional partitions for different file systems i.e. HFS, NTFS, EXT, etc. Fig. 3.4 is an example from Microsoft's Disk Management showing multiple partitions for a single hard disk drive.

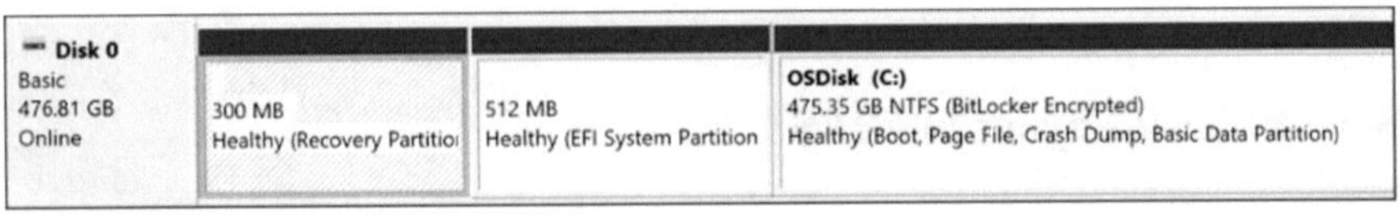

Disk 0
Basic
476.81 GB
Online
300 MB
Healthy (Recovery Partitio
512 MB
Healthy (EFI System Partition
OSDisk (C:)
475.35 GB NTFS (BitLocker Encrypted)
Healthy (Boot, Page File, Crash Dump, Basic Data Partition)

Fig. 3.4: Disk Partitioned and on the C: Volume formatted with the New Technology File System (NTFS)

> **Important**
>
> NAND flash memory-based storage devices have different characteristic according to their internal geometry and compared to a traditional hard disk, which stores data on rotating disks using a magnetic record.

3.3.1 Creation of F2FS partitions with Mkfs.f2fs

F2FS file systems are usually created with a special tool called *Mkfs.f2fs*. It can be used to create a F2FS file system (usually in a disk partition).

"The mkfs.f2fs is for the use of formatting a partition as the f2fs filesystem, which builds a basic on-disk layout." [89]

It is normally operated from the command line. The most important parameters are summarized in Table 3.2. If you prefer a graphical user interface, you can alternatively use the gparted program under Linux to create an F2FS partition (see Fig. 3.5).

Fig. 3.5: Using GParted in Kali Linux to Format the USB Flash Drive to F2Fs

Table 3.2: Mkfs.f2fs Command Options

Command Option	Description
-l [label]	Give a volume label, up to 512 unicode name.
-a [0 or 1]	Split start location of each area for heap-based allocation. 1 is set by default, which performs this.
-o [int]	Set overprovision ratio in percent over volume size. 5 is set by default.
-s [int]	Set the number of segments per section. 1 is set by default.
-z [int]	Set the number of sections per zone. 1 is set by default.
-e [str]	Set basic extension list. e.g. "mp3,gif,mov"
-t [0 or 1]	Disable discard command or not. 1 is set by default, which conducts discard.

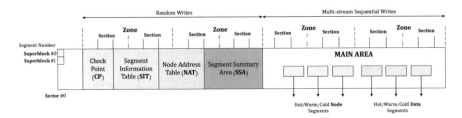

Fig. 3.6: Flash-Friendly File System Representation of How it appears Physically on the Disk [45]

3.3.2 F2FS on Disk

The F2FS is split into blocks that are 4K in size. Blocks are collected into *segments*. A segment is 512 blocks or 2MB in size. Each *section* is comprised of several consecutive segments. A *zone* is comprised of a series or set of sections. An *area* is comprised of multiple sections. The default size when using the *mkfs* utility is 2^0. Hence, there is one segment per section. A *volume* is comprised of six areas. The structure is depicted in Fig. 3.6. As mentioned, F2FS is split into six areas in total. Each is briefly described below and further discussed in this chapter:

- **Superblock (SB)**: holds the partition information and F2FS parameters; it is unchangeable.
- **Check Point (CP)**: represents the file system status; bitmaps for SIT and NAT; orphan inode list; summary entries of the active segment.
- **Segment Information Table (SIT)**: contains the valid segments and bitmap information in the Main Area.
- **Node Address Table (NAT)**: a block address table.
- **Segment Summary Area (SSA)**: summary entries representing the owner information including parent inode number and node/data offset.
- **Main Area**: node blocks store indices of data blocks; a data block contains directory or user file data.

As pointed out, F2FS divides the drive into six different, consecutive areas. At the beginning of the partition, we find the Superblock (SB). This is followed by a second copy of the Superblock. It is used if the first Superblock becomes corrupt. The Checkpoint (CP) region follows this. This region contains, among other things, information on the active segments and orphaned or expired nodes. Next comes the segment information table (SIT). It provides information about the blocks stored in the main area and their status (active or inactive). It is in turn followed by the Node Address Table (NAT), which can query the addresses of the respective active nodes. The following Segment Summary Area (SSA) provides information about which node owns which blocks. The first five blocks thus represent the metadata of the partition. The Main Area (MA), as the sixth region, contains the actual data blocks. Next comes the segment information table (SIT). It provides information about the blocks stored in the main area and their status (active or inactive). It is in turn followed by the Node Address Table (NAT), which can query the addresses of the respective active nodes. The following Segment Summary Area (SSA) provides information about which node owns which blocks. The first five blocks thus represent the metadata of the partition. The Main Area as the sixth region contains the actual data blocks with the files and directories.

Superblock

For the F2FS file system, the start of the logical partition is the Superblock. Fig. 3.6 identifies that there is superblock 0 and 1 that is in place as a redundancy in case there is a failure. Like other terms (inode, dentry, etc.) in this chapter, Superblock is based on Unix and not unique to F2FS. The Superblock (SB) [45]:

- is located at the beginning of the partitions.
- two copies exist, as redundancy for failure.
- includes basic partition information.
- includes several default parameters of F2FS.

The most important data fields of the Superblock are shown in Fig. 3.7. Like many binary formats, the Superblock starts with a Magic (Header). An example taken from a *Huawei P9* is given in Fig. 3.8. In this case, it is Hex 1020F5F2.

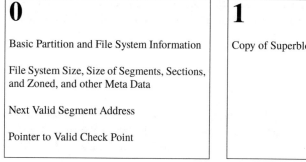
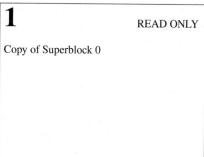

Fig. 3.7: F2FS Superblock the Starting Point and Backup Copy

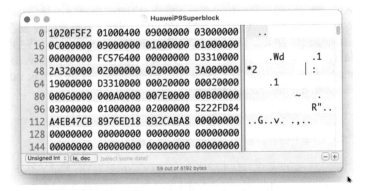

Fig. 3.8: Huawei P9 Extraction Showing the Start of a Superblock

Zone

A zone contains several sections for easier management. The default number of sections in a zone is 1, but there may be any number of sections in a zone. The purpose of zones is to separate into different parts of the device the six open sections in the device. Flash drives are often made from a number of sub-devices. Each sub-device can process Input/Output (IO) requests. These requests can be processed independently and hence processed in parallel. Therefore, the six open sections can process requests and write in parallel [8]. One of the issues with NAND Flash memory is writing to an erase block first. F2FS uses zones, and each zone has its own erase block.

Section and Segment

Fragmentation is an issue any file system wants to avoid. F2FS uses sections to organize and keep blocks together in segments. 512 blocks make up a segment (2MB). These segments contain such things as Checkpoint, Tables, and the Main Area.

Check Point (CP)

If you have used and installed Microsoft Windows, then you may have seen the term restore point before. The idea is you can have a restore point in case an application install goes wrong, or there is some other issue. F2FS also has a built-in feature to manage this called the Checkpoint. The Checkpoint also has NAT and SIT Journaling, which will be discussed in the Cleaning section (see 3.4.6).

0 LATEST STABLE VERSION	**1** LAST STABLE VERSION
File System Status	File System Status
BitMaps: Valid NAT & Valid SIT	BitMaps: Valid NAT & Valid SIT
Orphaned inode Lists	Orphaned inode Lists
Active Segments	Active Segments

Fig. 3.9: F2FS Checkpoint Current and Last Stable Versions

Segment Information Table (SIT)

The Segment Info Table (SIT) assists in identifying blocks that are in use "Valid" and those that are "Invalid" i.e. containing deleted data and may be cleaned. The SIT also tracks when a segment is empty of valid blocks and can be reassigned with live data.

Node Address Table (NAT)

The Node Address Table is for addressing the Main Area node blocks. The structure of the NAT contains the latest version, the inode number and the block address. There are three types of nodes: *inode*, *direct node*, and *indirect node*. Table 3.3 depicts the concept of the Node Address Table (NAT), which is used to read from the device. Each unique node is assigned a node ID (see sect. 3.4.1), which is recorded in the table, along with the physical on-disk location (block address).

Table 3.3: NAT Example Table

node ID	block address
0	addr0
. . .	addr. . .
, N	addrN

 Important

The term *inode* stands for *index node*. This forms the basic data structure for managing file systems with Unix-like operating systems. Each node is uniquely identified within a file system by its *inode number*. Each name entry in a directory refers to precisely one inode. This contains the file's metadata and refers to the data of the file or the file list of the directory.

Segment Summary Area (SSA)

Like the NAT, the Segment Summary Area (SSA) is concerned with the Main Area portion. The area deals with "Valid" Blocks of data in the Main Area. As was mentioned with the Log-Structured File System, when data can be removed, i.e. cleaned, this will probably cause fragmentation.

The valid blocks that may now be fragmented from each other can be copied and moved so they are all together. Speeding up the process to get to the data as it is all together and not spread across the drive in different locations.

"The Segment Summary Area (SSA) stores summary entries representing the owner information of all blocks in the Main area, such as parent inode number and its node/data offsets. The SSA entries identify parent node blocks before migrating valid blocks during cleaning" [45].

Updates to the SIT and NAT

When data is updated it is not until a new check point is created that the changes are made to the Node Address Table(NAT) and Segment Info Table (SIT). Until this occurs, the updated information is;

- held in memory.
- if only a few updates, they can be written into Segment Summary blocks.
- updated info is written into the Checkpoint block for when the checkpoint is created.

Shadow Copy

If you have been doing computer forensics, you are probably aware of, or at least heard, the term shadow copy or Volume Shadow Copy. This saves data by creating a snapshot as a safety net. F2FS does look for and use the last valid checkpoint. There are two Checkpoints. One is for identifying the most recent live or valid data. The second one is the shadow copy. Both the NAT and SIT also use shadow copies.

Main Area

The Main Area is where the blocks that contain file data are located. As F2FS uses different sections, it allows for the data (e.g. directory or file content) to be kept separate from the node (e.g. the indexing information) [8]. The six active logs in the Main Area are managed using the following temperature-based categorisations, which are based on several strategies (Fig 3.4, according to [45]):

Each block in the Main Area is 4KB, and each is allocated by its type: data or node. In the Main Area, there are three data blocks and three node blocks. Data blocks contain either a directory or user file data whereas a node block contains either an inode or indices of the data blocks. Data/node blocks cannot be stored in sections at the same time [45]. F2FS implements a search functionality i.e., a file *lookup operation* using the following set of steps outlined by [45], which assumes the file /dir/file. Fig. 3.10 and Table 3.5 identify the steps for the F2FS's lookup operation.

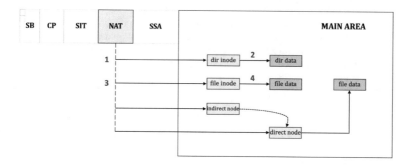

Fig. 3.10: F2FS File Lookup

Thus, we traverse through the file system tree with every file request. The starting point of our search is always Node Address Table.

3.4 File Structure of F2FS

3.4.1 Node Structure

File systems like the Log-Structured FS (LFS) use the index node (to identify the physical location of nodes), one large log, and updating direct and indirect nodes caused issues, such as the Wandering Tree (see sect. 3.2.3).

F2FS uses the Node Allocation Table (NAT) for finding the physical location of the nodes. The node blocks themselves have a Node ID. Following is a breakdown of the three types of node blocks, as recorded by The Linux Kernel Archives [89]:

Table 3.4: Temperature-based Categorisations of Main Area Blocks

Temperature	Node Block	Data Block
Hot	Direct node blocks of directories	Dentry blocks
Warm	Direct node blocks except those allocated as 'Hot'	Data blocks except those allocated as 'Hot' and 'Cold'
Cold	Indirect node blocks	Multimedia data or migrated data blocks

Table 3.5: F2FS File Lookup Operation

Step	Description
1	A block is read to obtain root inode. The block location is collected from the Node Address Table (NAT).
2	Searches for a directory entry- `dir`- inside the root inode block from the data blocks. The corresponding inode number for the directory is obtained.
3	The inode number is translated into a physical location. This location is obtained using the Node Address Table (NAT).
4	The inode named `dir` is collected by reading the corresponding block.
5	The directory entry named `file` is identified in the `dir` inode. The inode for file is translated into a physcial location and the corresponding block is read to obtain the inode of `file`. The data stored in the Main Area, and various indices from the corresponding file structure, can then be retrieved.

- **inode**: 4KB assigned to each inode block. Each comprises of 923 data block indices.
- **direct node**: There are two direct node pointers.
- **indirect node**: There are two indirect node pointers and one double indirect node pointer.

Whether it is a direct or indirect node: In both cases, these contain references to 1018 data blocks [89]. The NAT is used by F2FS to map all node blocks using translation. The pointer-based file indexing system, which uses both direct and indirect node blocks in addition to the Node Address Table, is considered to prevent the 'wandering tree' problem [45, 89]. Unlike traditional LFS design, F2FS avoids the problem by updating a single direct node block and its corresponding entry in the Node Address Table. This update process prevents the "the propagation of node updates caused by leaf data writes" [89]. This is dissimilar to the traditional LFS design where both direct and indirect pointer blocks are updated recursively and cause a snowball/chain (i.e. wandering tree) effect, which is inefficient [45]. The comparisons are documented in Table 3.6.

Table 3.6: Comparison of an Updated File Between LSFS and F2FS

Description	LSFS	F2FS
Data is Updated	Direct and Indirect pointer blocks are updated recursively.	Only updates one direct node block and its NAT entry.
If the file is larger than 4GB	Updates one more pointer block for a total of three.	Still updates only one.

The **Index Node (inode) Block** does not have the physical address for a file. Instead, it has the points to direct or indirect pointers with the node number. Fig. 3.11

demonstrates the structure of the inode block. The figure also depicts the use of several pointers in an inode block:

- direct pointers to the file's data blocks.
- two single indirect pointers.
- two double-indirect pointers.
- one triple-indirect pointer.

F2FS also reserves 200 bytes in an inode block to store extended attributes. If a file is very small, it can be saved directly in the inode. This procedure is also called in-lining. In this case, however, the file size must be less than 3,692 bytes. We can also inline extended attributes [45].

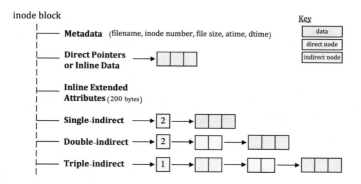

Fig. 3.11: Index Node (inode) Block

A **Direct Node Block** has the physical block address of the file and is updated when a file is updated. This Direct Node address is updated in the Node Address Table (NAT). When a file is updated, the **Indirect Node Block** is not, since it does not have the physical address. Instead, indirect node blocks hold identifiers (node IDs) that locate another node block, following the pointer-based structure.

3.4.2 File Creation and Management

File systems are different and use different ways of managing file locations. In FAT32, a file name is altered when deleted, replacing the first character with a hex $E5$ character. The filename itself is not part of the file but rather stored as a new directory entry. At which the front of a real Library, you go to the card to look up the book name or author. The card points you to where you will find the book. F2FS has directory entries also, and these are called *dentries*. Like the Library analogy and other file systems, the system has the file information, including the inode number.

Directory Structure

Directory Entry or *Dentry* keeps track of the index nodes (inodes) and occupies 11 bytes. A dentry contains a bitmap and two arrays of slots and names (see Fig. 3.12). A bitmap entry identifies if a slot is "Valid". Each slot includes the (1) hash value of the file name (1 byte), (2) inode number (4 bytes), (3) length of the file name (4 bytes) and (4) file type (directory, symlink, regular file . . . - 1 byte).

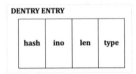

Fig. 3.12: F2FS Dentry Entry Structure

To manage a large volume of dentries and improve efficacy, multi-level hash tables are utilised by the F2FS file system. Each level has a hash table with a dedicated number of hash buckets. Several steps occur when F2FS looks up file names in a directory (see Table 3.7).

Table 3.7: F2FS Multi-level Hash Tables

Step	Description
1	Calculates the hash value of the file name.
2	Traverses the hash tables incrementally starting at level 0 until it reaches the maximum level which has been allocated and recorded in the inode.
3	Scans one bucket at each level (level 0 through to level N), resulting in an O(log(# of dentries)) complexity.
4	For speed and efficacy, F2FS compare the bitmap, hash value and file name to find a dentry.

In addition, for example, there is a requirement for larger directories in server environments. The F2FS file system can be configured in the first instance to allocate space for many dentries [45]. "With a larger hash table at low levels, F2FS reaches to a target dentry more quickly." [45] A bucket (see Fig. 3.13) consists of two or four dentry blocks.

Fig. 3.13: F2FS Bucket Structure

A dentry block consists of 214 dentry slots and file names. In order to determine whether a dentry is valid, a bitmap is used again. Due to the described properties, a dentry block is always exactly 4 KB in size. This value is determined as follows:

```
Dentry Block (4 K) =
bitmap (27 bytes) + reserved (3 bytes) +
dentries (11 * 214 bytes) + file name (8 * 214 bytes).
```

Fig. 3.14 depicts the structure of a dentry block. To clarify, deleted directories and entries can be recognised because they are marked as invalid in the bitmap. The dentry concerned is thus free and can be used otherwise.

Fig. 3.14: F2FS Dentry Block Structure

3.4.3 Fsck.f2fs Identifying Files

In Kali Linux, using Fsck.f2fs on the USB Flash Drive, we could see the folder and files that were not deleted. Note the inode identifiers in bold. Any deleted folder or deleted files are not displayed. You should start to see terms that you are now familiar with. In the example above, the file *pngpicture.png* was found with the inode id $0x6$. The Fsck.f2fs tool automatically scans for file system errors and corrects them [94]. The following listing shows an example of the output of the programme for a flash stick:

```
(ccurrier@kali)$ sudo fsck.f2fs -t /dev/sdb1
Info: [/dev/sdb1] Disk Model: Flash Disk
Info: Segments per section = 1
Info: Sections per zone = 1
Info: sector size = 512
Info: total sectors = 30717952 (14999 MB)
Info: MKFS version
  "Linux version 5.10.0-kali3-amd64 (devel@kali.org) (gcc-10 (Debian 10.2.1-6)
     10.2.1 20210110"
```

```
. . .
Info: superblock features = 0 :
Info: superblock encrypt level = 0, salt = 00000000000000000000000000000000
Info: total FS sectors = 30717952 (14999 MB)
Info: CKPT version = 373c4953
Info: Checked valid nat_bits in checkpoint
Info: checkpoint state = c5 :  nat_bits crc compacted_summary unmount
|-- folder <ino = 0x4>, <encrypted (0)>
|   |-- pngpicture.png <ino = 0x6>, <encrypted (0)>
|   '-- textstays <ino = 0xa>, <encrypted (0)>
|-- dump_sit <ino = 0x5>, <encrypted (0)>
[FSCK] Unreachable nat entries                          [Ok..]  [0x0]
[FSCK] SIT valid block bitmap checking                  [Ok..]
[FSCK] Hard link checking for regular file              [Ok..]  [0x0]
[FSCK] valid_block_count matching with CP               [Ok..]  [0xa0]
[FSCK] valid_node_count matching with CP (de lookup)    [Ok..]  [0x5]
[FSCK] valid_node_count matching with CP (nat lookup)   [Ok..]  [0x5]
[FSCK] valid_inode_count matched with CP                [Ok..]  [0x5]
[FSCK] free segment_count matched with CP               [Ok..]  [0x1d0f]
[FSCK] next block offset is free                        [Ok..]
[FSCK] fixing SIT types
[FSCK] other corrupted bugs                             [Ok..]
Done: 2.829615 secs
```

3.4.4 Metadata

The term metadata should be familiar to forensic examiners, usually referred to simply as data about data. Consider the properties of a file. In F2FS, three types of nodes are used that hold information about actual files.

There are index nodes referred to as inodes , direct nodes and indirect nodes. An inode consists of forensically important information, such as file size, allocated blocks, ownership (e.g., UID and GID) and Modified, Accessed and Changed (MAC) times [95]. These three timestamps are important and can tell us the following information when the file or directory is:

- Modified: updated when the file or directory is written.
- Accessed: updated when the file or directory is read.
- Changed: updated when the inode is modified.

The MAC-timestamps are all time specifications in *ms* (Unix epoch) and can easily be converted to a readable format with an appropriate converter. In the below *.png* file example, which we have already seen briefly in the last section, you can see some of the metadata for the file to include timestamps, file name, and file size.

```
[print_node_info: 353] Node ID [0x6:6] is inode
i_mode                  [0x     81a4 : 33188]
i_links                 [0x        1 : 1]
i_size                  [0x     3c41f : 246815]
i_blocks                [0x       3e : 62]
i_atime                 [0x606db122 : 1617801506]
i_atime_nsec            [0x24990b38 : 614009656]
i_ctime                 [0x606db114 : 1617801492]
i_ctime_nsec            [0x2bc016f9 : 734009081]
```

```
i_mtime              [0x606b7024 : 1617653796]
i_mtime_nsec         [0x ad1c7fa : 181520378]
i_generation         [0xd0856627 : 3498403367]
i_namelen            [0x      e : 14]
i_name               [pngpicture.png]
```

3.4.5 Multi-Head Logging

What is Multi-Head logging, and what does it have to do with Hot/Warm/Cold Data? The historical origin of the terms "hot" and "cold" goes back to the different data storage devices and their vibration. Hot data was located near the heat of spinning drives and CPUs, while cold data was stored on a tape or drive far from the data centre floor.

Wait, what is Hot/Warm/Cold Data? This involves the frequency of writes to the Main Area to both the Node and Data segments (see Fig.3.15). In the case of F2FS, the blocks that are updated particularly frequently are designated as warm. The direct blocks reference a block by its actual physical address on the disk. On the other hand, indirect blocks are assigned to the "cold" category. This is because they have only logical NodeID. This logical address must be adjusted or changed much less frequently during updates. Again, we distinguish between node blocks (containing linking and meta information) and data blocks (the actual data content). The Log-Structured File System uses a single log area, while F2FS splits this into six types of logs in the Main area split between node segments and data. Refer back to Table 3.4 for descriptions of Hot, Warm and Cold Node and Data Segments. See Table 3.8 for further descriptions.

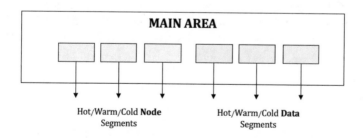

Fig. 3.15: Node and Data Segments in the Main Area [45]

In looking at F2FS resources, you will find benchmark testing that shows 2, 4, and 6 logs utilized for writing. You may be thinking of a standard log file, but this refers to multiple writing schemes. Six logs are the default value.

Table 3.8: Additional description of why Block Types are assigned a certain temperature [45]

Description	|LSFS|	F2FS
Direct Node Blocks	Hot	Updated frequently as they have the physical address.
Indirect Node Blocks	Cold	Has only the node number and are only created or updated when a dedicated node block is added or removed.
Directory Direct Node and Data Blocks	Hot	Different write patterns compared to blocks for regular files.
Data Blocks	Cold	Valid for extended period of time.

3.4.6 Cleaning

Deleted data is never meant to be stored permanently, no matter the operating system. This data that is once allocated goes unallocated. This data is available to be overwritten.

However, the F2FS file system allows the system to be cleaned. The idea behind this is performance. So that when data is deleted, the system can clean and defragment the live or valid data. Cleaning could be initiated by the user in the device settings, initiated due to a lack of free sections, or part of a regular background cleaning. The cleaning process is divided into three steps (see Table 3.9). First of all, the section to clean must be selected. Different selection strategies are used for this purpose. The selection of the target section is followed by identifying the invalid blocks. For this, the bitmap can inside the SIT is used. The cleanup process ends with the creation of a new checkpoint to free the blocks that have been released in the meantime for reallocation.

Adaptive Logging

You just read about the two, four, and six multi-head logging options to handle different types of data based on their frequency of writes. The Adaptive logging has to do with where the writes will occur and possibly involve the cleaning process in F2FS. The Log Structured File System used two logging features:

- Normal: Uses clean segments, and the data is written in order.
- Threaded: Looks for invalid data areas to write data to.

So F2FS is using a dynamic approach with Adaptive Logging. There are two strategies based on the presented circumstances. See Table 3.10 and the illustration (Fig. 3.16) below.

Table 3.9: Cleaning Process: Three Steps [45]

Step	Title	Description
1	Victim Selection	Identify a victim section among non-empty sections. Two policies: • Greedy Policy – foreground cleaning to minimize the latency visible to applications. Selecting section with the smallest number of valid blocks. Migrating valid blocks. • Cost Benefit Policy – Selects victim section not only on its utilization but also its "age"*.
2	Valid Block Identification & Migration	Victim selected. Need to identify valid blocks in the section quickly. A validity bitmap per segment is in the **SIT**. F2FS retrieves parent node blocks containing their indices from the **SSA** information. If the blocks are valid, F2FS migrates them to other free logs. For background cleaning, F2FS does not issue actual I/Os to migrate valid blocks. Instead, F2FS loads the blocks into page cache and marks them as dirty. Then, F2FS just leaves them in the page cache for the kernel worker thread to flush them to the storage later.**
3	Post-Cleaning Process	All valid blocks have been migrated. Victim selection registered as a new free section, an F2FS 'pre-free' section. Checkpointing occurs where the section is made a free section and it can be reallocated. This process is used to manage any loss of data referencing by checkpoints due to for example, unexpected power outages that may result in pre-free sections being reused before checkpointing.

As long as the data medium still has sufficient storage space, the append logging known from LSF is used. In this mode, only clean segments that are not yet occupied are written to. Remember: Sequential writes are always preferable to random writes in flash memory. In Threaded Logging mode, the whole thing is reversed. Now the remaining invalid blocks in dirty segments are collected, written. So now the remaining gaps are being used. F2FS automatically switches between the two modes depending on the remaining free memory. This is an attempt to achieve the best possible write performance.

Roll-Back Recovery

F2FS uses checkpoints to ensure integrity in the event of power failures or other disruptions. A Checkpoint uses not only the checkpoint but also both the Node Address Table (NAT) and the Segment Info Table (SIT). There is NAT and SIT journaling and bitmap addressing the valid NAT and SIT within the checkpoint.

Table 3.10: F2FS Adaptive Logging [45]

Title	Description
Append Logging	Writing to clean segments.
	Need cleaning operations if there is no free segment.
	Cleaning causes mostly random read and sequential writes.
	Node is always written with append logging policy.
Thread Logging	Lower than %5 of total sections by default.
	Writing to Dirty segments.
	Reuse invalid blocks in dirty segments. No need to clean.
	Cause random writes.
	F2FS gracefully gives up normal logging and turns to threaded logging for higher sustained performance.

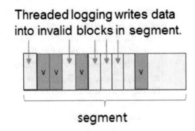

Threaded logging writes data into invalid blocks in segment.

segment

Fig. 3.16: Threaded Logging is tactical in going after invalid blocks in a segment

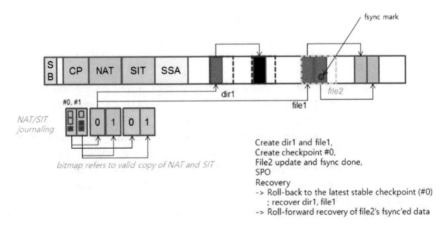

Fig. 3.17: F2FS Index Structure (Source: [46])

If there is a disruption of a power issue then F2FS can do a rollback recovery using the most recent valid Checkpoint (see Fig. 3.17). Earlier checkpoints were discussed, and F2FS has two to maintain a stable one. The header and footer identify the stable

Checkpoint is the same. There is also a version number if both checkpoint headers and footers match. In this instance, the file system will choose the most recent Checkpoint. F2FS does not always need to rely on the Checkpoint for recovery when *fsync()* is involved. F2FS focuses on the data blocks and direct node blocks (which are marked). The Roll-Forward Recovery Procedure consists of the following steps according to Lee et al. [45]:

1. Search marked Direct Node Blocks.
2. Per marked Node Block, identify old and new Data Blocks by checking the difference between the current and previous node block.
3. Update SIT: Invalidate old Data Blocks.
4. Replay new data writes; update NAT and SIT accordingly.
5. Create Checkpoint.

> **Important**

Under Linux/Unix, the C function *fsync()* from the standard library transfers changed buffered data from the working memory to the file on the physical device. The call blocks until the device have reported that the transfer is complete. Of course, the buffer should only be flushed occasionally to avoid stress for the hardware.

3.5 Forensic Analysis

The Flash-Friendly File System (F2FS) is made for removable media and used with some Android devices, or maybe changed over from another Android (Linux) based File System such as EXT. You will find plenty of videos on how to change the File System on an Android device and speed comparisons between F2FS and other file systems. In this section, we want to turn to how to read and acquire F2FS-formatted memory sticks or even SSDs. This section will talk about forensic analysis of the different F2FS formatted devices.

3.5.1 F2FS Sample Dataset

The examples discussed in this chapter with the associated binaries can be found at github.com under the following link: https://github.com/Xamnr/F2FS. For the examples, three different drives were analysed: 1) the memory of a Huawei P9, 2) the content of a USB memory stick, and 3) an SSD. All three volumes were formatted with F2FS. The volumes were filled with text documents, image and video files. Afterwards, some of the files were deleted. The first example comes up with a binary file of a HuaweiP9 Superblock <File:HuaweiP9Superblock> and Checkpoint <File:HuaweiP9Checkpoint.zip>.

Beyond this, for USB flash drive three extracts had been made:

1. BASE: Formatted F2FS
2. ADDED: Two Folders created. One folder and four test files created. 2 png files and 2 text files.
3. DELETED: 1 png (Moved) and 1 text file (copied). i png deleted and deleted test folder.

The second example contains a sample of a USB flash drive. A total of 2 folders and four files were added to the drive:

```
<ADDED EXTRACTION>
    |-- folder
    |-- Test
            |-- pngpicture.png
            |-- pngtodelete.png
            |-- textstays
            |-- texttodeletediconderoga
```

The third example contains the formerly added files, but this time some of them had been deleted:

```
<DELETED EXTRACTION>
    |-- folder
            |-- pngpicture.png <moved>
            |-- textstays <copied>

    deleted:
            |-- pngtodelete.png
            |-- textstays
            |-- texttodeletediconderoga
```

The example is completed by three dumps from the NAT, SIT and SSA region of the flash drive.

3.5.2 F2FS and Windows

The main issue for forensics as it relates to F2FS is that Microsoft Windows does not recognize F2FS formatted devices. Windows sees the USB Device itself but does not recognize the partition.

Fortunately, at least forensic tools should recognize the device (as shown below with MSAB's XRY) and be able to do extractions. Best practice is to use a write blocker for the media. Once the drive has been detected, the analysis process with XRY is quite straightforward.

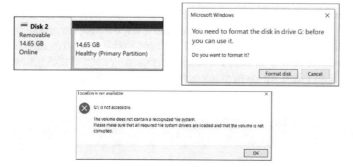

Fig. 3.18: F2FS formatted USB drive connected to a Microsoft Windows 10 computer

Fig. 3.19: MSAB's XRY 9.3 showing the Disk Connection Options

3.5.3 Data-Extraction with XRY

The first step is, of course, to establish a connection to the device and the storage medium. For Android devices it will depend on whether the mobile device is supported by model or by a generic one (see Fig. 3.19). Mobile Device support may not include all options such as Logical and Physical extraction, but rather only one. Remember Micro SD Cards inserted into the mobile device should be removed at some point and done separately.

The forensic tool(s) should be able to image the mobile device and/or the removable media without an issue. Since F2FS is made for Flash memory it could be found on Solid State Drives as well. After we have successfully read in the flash drive, the next step is to analyse the data it stores. For an example, we read the internal memory of a Huawei P9 that was formatted with F2FS. The actual extraction was carried out using the software XAMN. Fig. 3.20 shows the result for of our example drive. Obviously, in addition to some regular files, deleted file artefacts were also found during the scan process. The F2FS formatted Flash drive also had deleted files that were retrieved as well. Remember recovering deleted files relies on a lot of variables, but at least we know it is possible with the F2FS file system.

Fig. 3.20: MSAB's XAMN Showing that the extraction did decode data from the Huawei P9 cell phone Including deleted files

The header of the checkpoint area is initially less interesting from a forensic point of view (see Table 3.12). It only contains information about the number of available segments.

3.5.4 Superblock Examination

After successfully making a forensically sound copy of the medium to be examined, we can begin the actual analysis. Our investigation should also begin here since an F2FS partition starts with the Superblock(SB). In this region, important information about the structure of the rest of the file system can be found.

As examiners we commonly see the file system as raw data with our tools as seen in Fig. 3.21. Can we make sense of this data? In researching F2FS, a resource that describes the Superblock data structure was found [1]. This data was used to create Tables 3.11 and 3.12 for the Superblock and the Checkpoint, respectively[2].

---

[1] www.programmersought.com/article/49182049693/

[2] * Offset 3204+ Kernel Information and more: Linux version 5.10.0-kali3-amd64 (devel@kali.org) (gcc-10 (Debian 10.2.1-6) 10.2.1 20210110, GNU ld (GNU Binutils for Debian) 2.35.1) #1 SMP Debian 5.10.13-1kali1 (2021-02-08)

```
☑ Superblock Area
                                                                                  ...
Address        Hex                                                      ASCII
               00 01 02 03 04 05 06 07 08 09 10 11 12 13 14 15
..........0000 10 20 F5 F2 01 00 0E 00 09 00 00 00 03 00 00 00   ð ð|
..........0016 0C 00 00 00 09 00 00 00 01 00 00 00 01 00 00 00
..........0032 00 00 00 00 00 97 3A 00 00 00 00 00 15 1D 00 00          :
..........0048 4A 1D 00 00 02 00 00 00 02 00 00 00 22 00 00 00   J              "
..........0064 0F 00 00 00 15 1D 00 00 00 02 00 00 00 02 00 00
..........0080 00 06 00 00 00 0A 00 00 00 4E 00 00 00 6C 00 00              N     l
..........0096 03 00 00 00 01 00 00 00 02 00 00 00 AB 5C 97 4A           «\ J
..........0112 FA 45 4F 19 B0 6F DD 47 4C 22 C4 3E 00 00 00 00   úFO 'oÿGL "A>
..........0128 00 00 00 00 00 00 00 00 00 00 00 00 00 00 00 00
```

Fig. 3.21: Viewing the USB Flash Drive's F2FS Superblock with MSAB's XAMN

The Superblock (SB) provides us with important information about the structure of the partition and the exact location of NAT, SIT, SSA and MAIN area. The values given are to be understood as multiples of the block size. In our example, the SIT starts at block no. 1536. The correct address is obtained when we multiply this number by the block size. In our case, the SIT thus starts at byte 6,291,456 (1536*4096). The total size of the SIT can again be determined via the 4-byte value at offset 56. In our case, this is $hx02000000$. Since this is a little-endian (LE) value with the least significant bit on the far left, the size is 2. Incidentally, all other header fields are also LE values. The node ID of the root directory can also be determined in the superblock (offset 96).

If your forensic tool supports viewing the raw data then that is a start. Hopefully the tool has options to translate the code such as showing the bit options i.e. 16 or 32, Little or Big Endian, and others such as the GUID. If your tool does not have these options then you can use the HxD Hex Editor/Viewer with the Inspector feature. HxD can be found here mh-nexus.de/ or for English mh-nexus.de/en/.

❗ **Remember**

HxD is an editor, so work off of a copy of the file.

3.5.5 Examine NAT, SIT & SSA with Linux

Since F2FS was developed specifically for use with Linux or Android, it is obvious to conduct an investigation with this system as well. This section will show the forensic analysis of F2FS with open-source digital forensic tools if you are inclined to use Linux, i.e. Kali, Santoku, or another forensic type, and command line. Then you may

---

Source: www.programmersought.com/article/49182049693/
Source: www.programmersought.com/article/37962049663

Table 3.11: Super Block (USB Flash Drive) Example Values

Offset (decimal)	Bytes	Description	Hex	ASCII	Value	Format
0	4	Magic Number	10 20 F5 F2	10 20 F5 F2	1020F5F2	N/A
4	2	Major Version	01 00	..	1	In 16 LE)
6	2	Minor Version	0E 00	..	14	Int 16 LE
8	4	Log 2 Sector size in bytes	09 00 00 00	....	9	Int 32 LE
12	4	Log 2 Sectors per block	03 00 00 00	....	3	Int 32 LE
16	4	Log 2 Block Size in bytes	0C 00 00 00	....	12	Int 32 LE
16	4	Log 2 Block Size in bytes	0C 00 00 00	....	12	Int 32 LE
20	4	Log 2 Blocks per Segment	09 00 00 00	....	9	Int 32 LE
24	4	Segments per Sector	01 00 00 00	....	1	Int 32 LE
28	4	Sections per Zone	01 00 00 00	....	1	Int 32 LE
32	4	Checksum offset inside super block	00 00 00 00	....	0 Int 32 LE	
36	8	Total # of User Blocks	00 97 3A 00 00 00 00 00	.-:.....	3839744[3]	Int 64 LE
44	4	Total # of Sections	15 1D 00 00	....	7445	Int 32 LE
48	4	Total # of Segments	4A 1D 00 00	J...	7489	Int 32 LE
52	4	Segments for Checkpoint	02 00 00 00	....	2	Int32 LE
56	4	# of Segments for SIT	02 00 00 00	....	2	Int32 LE
60	4	# of Segments for NAT	22 00 00 00	"...	34	Int 32 LE
64	4	# of Segments for SSA	0F 00 00 00	....	15	Int 32 LE
68	4	# of Segments for Main	15 1D 00 00	....	7445	Int 32 LE
72	4	Start Block address of Segment 0	02 00 00 00	....	2	Int 32 LE
76	4	Start of block address for Checkpoint	00 02 00 00	....	512	Int 32 LE
80	4	Start block address of SIT	00 06 00 00	....	1536	Int 32 LE
84	4	Start block address of NAT	00 0A 00 00	....	2560	Int 32 LE
88	4	Start block address of SSA	00 4E 00 00	.N..	19968	Int 32 LE
92	4	Start block address Main	00 6C 00 00	.l..	27648	Int 32 LE
96	4	Root inode number	03 00 00 00	....	3	Int 32 LE

want to (write-protected, of course) gather additional system information about the removable media (USB Flash Drive in this case). You could mount the dd(bin) image as well. You will find F2FS Tools in the official Linux kernel GitHub repository [4]. Alternatively, you can install the necessary tools via package management. Under Ubuntu, for example, the following command can be used for this purpose:

```
# sudo apt-get install f2fs-tools
```

File system information can be dumped from the device using the F2FS Tools dump function. The primary interest is obtaining data from the NAT, SIT, and SSA. However, we can also use it to obtain a file if we want to. The dump.f2fs shows the on-disk inode information using the inode number and a dump of all SSA and SIT entries to file recognised by dump_ssa and sump_sit. On the web page of the

---

[4] http:// git.kernel.org/pub/scm/linux/kernel/git/jaegeuk/f2fs-tools.git

Table 3.12: Checkpoint (USB Flash Drive) Example Values

Offset (decimal)	Bytes	Description	Hex	ASCII	Value	Format
0	8	CP version for comparing old and new	41 49 3C 37 00 00 00 00	AI<7	926697793	Int 64 LE
8	8	# of User Blocks	00 3A 38 00 00 00 00 00	:8	3684864	Int 64 LE
16	8	# of Valid blocks in Main Area	42 00 00 00 00 00 00 00	B	66	Int 64 LE
24	4	# of Reserved segments for garbage cleaning (GC)	81 00 00 00	....	129	Int 32 LE
28	4	# of overprovision segments	F8 00 00 00	Ø	248	Int 32 LE
32	4	# of free segments in Main area	0F 1D 00 00	....	7439	Int 32 LE

Fig. 3.22: HxD with color coded selections of Superblock to match table data 3.11

the Linux Kernel Organisation [89] all options can be retrieved, with which the command can be executed (see Table 3.13).

Table 3.13: Usage: dump.f2fs command options

Command Option	Description
-d	debug level [default:0]
-i	inode no (hex)
-n	NAT dump nid from #1 #2 (decimal), for all 0 -1
-s	SIT dump segno from #1 #2 (decimal), for all 0 -1
-S	Sparse_mode
-a	SSA dump segno from #1 #2 (decimal), for all 0 -1
-b	Blk_addr (in 4 KB) Block Address
-V	Print the version number and exit

The tool can also be run without special parameters. In this way, information about the size of the disk and the sector size can be determined first of all. A typical output of the dump.f2fs command results without any options where /dev/sdb1 is the USB Flash Drive looks like this:

```
#sudo dump.f2fs /dev/sdb1
Info: [/dev/sdb1] Disk Model: Flash Disk
Info: Segments per section = 1
Info: Sections per zone = 1
Info: sector size = 512
Info: total sectors = 30717952 (14999 MB)
Info: MKFS version
"Linux version 5.10.0-kali3-amd64 ..."
...
Info: superblock features = 0 :
Info: superblock encrypt level = 0, salt = 0000000000000000000000000
Info: total FS sectors = 30717952 (14999 MB)
Info: CKPT version = 373c4953
Info: checkpoint state = c5 :  nat_bits crc compacted_summary unmount
Done: 0.177078 secs
```

Node Allocation Table (NAT) Data

In section 3.3.2 we have already learned about the task and function of the Node Allocation Table. With dump.f2fs we can output the contents of the table for our disk. The output of command sudo dump.f2fs -n 0~-1 /dev/sdb1 for our example is shown in Table 3.14. Remember: All the node blocks are mapped by NAT. Hence, the position of each node is translated by the NAT table. Apparently there are exactly 4 valid direct accounts on the device. In addition to the logical node ID, the block address is also specified. Since the default block size is 4 KB by default, we can thus determine the exact physical on-disk location of the node.

Table 3.14: Example for a Node Allocation Table (NAT)

nid: 3	ino: 3	offset:0	blkaddr: 27666	pack:1
nid: 4	ino: 4	offset:0	blkaddr: 27661	pack:1
nid: 6	ino: 6	offset:0	blkaddr: 28167	pack:1
nid: 10	ino: 10	offset:0	blkaddr: 28167	pack:1

Show the Segment Info Table (SIT) Data

The second important data structure besides the NAT is the Segment Information Table. The term segment here means a contiguous lump of disk blocks. Normally 512 continuous Blocks grouped into one segment. As already discussed in section XX, a segment is assigned a sector by default. For our example USB stick, the command would look like this: sudo dump.f2fs -s 0~-1 /dev/sdb1. The (shortened) output in this case looks like this:

```
segment_type(0:HD, 1:WD, 2:CD, 3:HN, 4:WN, 5:CN)

segno:0                 vblocks:2        seg_type:3        sit_pack:1
00   00   02   80   00   00   00   00   00   00   00   00   00   00   00   00
00   00   00   00   00   00   00   00   00   00   00   00   00   00   00   00
00   00   00   00   00   00   00   00   00   00   00   00   00   00   00   00
00   00   00   00   00   00   00   00   00   00   00   00   00   00   00   00
segno:1                 vblocks:3        seg_type:4        sit_pack:1
02   50   00   00   00   00   00   00   00   00   00   00   00   00   00   00
00   00   00   00   00   00   00   00   00   00 00   00   00   00   00   00
...
segno:7444              vblocks:0        seg_type:0        sit_pack:1

valid_blocks:[0xa0]        valid_segs:5 free_segs:7440
```

The result is a bitmap for valid blocks inside the different segments. The segment summary contains 512 entries, which is the 2MB segment size. A summary entry for a 4KB-sized block in a segment contains the. The first segment with number 0 seems to have 2 valid block. It is a hot data block with directory entries inside (seg_type=3). In contrast, the second segment contains Data blocks (seg_type=4). There are a total of 160($hxA0$) valid blocks on the F2FS partition that are stored in 5 valid segments.

Look inside the Segment Summary Area (SSA) Data

A look at the SSA allows us to find out who exactly owns each block. For example, to get an insight into the segment with the number 0, we can use the following command: sudo dump.f2fs -a 0~-1 /dev/sdb1

```
segno: 0, Current Node
[ 0: 3][ 1: 3][ 2: 4][ 3: 5][ 4: 5]
[ 5: 5][ 6: 5][ 7: 5][ 8: 4][ 9: 4]
[10: 5][11: 5][12: 4][13: 4][14: 5]
[15: 5][16: 3][17: 5][18: 3][19: 3]
[20: 4][21: 3][22: 4][23: 3][24: 3]
[25: 0][26: 0][27: 0][28: 0][29: 0]
...
```

As clearly seen, the blocks with the numbers 0 and 1 from segment no 0 both belong to the node with the node ID 3. The third block belongs to the node with the number 4 and so on.

Obtain a file by it's node ID

If you recall earlier the linux command sudo fsck.f2fs -t /dev/sdb1 obtained some data including the files and their node identifiers.

```
|-- folder <ino = 0x4>, <encrypted (0)>
|    |-- pngpicture.png <ino = 0x6>, <encrypted (0)>
|    '-- textstays <ino = 0xa>, <encrypted (0)>
```

In order to get the file, again we can to use the linux command line with the F2fs.dump command. Your forensic tools or even Linux should do this for you, but just to reinforce how this F2FS directory works with nodes you could use the command:

```
#sudo dump.f2fs -i 0x6 /dev/sdb1

Info: [/dev/sdb1] Disk Model: Flash Disk
Info: Segments per section = 1
Info: Sections per zone = 1
Info: sector size = 512
Info: total sectors = 30717952 (14999 MB)
...
[print_node_info: 353] Node ID [0x6:6] is inode
i_mode                     [0x    81a4 : 33188]
i_advise                   [0x       3 : 3]
i_uid                      [0x       0 : 0]
i_gid                      [0x       0 : 0]
i_links                    [0x       1 : 1]
i_size                     [0x    3c41f : 246815]
i_blocks                   [0x      3e : 62]
i_atime                    [0x606db122 : 1617801506]
i_atime_nsec               [0x24990b38 : 614009656]
i_ctime                    [0x606db114 : 1617801492]
i_ctime_nsec               [0x2bc016f9 : 734009081]
i_mtime                    [0x606b7024 : 1617653796]
i_mtime_nsec               [0x ad1c7fa : 181520378]
i_generation               [0xd0856627 : 3498403367]
i_current_depth            [0x       0 : 0]
i_xattr_nid                [0x       0 : 0]
i_flags                    [0x       0 : 0]
i_inline                   [0x       1 : 1]
i_pino                     [0x       4 : 4]
i_dir_level                [0x       0 : 0]
i_namelen                  [0x       e : 14]
i_name                     [pngpicture.png]
i_ext: fofs:0 blkaddr:ef400 len:3d
i_addr[0x0]                [0x   ef400 : 979968]
i_addr[0x1]                [0x   ef401 : 979969]
i_addr[0x2]                [0x   ef402 : 979970]
i_addr[0x3]                [0x   ef403 : 979971]
...
i_addr[0x3b]               [0x   ef43b : 980027]
i_addr[0x3c]               [0x   ef43c : 980028]
```

```
i_nid[0]                    [0x      0 : 0]
i_nid[1]                    [0x      0 : 0]
i_nid[2]                    [0x      0 : 0]
i_nid[3]                    [0x      0 : 0]
i_nid[4]                    [0x      0 : 0]

Do you want to dump this file to ./lost_found/? [Y/N] Y
Info: checkpoint state = c5 :
nat_bits crc compacted_summary unmount
Done: 3.409981 secs
```

We can thus query important meta-information about the file. In addition to file names (*pngpicture.png*) and size, the MAC timestamps are displayed. The number and concrete address of the blocks and the size of the file are printed out. The file occupies a total of 63 blocks. With a block size of 4096 bytes, this corresponds to 258.048 bytes. The actual size of the file is somewhat smaller, with 246.815 bytes.

3.5.6 Carving for artefacts with XAMN

XAMN is an intuitive tool that helps you find and analyse data faster and easier, we can even find a formerly deleted audio file (Fig. 3.23). For the file content search, all three samples of the dataset were first loaded for analysis with XAMN.

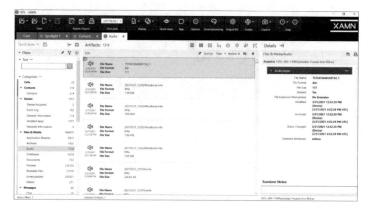

Fig. 3.23: MSAB's XAMN Spotlight showing a deleted audio file

First of all, it can be noted, that the program is able to detect F2FS partitions and their regions. Each region can be called individually and its content can be examined separately.

Looking at the screen capture on the left you should recognize the F2FS Areas. Or more importantly that you are dealing with a Flash-Friendly File System. Both the Superblock and Checkpoint Area are highlighted.

The files themselves and their meta information must be located in the Main Area of the disk. Accordingly , we checked to see if there were any references to the files added or deleted in the examples. A search for the PNG picture file name resulted in two hits (see Fig. 3.24). A simple search with a hex editor should give the same result. But also the names of the image data could be found (see Fig. 3.25). This appears to be the contents of the directory. In addition, a dot '.' and then two dots '..' are recognizable in the dump. Presumably these stand, as usual in Linux for the current directory or for the parent directory entry.

Fig. 3.24: MSAB's XAMN Elements showing the "pngpicture" search results

We are then able to find all four file names together in both the ADDED and DELETED extractions.

Even more, all three samples of the USB flash device could be successfully imported into XAMN. A look at the file tree shows that all file artefacts were found for the three scenarios (1..BASE,2..ADDED,3..DELETED). The correct directory structure could also be reconstructed. In addition to the regular files, the moved or deleted files are displayed as well (Fig. 3.26).

..00114325840	00	00	00	00	00	00	00	00	00	00	00	00	2E	00	00	00	.
..00114325856	00	00	00	00	2E	2E	00	00	00	00	00	00	70	6E	67	70	.. pngp
..00114325872	69	63	74	75	72	65	2E	70	6E	67	00	00	70	6E	67	74	icture.png pngt
..00114325888	6F	64	65	6C	65	74	65	2E	70	6E	67	00	74	65	78	74	odelete.png text
..00114325904	73	74	61	79	73	00	00	00	00	00	00	00	74	65	78	74	stays text
..00114325920	74	6F	64	65	6C	65	74	65	74	69	63	6F	6E	64	65	72	todeleteticonder
..00114325936	6F	67	61	00	00	00	00	00	00	00	00	00	00	00	00	00	oga
..00114325952	00	00	00	00	00	00	00	00	00	00	00	00	00	00	00	00	

Fig. 3.25: Found all four file names together in the extraction notice the ".." and "." Before the data

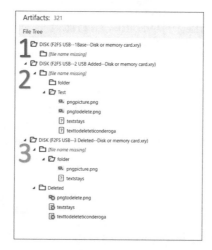

Fig. 3.26: File Tree showing the three USB Flash Drive Extractions

PNG File Signature Analysis

In the normal logging, blocks are written to clean unused segments. Thus there is a good chance that blocks occupied by a file are also written together on the volume. In our example, among other things, two .png image files were uploaded to the disk and then deleted again. This raises the question of whether we can recover the file contents using carving? We want to see and know about the ability to carve the PNG Files. Keep in mind the Cleaning ability of F2FS would most likely cause additional changes.

It is often assumed by laymen that once files have been deleted they cannot be recovered - neither in whole nor in part. This (careless) assumption is found especially often with respect to Unix. The possibilities of finding data fragments at different places of the file system or the hard disk can be used in an investigation. Often these individual fragments can be put together to a file with the method called file *Carving* or at least essential information can be extracted. In our example we want to search for the two image files in *png* format. Binary formats of image files often start with a magic number by which we can recognize the file. Referring to Gary Kessler's File Signature website: www.garykessler.net/library/file_sigs.html, a search for "PNG" resulted in the following hits (Trailer means the end of the file):

Table 3.15: PNG File Signature as shown from Gary Kessler's website

Description	Result
File Header (Hex)	89 50 4E 47 0D 0A 1A 0A
File Header (ASCII)	‰PNG...
File Description	Portable Network Graphics file
File Extension	PNG
File Trailer or Footer (Hex)	49 45 4E 44 AE 42 60 82
File Trailer or Footer (ASCII)	IEND®B'...

Knowing both the Header and footer gave us a few options. We decided to use a Global Regular Expression (GREP) to see if we could recover the complete file from file header to footer (or trailer). To verify the file header and footer is correct. We can look at the extraction and pick a PNG file and view the raw file data. As you can see below (see Fig. 3.27 and 3.28) both the header and the footer look good.

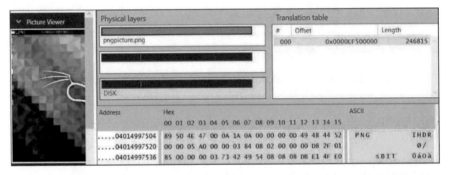

Fig. 3.27: MSAB's XAMN Source Mode showing the PNG File Header (Hex): 89 50 4E 47 0D 0A 1A 0A

Excellent, now we can carve for the deleted png pictures to see if we can find them. A search for file headers in both the Added data USB and the Deleted USB resulted in 101 png file header hits for both of them. Note the deleted png file carved below. The forensic Analysis Tool used below (see Fig. 3.30 and 3.31) was able to find the deleted files and present them.

A search for Test did reveal a hit with the word Folder and Test (the two folders on the USB Flash Drive). Note the red characters are showing that these are different by comparison with the other extraction or extractions.

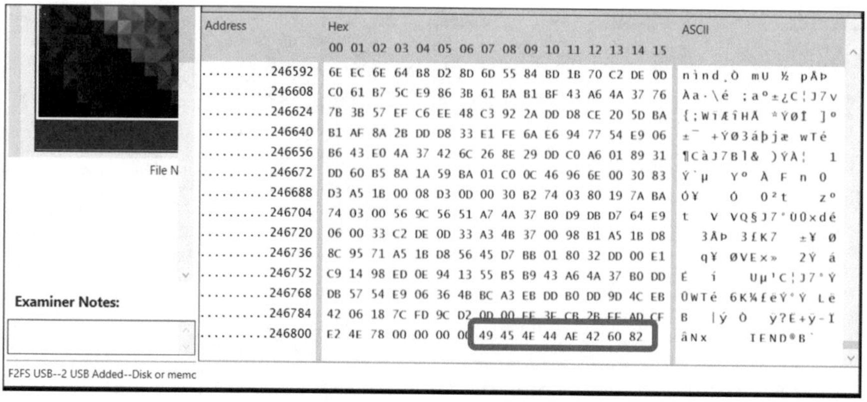

Fig. 3.28: MSAB's XAMN Source Mode showing the PNG File Footer (Hex): 49 45 4E 44 AE 42 60 82

Fig. 3.29: MSAB's XAMN Elements showing the PNG file header search and the deleted PNG File

3.5.7 Node Allocation Table (NAT) Comparisons

The changes made to samples 2 (ADDED) and 3 (DELETED) must also have led to a change in the Node Access Table (NAT). Blocks must have become invalid or new blocks must have been occupied on the data carrier as a result of deleting or moving files. For the examination with XAMN we must first open in the NAT area. Then we can compare the two areas with each other. The results are shown in Fig. 3.32 for the ADDED sample and in Fig. 3.33 for the DELETED sample. The only differences in the NAT area was found between the USB Flash Drive, with Data Added and when data was moved/deleted; these are shown in red.

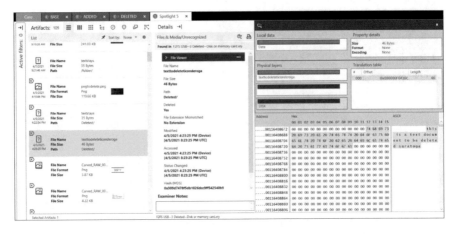

Fig. 3.30: MSAB's XAMN showing the Deleted Text File

Fig. 3.31: MSAB's XAMN showing the Deleted PNG File

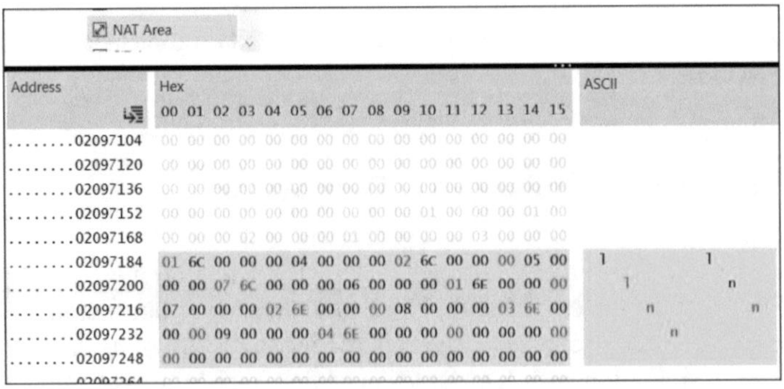

Fig. 3.32: USB Flash Drive NAT bytes in red are different when compared with the DELETED sample's NAT

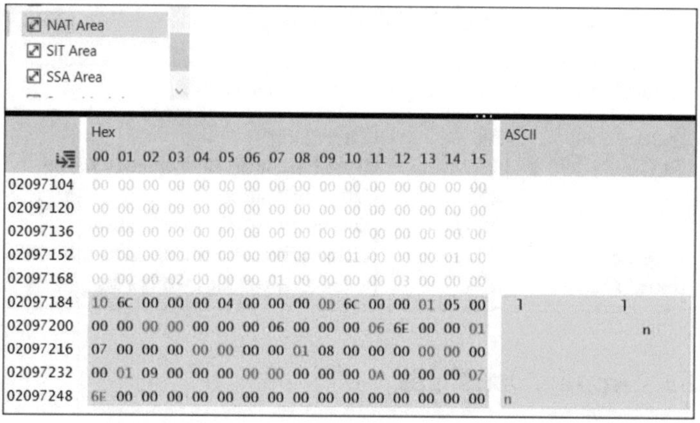

Fig. 3.33: USB Flash Drive NAT bytes in red are different when compared with the ADDED sample's NAT

Additional Data Structure

In addition to the works in this chapter, a F2FS forensic paper [96], in Chinese, was found and the following data structure tables (Table 3.16 and 3.17) are included as they may be deemed useful. For convenience a copy of the the original and the translated version using Google Translate (accuracy cannot be guaranteed) can be found here: http://github.com/Xamnr/F2FS.

Table 3.16: Common file metadata information data structure [96]

Intra-block Offset	Byte Length	Content Description
0x10	8	File size
0x20	24	Timestamp
0x5C	255	File name
0x168	3692	923 group index address
0x0FE8	20	File identification number id
0x0FEC	20	File node number ino

Table 3.17: Data structure of catalog file metadata information block [96]

Intra-block Offset	Byte Length	Content Description
0x20	24	Timestamp
0x58	4	Byte length of the directory name
0x5C	255	Directory name
0x168	3692	Directory subfile information
0x0FE8	20	Catalog file identification number nid
0x0FEC	20	Catalog file node number ino

3.6 F2FS - Application fields

One of the largest Android Manufacturers Samsung and the original creator of the Flash-Friendly File System (F2FS) is using F2FS in combination with UFS in some of their devices over using EXT, such as the Galaxy Note 10 and Galaxy Tab S6. Early on Motorola and Google used F2FS. Huawei and ZTE have also used F2FS on some of their devices.

An interesting, albeit dated article that is of interest entitled "Drone Forensic Analysis Using Open Source Forensic Analysis Using Open Source Tools" [94]. Drones use flash media, many have removable media, so it is not a surprise to see the connection. What is interesting is the mounting of the DD image to use the F2FS Tools. Working off a copy of the dd image would be advised. There are certainly a lot of developments in F2FS, including last year with Linux 5.11 and encryption.

3.7 Conclusion

The Flash-Friendly File System (F2FS) has been around for some time and as you can see still may be used. You have seen that it was specific for Flash memory and that this includes some mobile devices. With regards to the Android mobile devices the user may elect to use F2FS over EXT4 if that is an option. Forensic Tools should be able to handle the Flash-Friendly File System, so test them to be sure. The issue is will we find the data that has been deleted. As you saw recovering deleted files is a possibility, however, not a certainty as there are so many variables involved.

Acknowledgements Many thanks to Changman Lee, Dongho Sim, Joo-Young Hwang, and Sangyeun Cho, Samsung Electronics Co., Ltd. for their documentation and the 2015 USENIX Conference presentation by Joo-Young Hwang entitled: "F2FS: A New File System for Flash Storage" [45] and to Neil Brown for his 2012 article "An f2fs teardown" [8].

Chapter 4
QNX6

Conrad Meyer

Abstract The QNX6 filesystem is present in Smartphones delivered by Blackberry (e.g. Devices that are using Blackberry 10) and modern vehicle infotainment systems that use QNX as their operating system. In 2015 QNX as an OS was used in over 50 million vehicles [6] and can hence be considered as one of the most important operating systems in the automotive world. Today's digital forensics tools don't recover a lot from this filesystem, have difficulties with different block sizes, or even don't support the filesystem at all. So it's crucial for the forensic examiner to understand the principles of this filesystem used. This chapter gives an overview of how the filesystem generally stores the files and metadata to give the examiner the chance to get the most information out of the evidence.

4.1 Introduction

This chapter gives an insight into the different structures and principles of the QNX6 filesystem developed by QNX.The filesystem was first introduced within QNX Neutrino 6.4 real-time operating system, which today is owned and developed by Blackberry. It is a power-safe file system [7] and can withstand a sudden loss of power without corrupting or losing data. This property is especially useful for the forensic examiner, as it can easily happen that evidence (e.g. a vehicle or smartphone) loses its power supply due to a battery pack running empty.

Conrad Meyer

Central Office for Information Technology in the Security Sector (ZITiS), Zamdorfer Straße 88, Munich, Bavaria e-mail: conrad.meyer@zitis.bund.de

© The Author(s) 2022

C. Hummert, D. Pawlaszczyk (eds.), *Mobile Forensics – The File Format Handbook*, https://doi.org/10.1007/978-3-030-98467-0_4

Table 4.1: Standard Parameters of the QNX6 Filesystem

Parameter	Value	Remark
Max physical Size	2 TB 2	
Supported Standard Logical Blocksizes	512, 1024, 2048, 4096 Bytes	
Max Filename Length	510 bytes	UTF-8

Table 4.1 shows the standard values that are regularly used when formatting a volume with the QNX6 filesystem. Note, that especially in-car infotainment systems, those values can be different (e.g. larger blocksize). All the addressing inside the filesystem is based on the blocksize, extracted out of the superblock.

The following sections will give the reader an insight into the binary structures of the most important parts of the filesystem, like a superblock or inode and some basic knowledge about the mechanism when files are deleted.

4.2 QNX6 Filesystem Structure

To understand the principle behaviour and main functions of the QNX6 filesystem, the following chapter shows the structure of a volume and how files, directories and metadata are linked. Volumes can be formatted in QNX6 in little-endian or big-endian style. All the examples in the following show a QNX6 Volume formatted with little endianness. Fig. 4.1 shows the main parts of a QNX6 filesystem and their standard size and addresses. The system area contains the Bitmap of the allocated

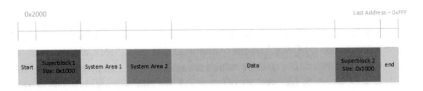

Fig. 4.1: Layout of a QNX6 filesystem volume

and unallocated Blocks of the Filesystem. Each bit represents a Block. Suppose the volume is formatted in the standard way. In that case, the volume will start with a volume boot record, which contains standard ASCII coded bootloader messages (Fig. 4.2), already giving a hint that the Volume is formatted with QNX.

! **Attention**

Sometimes, on non standard volumes a partition directly starts with the Superblock.

Offset	0	1	2	3	4	5	6	7	8	9	A	B	C	D	E	F	ANSI ASCII
00000000	EB	10	90	00	20	60	D2	00	10	00	00	00	D8	3F	06	00	ë `Ò ø?
00000010	00	80	FA	31	C0	8E	D0	BC	00	20	B8	C0	07	50	B8	36	€úlÀŽÐ¼ ¸À P¸6
00000020	01	50	CB	00	00	00	00	00	00	00	00	00	00	00	00	00	PË
00000030	00	00	66	90	00	00	00	00	00	00	00	00	8D	B4	00	00	f ´
00000040	10	00	00	00	00	00	00	00	00	00	00	00	00	00	00	00	
00000050	00	00	00	00	00	00	00	00	00	00	00	00	00	00	00	00	
00000060	FF	FF	00	00	00	93	00	00	FF	FF	00	00	00	93	00	00	ÿÿ " ÿÿ "
00000070	00	00	00	00	00	00	00	00	00	00	00	00	00	00	00	00	
00000080	00	00	00	00	00	00	00	00	00	00	00	00	00	00	00	00	
00000090	18	00	90	7C	00	00	00	00	FF	FF	00	00	00	9B	CF	00		ÿÿ ›Ï
000000A0	FF	FF	00	00	00	93	CF	00	0D	0A	51	4E	58	20	76	31	ÿÿ "Ï QNX v1
000000B0	2E	32	62	20	42	6F	6F	74	20	4C	6F	61	64	65	72	00	.2b Boot Loader
000000C0	0D	0A	55	6E	73	75	70	70	6F	72	74	65	64	20	42	49	Unsupported BI
000000D0	4F	53	00	0D	0A	52	41	4D	20	45	72	72	6F	72	00	0D	OS RAM Error
000000E0	0A	44	69	73	6B	20	52	65	61	64	20	45	72	72	6F	72	Disk Read Error
000000F0	00	0D	0A	4D	69	73	73	69	6E	67	20	4F	53	20	49	6D	Missing OS Im
00000100	61	67	65	00	0D	0A	49	6E	76	61	6C	69	64	20	4F	53	age Invalid OS
00000110	20	49	6D	61	67	65	00	0D	0A	55	6E	73	75	70	70	6F	Image Unsuppo
00000120	72	74	65	64	20	4D	75	6C	74	69	2D	42	6F	6F	74	00	rted Multi-Boot
00000130	3A	20	00	0D	0A	00	0E	1F	88	16	11	00	FB	FC	F6	06	: ˆ ûüö
00000140	03	00	02	74	03	E8	3F	00	F6	06	03	00	01	75	06	BE	t è? ö u ¾
00000150	A8	00	E8	3C	00	BB	AA	55	B4	41	CD	13	72	21	81	FB	¨ è< »ªU´AÍ r! û
00000160	55	AA	75	1B	F6	C1	01	74	16	B8	00	02	50	8E	C0	B8	Uªu öÁ t ¸ PŽÀ¸
00000170	00	02	50	66	31	C0	89	C7	BB	08	00	E8	40	00	CB	BE	Pf1À‰Ç» è@ Ë¾
00000180	C0	00	E8	0C	00	EB	53	B4	0F	CD	10	83	E0	7F	CD	10	À è ëS´ Í ƒà Í
00000190	C3	AC	08	C0	74	09	BB	07	00	B4	0E	CD	10	EB	F2	C3	Ã¬ Àt » ´ Í ëòÃ
000001A0	66	03	06	04	00	BE	40	00	89	5C	02	89	7C	04	8C	44	f ¾@ ‰\ ‰| ŒD
000001B0	06	66	89	44	08	8A	16	11	00	B4	42	CD	13	C3	56	E8	f‰D Š ´BÍ ÃVè
000001C0	DE	FF	72	02	5E	C3	BE	DF	00	E8	C5	FF	EB	0C	E8	CF	Þÿr ^Ã¾ß èÅÿë èÏ
000001D0	FF	73	06	F6	C4	10	75	EE	F9	C3	F4	EB	FD	00	00	00	ÿs öÄ uîùÃôëý
000001E0	00	00	00	00	00	00	00	00	00	00	00	00	00	00	00	00	
000001F0	00	00	00	00	00	00	00	00	00	00	00	00	00	00	55	AA	Uª

Fig. 4.2: Sector 0 of a QNX6 Partition/Volume

In the following, we will have a closer look at all the structures above. We will follow those structures to construct a file and its metadata out of the filesystem information. The example filesystem is in little-endian mode.

4.2.1 Superblock

The filesystem maintains two Superblocks or global root blocks. One of those blocks, called the working Superblock, manages the modified data, while the other one, the stable Superblock, consists of the original version of all the blocks. Which Superblock is the active one is determined by the 64-bit long serial number. The Superblock with the higher serial is the active one. After all, active write operations are done, and the integrity is checked, the former working superblock becomes the new stable one by updating the serial number (old superblock serial +1).

The superblock contains the global information of the filesystem. Table 4.2 contains the offset address of the main features of the Superblock.

Table 4.2: Main Features and their Offset in the QNX6 superblock

Parameter	Offset in Superblock	Size (bytes)
Serialnumber	0x8	8
creation timestamp	0x10	8
last access timestamp	0x14	8
Volume ID	0x20	16
Blocksize	0x30	4
Root Inode Inodes	0x48	array 16 x 4 bytes
Root Inode bitmap	0x98	array 16 x 4 bytes
Root Inode longfilenames	0xE8	array 16 x 4 bytes

! Attention

When used with the standard driver issued by Blackberry and the default settings, you can determine the last access to the filesystem by selecting the stable superblock (highest serial) and checking the access timestamp (assuming that system time is used was valid). However, some non-standard drivers don't touch this timestamp, so for reliable results, you have to test the drivers from the System where the image originated in each case!

The superblock contains three root inodes that point to the main parts of the filesystem. The first array root inode contains the pointers to the inodes that contain the data (files, directories, data). The second one contains the pointers to the bitmap of the allocated blocks, and the third one is the pointers to the long filenames (filenames > 27 utf8 characters, up to 510 characters). The data inside those root inodes is shown in Table 4.3. Those root inodes contain pointers to the corresponding filesystem parts. If the level parameter is zero, the root inode has 16 direct pointers. By adding another level, indirect pointers are added, as shown in Fig. 4.4. Each indirect pointer then points to a block containing inodes or indirect 32-bit pointers, depending on the defined number of levels. The actual data is always at the lowest level of the tree. Given the value of blocks that such a tree can address is 16 * (block size in bytes / 4) ^{level} So, for example, with a level value of 2, and a block size of 1024 bytes, already 1,048,576 blocks can be addressed.

```
Offset      0  1  2  3  4  5  6  7   8  9  A  B  C  D  E  F       ANSI ASCII
00002000   22 11 19 68 46 DA 79 9A  23 00 00 00 00 00 00 00    "  hFÚyš#
00002010   1E 00 00 00 43 94 6C 60  00 01 00 00 04 00 03 00       C"l`
00002020   94 08 BE 35 56 35 4F 2B  8C 24 B2 EB CB 2A 42 90    █ ¾5V5O+Œ$²ëË*B
00002030   00 10 00 00 00 19 00 00  A7 16 00 00 F8 C7 00 00        §   øÇ
00002040   7E 7F 00 00 01 00 00 00  00 80 0C 00 00 00 00 00    ~       €
00002050   CD 00 00 00 FF FF FF FF  FF FF FF FF FF FF FF FF    Í   ÿÿÿÿÿÿÿÿÿÿÿÿ
00002060   FF FF FF FF FF FF FF FF  FF FF FF FF FF FF FF FF    ÿÿÿÿÿÿÿÿÿÿÿÿÿÿÿÿ
00002070   FF FF FF FF FF FF FF FF  FF FF FF FF FF FF FF FF    ÿÿÿÿÿÿÿÿÿÿÿÿÿÿÿÿ
00002080   FF FF FF FF FF FF FF FF  FF FF FF FF FF FF FF FF    ÿÿÿÿÿÿÿÿÿÿÿÿÿÿÿÿ
00002090   01 01 00 00 00 00 00 00  FF 18 00 00 00 00 00 00           ÿ
000020A0   00 00 00 00 01 00 00 00  FF FF FF FF FF FF FF FF        ÿÿÿÿÿÿÿÿ
000020B0   FF FF FF FF FF FF FF FF  FF FF FF FF FF FF FF FF    ÿÿÿÿÿÿÿÿÿÿÿÿÿÿÿÿ
000020C0   FF FF FF FF FF FF FF FF  FF FF FF FF FF FF FF FF    ÿÿÿÿÿÿÿÿÿÿÿÿÿÿÿÿ
000020D0   FF FF FF FF FF FF FF FF  FF FF FF FF FF FF FF FF    ÿÿÿÿÿÿÿÿÿÿÿÿÿÿÿÿ
000020E0   00 01 00 00 00 00 00 00  00 B0 03 00 00 00 00 00        °
000020F0   73 7F 00 00 FF FF FF FF  FF FF FF FF FF FF FF FF    s   ÿÿÿÿÿÿÿÿÿÿÿÿ
00002100   FF FF FF FF FF FF FF FF  FF FF FF FF FF FF FF FF    ÿÿÿÿÿÿÿÿÿÿÿÿÿÿÿÿ
00002110   FF FF FF FF FF FF FF FF  FF FF FF FF FF FF FF FF    ÿÿÿÿÿÿÿÿÿÿÿÿÿÿÿÿ
00002120   FF FF FF FF FF FF FF FF  FF FF FF FF FF FF FF FF    ÿÿÿÿÿÿÿÿÿÿÿÿÿÿÿÿ
00002130   01 01 00 00 00 00 00 00  00 00 00 00 00 00 00 00
00002140   FF FF FF FF FF FF FF FF  FF FF FF FF FF FF FF FF    ÿÿÿÿÿÿÿÿÿÿÿÿÿÿÿÿ
00002150   FF FF FF FF FF FF FF FF  FF FF FF FF FF FF FF FF    ÿÿÿÿÿÿÿÿÿÿÿÿÿÿÿÿ
00002160   FF FF FF FF FF FF FF FF  FF FF FF FF FF FF FF FF    ÿÿÿÿÿÿÿÿÿÿÿÿÿÿÿÿ
00002170   FF FF FF FF FF FF FF FF  FF FF FF FF FF FF FF FF    ÿÿÿÿÿÿÿÿÿÿÿÿÿÿÿÿ
00002180   00 01 00 00 00 00 00 00  00 00 00 00 00 00 00 00
00002190   00 00 00 00 00 00 00 00  00 00 00 00 00 00 00 00
000021A0   00 00 00 00 00 00 00 00  00 00 00 00 00 00 00 00
000021B0   00 00 00 00 00 00 00 00  00 00 00 00 00 00 00 00
000021C0   00 00 00 00 00 00 00 00  00 00 00 00 00 00 00 00
000021D0   00 00 00 00 00 00 00 00  00 00 00 00 00 00 00 00
000021E0   00 00 00 00 00 00 00 00  00 00 00 00 00 00 00 00
000021F0   00 00 00 00 00 00 00 00  00 00 00 00 00 00 00 00
```

Offset	Title	Value	
2000	Magic	22 11 19 68	
2004	Checksum	46 DA 79 9A	
2008	Serial	23 00 00 00 00 00 00 00	
2010	CTime	01.01.1970	00:00:30
2014	ATime	06.04.2021	17:02:59
2018	Flags	00 01 00 00	
201C	Version1	04 00	
201E	Version2	03 00	
2020	VolumeId	94 08 BE 35 56 35 4F 2B 8C 24 B2 EB CB 2A 42 90	
2030	BlockSize	00 10 00 00	
2034	Number of INodes	00 19 00 00	
2038	Free INodes	A7 16 00 00	
203C	Number of Blocks	F8 C7 00 00	
2040	Free Blocks	7E 7F 00 00	
2044	Allocation groups	01 00 00 00	

Root Node

Offset	Title	Value
2048	size	00 80 0C 00 00 00 00 00
2050	Pointer	CD 00 00 00 FF FF FF FF FF FF FF FF FF FF FF FF FF FF FF FF FF FF FF FF FF FF FF FF FF FF FF FF
2090	Levels	01
2091	Mode	01
2092	Spare	00 00 00 00 00 00

Fig. 4.3: An example of a QNX6 superblock.

Table 4.3: Structure of the root inodes

Parameter	Offset in root inode	Size (bytes)
Size	0x0	8
Pointer	0x8	array 16 x 4 bytes
Levels	0x48	1
Mode	0x49	1

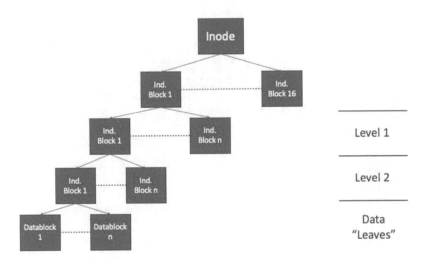

Fig. 4.4: Illustration of inode levels, here a level value of 3

4.2.2 Bitmap

The Bitmap block is used to determine whether a block in the filesystem is used or not. Each bit in the bitmap represents a block. A value of 0 means the Block is unused, 1 means that the Block is allocated. If the volume size is smaller than the bits available in the Bitmap Block, the unused bits are stuffed with ones. The bitmap incorporates two parts. First, system area 1 is split into two halves, where the upper half is used by superblock 1, and the lower half is used by superblock 2. This bitmap area contains the bitmap, inode and indirect addressing blocks of those structures. Second, the bitmap of the blocks that are not used for the filesystem structure (bitmap and inodes). The preallocation of the first system area block leads to the effect that each superblock always works on its own filesystem structure, and to the point that there is always a non-corrupted structure, even in the case of a sudden power loss (a superblock is just becoming the stable one, if all write operations are done, see sect. 4.2.1).

Fig. 4.5 depicts the end of the used space of the bitmap pointed to in the example superblock from Fig. 4.3. The bitmap comprises two blocks, starting at 0x3000, and the volume contains a total of 0xC7F8 blocks. In Fig 4.5, the stuffing of the unused space with ones therefore starts at 0x48FF: Bitmap starting address: 0x3000 + number of blocks 0xC8f8 divided by 8 (each Block represented by 1 bit).

Offset	0	1	2	3	4	5	6	7	8	9	A	B	C	D	E	F	ANSI ASCII
000037F0	00	00	00	00	00	00	00	00	00	00	00	00	00	00	00	00	
00003800	00	00	00	00	00	00	00	00	00	00	00	00	00	00	00	00	
00003810	00	00	00	00	00	00	00	00	00	00	00	00	00	00	00	00	
00003820	00	00	00	00	00	00	00	00	00	00	00	00	00	00	00	00	
00003830	00	00	00	00	00	00	00	00	00	00	00	00	00	00	00	00	
00003840	00	00	00	00	00	00	00	00	00	00	00	00	00	00	00	00	
00003850	00	00	00	00	00	00	00	00	00	00	00	00	00	00	00	00	
00003860	00	00	00	00	00	00	00	00	00	00	00	00	00	00	00	00	
00003870	00	00	00	00	00	00	00	00	00	00	00	00	00	00	00	00	
00003880	00	00	00	00	00	00	00	00	00	00	00	00	00	00	00	00	
00003890	00	00	00	00	00	00	00	00	00	00	00	00	00	00	00	00	
000038A0	00	00	00	00	00	00	00	00	00	00	00	00	00	00	00	00	
000038B0	00	00	00	00	00	00	00	00	00	00	00	00	00	00	00	00	
000038C0	00	00	00	00	00	00	00	00	00	00	00	00	00	00	00	00	
000038D0	00	00	00	00	00	00	00	00	00	00	00	00	00	00	00	00	
000038E0	00	00	00	00	00	00	00	00	00	00	00	00	00	00	00	00	
000038F0	00	00	00	00	F0	FF	FF	FF	FF	FF	FF	FF	FF	FF	FF	FF	ðÿÿÿÿÿÿÿÿÿÿÿ
00003900	FF	FF	FF	FF	FF	FF	FF	FF	FF	FF	FF	FF	FF	FF	FF	FF	ÿÿÿÿÿÿÿÿÿÿÿÿÿÿÿÿ
00003910	FF	FF	FF	FF	FF	FF	FF	FF	FF	FF	FF	FF	FF	FF	FF	FF	ÿÿÿÿÿÿÿÿÿÿÿÿÿÿÿÿ
00003920	FF	FF	FF	FF	FF	FF	FF	FF	FF	FF	FF	FF	FF	FF	FF	FF	ÿÿÿÿÿÿÿÿÿÿÿÿÿÿÿÿ
00003930	FF	FF	FF	FF	FF	FF	FF	FF	FF	FF	FF	FF	FF	FF	FF	FF	ÿÿÿÿÿÿÿÿÿÿÿÿÿÿÿÿ
00003940	FF	FF	FF	FF	FF	FF	FF	FF	FF	FF	FF	FF	FF	FF	FF	FF	ÿÿÿÿÿÿÿÿÿÿÿÿÿÿÿÿ
00003950	FF	FF	FF	FF	FF	FF	FF	FF	FF	FF	FF	FF	FF	FF	FF	FF	ÿÿÿÿÿÿÿÿÿÿÿÿÿÿÿÿ
00003960	FF	FF	FF	FF	FF	FF	FF	FF	FF	FF	FF	FF	FF	FF	FF	FF	ÿÿÿÿÿÿÿÿÿÿÿÿÿÿÿÿ
00003970	FF	FF	FF	FF	FF	FF	FF	FF	FF	FF	FF	FF	FF	FF	FF	FF	ÿÿÿÿÿÿÿÿÿÿÿÿÿÿÿÿ
00003980	FF	FF	FF	FF	FF	FF	FF	FF	FF	FF	FF	FF	FF	FF	FF	FF	ÿÿÿÿÿÿÿÿÿÿÿÿÿÿÿÿ
00003990	FF	FF	FF	FF	FF	FF	FF	FF	FF	FF	FF	FF	FF	FF	FF	FF	ÿÿÿÿÿÿÿÿÿÿÿÿÿÿÿÿ
000039A0	FF	FF	FF	FF	FF	FF	FF	FF	FF	FF	FF	FF	FF	FF	FF	FF	ÿÿÿÿÿÿÿÿÿÿÿÿÿÿÿÿ

Fig. 4.5: An example of a QNX6 Bitmap

4.2.3 Inode

On the lowest level of the root inode tree, in the "leaves", the direct inode data is found. Depending on the level defined, also those inodes can address other indirect inode addressing blocks. An inode contains a vast amount of data useful for the forensic examiner, e.g. permissions, access time, change time, and modification time. Table 4.4 shows the offsets and the size of the various parameters in an inode.

Table 4.4: Structure of an inode

Parameter	Offset	Size (bytes)
size	0x0	8
uid	0x8	4
gid	0xC	4
ftime	0x10	4
mtime	0x14	4
atime	0x18	4
ctime	0x1C	4
mode	0x20	2
blockpointer	0x24	array 16 x 4 bytes
Levels	0x54	1
status	0x49	1 (see table 4.5)

Table 4.5: inode status byte

Value	Status
0x1	directory
0x2	deleted
0x3	normal

As QNX OS is in line with the POSIX standards; also the timestamps are. The epoch is the standard POSIX (or UNIX) epoch, the 01.01.1970, 00:00 UTC. From that epoch, the timestamps are counted in seconds. The modified timestamp (mtime) is the time of the last write operation on this specific file. The access timestamp (atime) tells the examiner the time the file was last read. The change timestamp (ctime) is changed when the permissions of a file are changed. So ctime can be changed without a change in atime. The timestamp ftime is not fully referenced in the POSIX standard. Like in many other filesystems, it is the timestamp when the file was created. The inode 1 always contains the root directory, and inode counting starts with 1.

! Attention

When it comes to timestamps, the forensic expert has to pay attention to the reliability of the timestamps given. This is especially true for QNX6. Not all timestamps are actualised on some systems, as with QNX with the standard QNX6 file-system driver. Whenever possible, tests with the system you are examining should be performed (e.g. changing permissions, modifying files, etc.)!

Offset	0 1 2 3 4 5 6 7	8 9 A B C D E F	ANSI ASCII
00006360	FF FF FF FF 00 03 00 00	00 00 00 00 00 00 00 00	ÿÿÿÿ
00006370	00 00 00 00 00 00 00 00	00 00 00 00 00 00 00 00	
00006380	00 10 00 00 00 00 00 00	00 00 00 00 00 00 00 00	
00006390	F8 03 00 00 4D 93 6C 60	13 94 6C 60 4D 93 6C 60	ø M"l`  "l`M"l`
000063A0	ED 41 03 00 72 7F 00 00	FF FF FF FF FF FF FF FF	íA r ÿÿÿÿÿÿÿÿ
000063B0	FF FF FF FF FF FF FF FF	FF FF FF FF FF FF FF FF	ÿÿÿÿÿÿÿÿÿÿÿÿÿÿÿÿ
000063C0	FF FF FF FF FF FF FF FF	FF FF FF FF FF FF FF FF	ÿÿÿÿÿÿÿÿÿÿÿÿÿÿÿÿ
000063D0	FF FF FF FF FF FF FF FF	FF FF FF FF FF FF FF FF	ÿÿÿÿÿÿÿÿÿÿÿÿÿÿÿÿ
000063E0	FF FF FF FF 00 03 00 00	00 00 00 00 00 00 00 00	ÿÿÿÿ
000063F0	00 00 00 00 00 00 00 00	00 00 00 00 00 00 00 00	
00006400	00 10 00 00 00 00 00 00	00 00 00 00 00 00 00 00	

Offset	Title	Value	
6360	Size	00 10 00 00 00 00 00 00	
6368	Uid	00 00 00 00	
636C	Gid	00 00 00 00	
6390	File time	01.01.1970	00:16:56
6394	Mod time	06.04.2021	16:58:53
6398	Access time	06.04.2021	17:02:11
639C	Change time	06.04.2021	16:58:53
63A0	Mode	ED 41	
63A2	ExtMode	03 00	

Blockptr

Offset	Title	Value
63A4	BlockPtr 0	72 7F 00 00
63A8	BlockPtr 1	FF FF FF FF
63AC	BlockPtr 2	FF FF FF FF
63B0	BlockPtr 3	FF FF FF FF
63B4	BlockPtr 4	FF FF FF FF
63B8	BlockPtr 5	FF FF FF FF
63BC	BlockPtr 6	FF FF FF FF
63C0	BlockPtr 7	FF FF FF FF
63C4	BlockPtr 8	FF FF FF FF
63C8	BlockPtr 9	FF FF FF FF
63CC	BlockPtr 10	FF FF FF FF
63D0	BlockPtr 11	FF FF FF FF
63D4	BlockPtr 12	FF FF FF FF
63D8	BlockPtr 13	FF FF FF FF
63DC	BlockPtr 14	FF FF FF FF
63E0	BlockPtr 15	FF FF FF FF

Offset	Title	Value
63E4	File levels	00
63E5	Status	03
63E6	Unkown	00 00
63E8	Zero	00 00 00 00 00 00 00 00 00 00 00 00 00 00 00 00 00 00 00 00 00 00 00 00

Fig. 4.6: An example of a QNX6 Inode.

4.2.4 Directories

Inodes with the status 0x3 point to a directory file system object that contains sub-directories and file entries with names shorter than 27 UTF-8 characters. An entry starts with the inode number of that entry, where you can find the metadata like timestamps and the pointers to the Data or other directories, followed by a name length field and the actual name. A directory always contains a "." and a ".." entry. The "." entry contains the inode number of the directory inode, and the ".." entry contains the inode number of the parent directory inode. In the example Fig. 4.7, those entries are both pointing to the same inode number because the directory shown is the root directory.

Table 4.6: Directory entry

Parameter	Offset	Size (bytes)
Inode number	0x0	4
Namelength	0x4	1
Name	0x5	up to 27

```
 Offset    0  1  2  3  4  5  6  7    8  9  A  B  C  D  E  F        ANSI ASCII
07F12FD0  00 00 00 00 00 00 00 00   00 00 00 00 00 00 00 00
07F12FE0  00 00 00 00 00 00 00 00   00 00 00 00 00 00 00 00
07F12FF0  00 00 00 00 00 00 00 00   00 00 00 00 00 00 00 00
07F13000  01 00 00 00 01 2E 00 00   00 00 00 00 00 00 00 00     .
07F13010  00 00 00 00 00 00 00 00   00 00 00 00 00 00 00 00
07F13020  01 00 00 00 02 2E 2E 00   00 00 00 00 00 00 00 00     ..
07F13030  00 00 00 00 00 00 00 00   00 00 00 00 00 00 00 00
07F13040  02 00 00 00 05 2E 62 6F   6F 74 00 00 00 00 00 00     .boot
07F13050  00 00 00 00 00 00 00 00   00 00 00 00 00 00 00 00
07F13060  03 00 00 00 03 62 69 6E   00 00 00 00 00 00 00 00     bin
07F13070  00 00 00 00 00 00 00 00   00 00 00 00 00 00 00 00
07F13080  04 00 00 00 03 65 74 63   00 00 00 00 00 00 00 00     etc
07F13090  00 00 00 00 00 00 00 00   00 00 00 00 00 00 00 00
07F130A0  05 00 00 00 04 69 6E 66   6F 00 00 00 00 00 00 00     info
07F130B0  00 00 00 00 00 00 00 00   00 00 00 00 00 00 00 00
07F130C0  06 00 00 00 03 6C 69 62   00 00 00 00 00 00 00 00     lib
07F130D0  00 00 00 00 00 00 00 00   00 00 00 00 00 00 00 00
07F130E0  07 00 00 00 03 6F 70 74   00 00 00 00 00 00 00 00     opt
07F130F0  00 00 00 00 00 00 00 00   00 00 00 00 00 00 00 00
07F13100  08 00 00 00 03 75 73 72   00 00 00 00 00 00 00 00     usr
07F13110  00 00 00 00 00 00 00 00   00 00 00 00 00 00 00 00
07F13120  1C 00 00 00 08 66 6C 61   73 68 2E 73 68 00 00 00     flash.sh
07F13130  00 00 00 00 00 00 00 00   00 00 00 00 00 00 00 00
07F13140  1D 00 00 00 13 66 6F 72   6D 61 74 41 70 70 43 68     formatAppCh
07F13150  6B 50 65 72 73 2E 73 68   00 00 00 00 00 00 00 00   kPers.sh
07F13160  1E 00 00 00 0E 66 6F 72   6D 61 74 42 6F 6C 6F 31     formatBolo1
07F13170  2E 73 68 00 00 00 00 00   00 00 00 00 00 00 00 00   .sh
07F13180  21 00 00 00 0E 66 6F 72   6D 61 74 42 6F 6C 6F 32   !   formatBolo2
07F13190  2E 73 68 00 00 00 00 00   00 00 00 00 00 00 00 00   .sh
07F131A0  00 00 00 00 00 00 00 00   00 00 00 00 00 00 00 00
```

Fig. 4.7: An example of a QNX6 directory. Here, the root directory is shown.

A long directory entry has a different structure (Table 4.7). It includes the Inode, in which the timestamps and pointers to the data are. Furthermore, the long filenames inode Number, where the entry's name is found, is noted in this structure. An example of a long filename/directory entry is displayed in Fig. 4.8.

Table 4.7: Long Directory entry

Parameter	Offset	Size (bytes)
Inode number	0x0	4
size	0x4	1
Long Filenames Inode Number	0x8	4
checksum	0x12	checksum

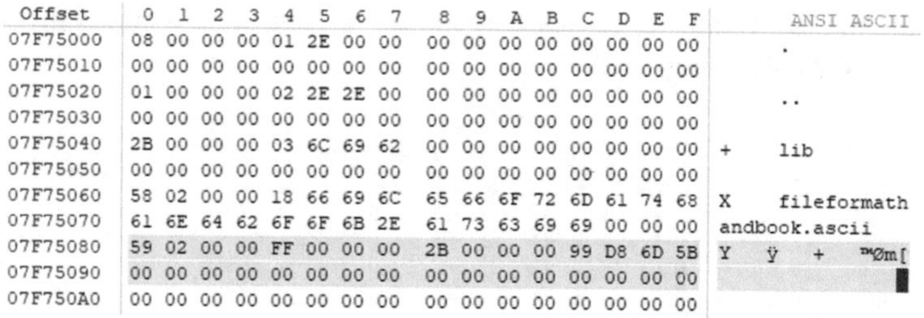

```
Offset    0  1  2  3  4  5  6  7   8  9  A  B  C  D  E  F    ANSI ASCII
07F75000  08 00 00 00 01 2E 00 00  00 00 00 00 00 00 00 00   .
07F75010  00 00 00 00 00 00 00 00  00 00 00 00 00 00 00 00
07F75020  01 00 00 00 02 2E 2E 00  00 00 00 00 00 00 00 00   ..
07F75030  00 00 00 00 00 00 00 00  00 00 00 00 00 00 00 00
07F75040  2B 00 00 00 03 6C 69 62  00 00 00 00 00 00 00 00   +   lib
07F75050  00 00 00 00 00 00 00 00  00 00 00 00 00 00 00 00
07F75060  58 02 00 00 18 66 69 6C  65 66 6F 72 6D 61 74 68   X   fileformath
07F75070  61 6E 64 62 6F 6F 6B 2E  61 73 63 69 69 00 00 00   andbook.ascii
07F75080  59 02 00 00 FF 00 00 00  2B 00 00 00 99 D8 6D 5B   Y  ÿ   +   ™Øm[
07F75090  00 00 00 00 00 00 00 00  00 00 00 00 00 00 00 00
07F750A0  00 00 00 00 00 00 00 00  00 00 00 00 00 00 00 00
```

Fig. 4.8: An example of a QNX6 inode entry of a long filename

4.2.5 Long Filenames Inode

If a file or directories length is longer than 27 UTF-8 characters, the name is stored in the long filenames node. Long filenames Inodes start counting with zero. The structure is shown in Table 4.8, an example is Fig. 4.9.

Table 4.8: Long Filenames Inode

Parameter	Offset	Size (bytes)
filename length	0x0	2
filename	0x2	up to 510 bytes

4.3 Example: Construction of a file

To understand how a file can be retrieved from the filesystem data, we will manually find the file /usr/fileformathandbook.ascii with its content and metadata by using the

Offset	0	1	2	3	4	5	6	7	8	9	A	B	C	D	E	F	ANSI ASCII
03221000	24	00	66	69	6C	65	66	6F	72	6D	61	74	68	61	6E	64	$ fileformathand
03221010	62	6F	6F	6B	76	65	72	79	6C	6F	6E	67	6E	61	6D	65	bookverylongname
03221020	2E	61	73	63	69	69	00	00	00	00	00	00	00	00	00	00	.ascii
03221030	00	00	00	00	00	00	00	00	00	00	00	00	00	00	00	00	

Fig. 4.9: An example QNX6 long filenames entry

filesystem information. We will begin the reconstruction from the root directory. As already mentioned in the previous chapter, inode 1 contains the root directory. From there, we will start finding the file in the filesystem structure. The first step is to determine the valid stable superblock by the serial number. The superblocks inode root block is shown in Fig. 4.10

Offset	0	1	2	3	4	5	6	7	8	9	A	B	C	D	E	F	ANSI ASCII
00002000	22	11	19	68	46	DA	79	9A	23	00	00	00	00	00	00	00	" hFÚyš#
00002010	1E	00	00	00	43	94	6C	60	00	01	00	00	04	00	03	00	C"l`
00002020	94	08	BE	35	56	35	4F	2B	8C	24	B2	EB	CB	2A	42	90	" ¾5V5O+Œ$²ëË*B
00002030	00	10	00	00	00	19	00	00	A7	16	00	00	F8	C7	00	00	§ øÇ
00002040	7E	7F	00	00	01	00	00	00	00	80	0C	00	00	00	00	00	~ €
00002050	CD	00	00	00	FF	FF	FF	FF	FF	FF	FF	FF	FF	FF	FF	FF	Í ÿÿÿÿÿÿÿÿÿÿÿÿ
00002060	FF	FF	FF	FF	FF	FF	FF	FF	FF	FF	FF	FF	FF	FF	FF	FF	ÿÿÿÿÿÿÿÿÿÿÿÿÿÿÿÿ
00002070	FF	FF	FF	FF	FF	FF	FF	FF	FF	FF	FF	FF	FF	FF	FF	FF	ÿÿÿÿÿÿÿÿÿÿÿÿÿÿÿÿ
00002080	FF	FF	FF	FF	FF	FF	FF	FF	FF	FF	FF	FF	FF	FF	FF	FF	ÿÿÿÿÿÿÿÿÿÿÿÿÿÿÿÿ
00002090	01	01	00	00	00	00	00	00	FF	18	00	00	00	00	00	00	ÿ

Fig. 4.10: Inode Root block used in the file reconstruction example

The root block tree has one level, meaning that we go on with the indirect inode block in the next step. The formula can easily calculate the physical address of those blocks:

$$blockaddress = blocknumber * blocksize + offset$$

On standard QNX6 Volumes, the offset is the superblock size + the offset of the beginning of the superblock. Thus, the first indirect inode block is located at 0xCD * 0x1000 + 0x3000 = 0xD0000, where 0xCD is the block number, 0x1000 the blocksize and 0x3000 the global offset due to the superblock with size 0x1000 and start at 0x2000. From the indirect inode (Fig. 4.11), we can retrieve the number 0x03, and by this, the address of the first inode block, which is located at 0x6000.

The first inode in this block is the root inode. If we take the first block pointer, 0x7F10, of this inode, we get the address of the root directory: 0x7F13000. This root directory, Fig. 4.13 is already familiar to us, as the second version of it is shown in Fig. 4.7, but this time, it is the root directory maintained by the first superblock.

In the root directory, we take the inode number for the /usr directory, 0x08. With this number, we go back to the first Inode Block, where the inode 8 is located at 0x6380 (0x6000, where inode 1 is located plus 7 * 0x80 offset, for the preceding inodes). From that inode (Fig. 4.14) we can then calculate the /usr directory offset in the way we already did for the root directory. The /usr directory is defined at block 0x7F72

```
Offset     0  1  2  3  4  5  6  7   8  9  A  B  C  D  E  F    ANSI ASCII
000D0000  03 00 00 00 CF 00 00 00  D0 00 00 00 D1 00 00 00        Ï     Ð     Ñ
000D0010  D2 00 00 00 D3 00 00 00  D4 00 00 00 D5 00 00 00     Ò    Ó    Ô    Õ
000D0020  0B 00 00 00 D7 00 00 00  0D 00 00 00 0E 00 00 00          ×
000D0030  DA 00 00 00 DB 00 00 00  DC 00 00 00 DD 00 00 00     Ú    Û    Ü    Ý
000D0040  13 00 00 00 DF 00 00 00  E0 00 00 00 16 00 00 00          ß    à
000D0050  17 00 00 00 18 00 00 00  19 00 00 00 1A 00 00 00
000D0060  1B 00 00 00 1C 00 00 00  1D 00 00 00 1E 00 00 00
```

Fig. 4.11: Indirect inode block

```
Offset     0  1  2  3  4  5  6  7   8  9  A  B  C  D  E  F    ANSI ASCII
00006000  00 10 00 00 00 00 00 00  00 00 00 00 00 00 00 00
00006010  1E 00 00 00 CC 43 6D 38  10 94 6C 60 0C 44 6D 38    ÌCm8 "l` Dm8
00006020  FD 41 09 00 10 7F 00 00  FF FF FF FF FF FF FF FF    ýA      ÿÿÿÿÿÿÿÿ
00006030  FF FF FF FF FF FF FF FF  FF FF FF FF FF FF FF FF    ÿÿÿÿÿÿÿÿÿÿÿÿÿÿÿÿ
00006040  FF FF FF FF FF FF FF FF  FF FF FF FF FF FF FF FF    ÿÿÿÿÿÿÿÿÿÿÿÿÿÿÿÿ
00006050  FF FF FF FF FF FF FF FF  FF FF FF FF FF FF FF FF    ÿÿÿÿÿÿÿÿÿÿÿÿÿÿÿÿ
00006060  FF FF FF FF 00 01 00 00  00 00 00 00 00 00 00 00    ÿÿÿÿ
00006070  00 00 00 00 00 00 00 00  00 00 00 00 00 00 00 00
00006080  00 10 00 00 00 00 00 00  00 00 00 00 00 00 00 00
00006090  1E 00 00 00 1E 00 00 00  1E 00 00 00 0C 44 6D 38                Dm8
```

Fig. 4.12: inode 1 which contains the pointers to the root diretory

```
Offset     0  1  2  3  4  5  6  7   8  9  A  B  C  D  E  F    ANSI ASCII
07F13000  01 00 00 00 01 2E 00 00  00 00 00 00 00 00 00 00    .
07F13010  00 00 00 00 00 00 00 00  00 00 00 00 00 00 00 00
07F13020  01 00 00 00 02 2E 2E 00  00 00 00 00 00 00 00 00    ..
07F13030  00 00 00 00 00 00 00 00  00 00 00 00 00 00 00 00
07F13040  02 00 00 00 05 2E 62 6F  6F 74 00 00 00 00 00 00    .boot
07F13050  00 00 00 00 00 00 00 00  00 00 00 00 00 00 00 00
07F13060  03 00 00 00 03 62 69 6E  00 00 00 00 00 00 00 00    bin
07F13070  00 00 00 00 00 00 00 00  00 00 00 00 00 00 00 00
07F13080  04 00 00 00 03 65 74 63  00 00 00 00 00 00 00 00    etc
07F13090  00 00 00 00 00 00 00 00  00 00 00 00 00 00 00 00
07F130A0  05 00 00 00 04 69 6E 66  6F 00 00 00 00 00 00 00    info
07F130B0  00 00 00 00 00 00 00 00  00 00 00 00 00 00 00 00
07F130C0  06 00 00 00 03 6C 69 62  00 00 00 00 00 00 00 00    lib
07F130D0  00 00 00 00 00 00 00 00  00 00 00 00 00 00 00 00
07F130E0  07 00 00 00 03 6F 70 74  00 00 00 00 00 00 00 00    opt
07F130F0  00 00 00 00 00 00 00 00  00 00 00 00 00 00 00 00
07F13100  08 00 00 00 03 75 73 72  00 00 00 00 00 00 00 00    usr
07F13110  00 00 00 00 00 00 00 00  00 00 00 00 00 00 00 00
07F13120  1C 00 00 00 08 66 6C 61  73 68 2E 73 68 00 00 00    flash.sh
07F13130  00 00 00 00 00 00 00 00  00 00 00 00 00 00 00 00
```

Fig. 4.13: Root Directory

which is at offset 0x7F75000. Here we see now our filename and the corresponding
inode Number, where the metadata and pointer to the file content is.

We see that the *fileformathandbook.ascii* file has the inode number 0x258. Knowing this, we have to find the offset where this inode is defined. With a block size of
0x1000 and an inode size of 0x80, each inode block contains 0x20 inodes, so the
inode we are looking for is the 24th inode in inode block number 19. Going back to
Fig. 4.11, the 19 inode block is at physical block 0xE0, calculated address 0xE3000

Offset	Title	Value	
6380	Size	00 10 00 00 00 00 00 00	
6388	Uid	00 00 00 00	
638C	Gid	00 00 00 00	
6390	File time	01.01.1970	00:16:56
6394	Mod. time	06.04.2021	16:58:53
6398	Access time	06.04.2021	17:02:11
639C	Change time	06.04.2021	16:58:53
63A0	Mode	ED 41	
63A2	ExtMode	03 00	

```
00006370  00 00 00 00 00 00 00 00   00 00 00 00 00 00 00 00
00006380  00 10 00 00 00 00 00 00   00 00 00 00 00 00 00 00
00006390  F8 03 00 00 4D 93 6C 60   13 94 6C 60 4D 93 6C 60   ø    M¨1`  ¨1`M¨1`
000063A0  ED 41 03 00 72 7F 00 00   FF FF FF FF FF FF FF FF   íA   r       ÿÿÿÿÿÿÿÿ
000063B0  FF FF FF FF FF FF FF FF   FF FF FF FF FF FF FF FF   ÿÿÿÿÿÿÿÿÿÿÿÿÿÿÿÿ
000063C0  FF FF FF FF FF FF FF FF   FF FF FF FF FF FF FF FF   ÿÿÿÿÿÿÿÿÿÿÿÿÿÿÿÿ
000063D0  FF FF FF FF FF FF FF FF   FF FF FF FF FF FF FF FF   ÿÿÿÿÿÿÿÿÿÿÿÿÿÿÿÿ
000063E0  FF FF FF FF 00 03 00 00   00 00 00 00 00 00 00 00   ÿÿÿÿ
000063F0  00 00 00 00 00 00 00 00   00 00 00 00 00 00 00 00
```

Fig. 4.14: Inode 8, which has the pointer to the /usr directory in our example

```
Offset     0  1  2  3  4  5  6  7   8  9  A  B  C  D  E  F   ANSI ASCII
07F75000  08 00 00 00 01 2E 00 00   00 00 00 00 00 00 00 00   .
07F75010  00 00 00 00 00 00 00 00   00 00 00 00 00 00 00 00
07F75020  01 00 00 00 02 2E 2E 00   00 00 00 00 00 00 00 00   ..
07F75030  00 00 00 00 00 00 00 00   00 00 00 00 00 00 00 00
07F75040  2B 00 00 00 03 6C 69 62   00 00 00 00 00 00 00 00   +    lib
07F75050  00 00 00 00 00 00 00 00   00 00 00 00 00 00 00 00
07F75060  58 02 00 00 18 66 69 6C   65 66 6F 72 6D 61 74 68   X    fileformath
07F75070  61 6E 64 62 6F 6F 6B 2E   61 73 63 69 69 00 00 00   andbook.ascii
07F75080  59 02 00 00 FF 00 00 00   2B 00 00 00 99 D8 6D 5B   Y  ÿ    +    ™Øm[
07F75090  00 00 00 00 00 00 00 00   00 00 00 00 00 00 00 00
```

Fig. 4.15: /usr directory with the entry of the file we are looking for

+ 0xB80 (24th inode in Block). In this inode, depicted in Fig. 4.16 we find all the relevant filesystem metadata for this file and the pointers to the filesystem content.

Following now the pointers to the content, beginning with 0x19D, we can retrieve the file block by block (Fig. 4.17).

After demonstrating the retrieval of the example file from the file system data, it is easy to understand the next section, which shows the possibilities to reconstruct deleted files.

4.4 Deleted Files

There are some possibilities to recover deleted files in a QNX6 Volume, depending, when the file or directory was deleted and what happened with the filesystem in the meanwhile. Deleting an entry (directory or file) in QNX6 means that the Status in

Offset	Title	Value	
E3B80	Size	9C 16 00 00 00 00 00 00	
E3B88	Uid	00 00 00 00	
E3B8C	Gid	00 00 00 00	
E3B90	File time	06.04.2021	16:57:31
E3B94	Mod. time	06.04.2021	17:02:39
E3B98	Access time	06.04.2021	17:02:56
E3B9C	Change time	06.04.2021	17:02:39
E3BA0	Mode	FD 81	
E3BA2	ExtMode	01 00	

Blockptr

Offset	Title	Value
E3BA4	BlockPtr 0	9D 01 00 00
E3BA8	BlockPtr 1	1C 32 00 00
E3BAC	BlockPtr 2	FF FF FF FF
E3BB0	BlockPtr 3	FF FF FF FF

```
000E3B60   FF FF FF FF 00 03 00 00   00 00 00 00 00 00 00 00   ÿÿÿÿ
000E3B70   00 00 00 00 00 00 00 00   00 00 00 00 00 00 00 00
000E3B80   9C 16 00 00 00 00 00 00   00 00 00 00 00 00 00 00   œ
000E3B90   FB 92 6C 60 2F 94 6C 60   40 94 6C 60 2F 94 6C 60   û'l`/"l`@"l`/"l`
000E3BA0   FD 81 01 00 9D 01 00 00   1C 32 00 00 FF FF FF FF   ý         2  ÿÿÿÿ
000E3BB0   FF FF FF FF FF FF FF FF   FF FF FF FF FF FF FF FF   ÿÿÿÿÿÿÿÿÿÿÿÿÿÿÿÿ
000E3BC0   FF FF FF FF FF FF FF FF   FF FF FF FF FF FF FF FF   ÿÿÿÿÿÿÿÿÿÿÿÿÿÿÿÿ
000E3BD0   FF FF FF FF FF FF FF FF   FF FF FF FF FF FF FF FF   ÿÿÿÿÿÿÿÿÿÿÿÿÿÿÿÿ
000E3BE0   FF FF FF FF 00 03 00 00   00 00 00 00 00 00 00 00   ÿÿÿÿ
000E3BF0   00 00 00 00 00 00 00 00   00 00 00 00 00 00 00 00
```

Fig. 4.16: Inode entry of our example file

```
Offset      0  1  2  3  4  5  6  7    8  9  A  B  C  D  E  F    ANSI ASCII
0019FFD0   00 00 00 00 00 00 00 00   00 00 00 00 00 00 00 00
0019FFE0   00 00 00 00 00 00 00 00   00 00 00 00 00 00 00 00
0019FFF0   00 00 00 00 00 00 00 00   00 00 00 00 00 00 00 00
001A0000   54 68 69 73 20 69 73 20   61 20 54 65 73 74 66 69   This is a Testfi
001A0010   6C 65 20 66 6F 72 20 74   68 65 20 46 69 6C 65 20   le for the File
001A0020   46 6F 72 6D 61 74 20 68   61 6E 64 62 6F 6F 6B 2E   Format handbook.
001A0030   20 54 68 69 73 20 54 65   73 74 66 69 6C 65 20 6A    This Testfile j
001A0040   75 73 74 20 72 65 70 65   61 74 73 20 74 68 65 20   ust repeats the
001A0050   73 61 6D 65 20 74 65 78   74 20 6F 76 65 72 20 61   same text over a
001A0060   6E 64 20 6F 76 65 72 20   61 67 61 69 6E 2E 20 54   nd over again. T
001A0070   68 69 73 20 69 73 20 61   20 54 65 73 74 66 69 6C   his is a Testfil
001A0080   65 20 66 6F 72 20 74 68   65 20 46 69 6C 65 20 46   e for the File F
001A0090   6F 72 6D 61 74 20 68 61   6E 64 62 6F 6F 6B 2E 20   ormat handbook.
001A00A0   54 68 69 73 20 54 65 73   74 66 69 6C 65 20 77 61   This Testfile wa
```

Fig. 4.17: Content of our example file

an Inode switches to "deleted" (see Table 4.5) and that the entries inode number is deleted from the directory as shown in Fig. 4.18. By this, it is not possible to recover a file by its name, because there is no link anymore between the filename and the inode containing the metadata and the pointers to the file content. If a directory is updated after a file was deleted (e.g. a new file is added), the filesystem driver moves the directory to another block. The filename is "lost" from the regular filesystem

Conrad Meyer

directory tree. Also, the blocks, which contain the content of the files are set to unused in the bitmap, which means, they are free to be overwritten by other data. Knowing this, there are still some possibilities to recover files, with and without their respective names.

Offset	0	1	2	3	4	5	6	7	8	9	A	B	C	D	E	F	ANSI ASCII
07FD7FF0	FF	FF	FF	FF	FF	FF	FF	FF	FF	FF	FF	FF	FF	FF	FF	FF	ÿÿÿÿÿÿÿÿÿÿÿÿÿÿÿÿ
07FD8000	08	00	00	00	01	2E	00	00	00	00	00	00	00	00	00	00	.
07FD8010	00	00	00	00	00	00	00	00	00	00	00	00	00	00	00	00	
07FD8020	01	00	00	00	02	2E	2E	00	00	00	00	00	00	00	00	00	..
07FD8030	00	00	00	00	00	00	00	00	00	00	00	00	00	00	00	00	
07FD8040	2B	00	00	00	03	6C	69	62	00	00	00	00	00	00	00	00	+ lib
07FD8050	00	00	00	00	00	00	00	00	00	00	00	00	00	00	00	00	
07FD8060	00	00	00	00	18	66	69	6C	65	66	6F	72	6D	61	74	68	fileformath
07FD8070	61	6E	64	62	6F	6F	6B	2E	61	73	63	69	69	00	00	00	andbook.ascii
07FD8080	00	00	00	00	FF	00	00	00	2B	00	00	00	99	D8	6D	5B	ÿ + ™Øm[
07FD8090	00	00	00	00	00	00	00	00	00	00	00	00	00	00	00	00	

Sector 261.823 of 409.568								Offset:				7FD7FFF				= 255 | Block:
07FD8000	08	00	00	00	01	2E	00	00	00	00	00	00	00	00	00	00	.
07FD8010	00	00	00	00	00	00	00	00	00	00	00	00	00	00	00	00	
07FD8020	01	00	00	00	02	2E	2E	00	00	00	00	00	00	00	00	00	..
07FD8030	00	00	00	00	00	00	00	00	00	00	00	00	00	00	00	00	
07FD8040	2B	00	00	00	03	6C	69	62	00	00	00	00	00	00	00	00	+ lib
07FD8050	00	00	00	00	00	00	00	00	00	00	00	00	00	00	00	00	
07FD8060	58	02	00	00	18	66	69	6C	65	66	6F	72	6D	61	74	68	X fileformath
07FD8070	61	6E	64	62	6F	6F	6B	2E	61	73	63	69	69	00	00	00	andbook.ascii
07FD8080	00	00	00	00	00	00	00	00	00	00	00	00	00	00	00	00	
07FD8090	00	00	00	00	00	00	00	00	00	00	00	00	00	00	00	00	
07FD80A0	00	00	00	00	00	00	00	00	00	00	00	00	00	00	00	00	
07FD80B0	00	00	00	00	00	00	00	00	00	00	00	00	00	00	00	00	

Fig. 4.18: Directory entry before (bottom) and after (top) deletion

The first possibility, if the file was just deleted recently, it may still be present in the non-active filesystem structure of the second superblock. If this is the case, the file can normally be fully recovered, even with its content (still, it is possible that the content is not original).

Second, you can parse the inodes to recover files with their metadata without the associated filename. This fact is quite problematic because the Blocks do not necessarily still contain the files original data.

In conclusion, we see that the reconstruction of files is sometimes possible. However, compared to some other filesystems (e.g. NTFS), there is a smaller possibility to recover deleted files from the filesystem information. In some special cases where you can prove the integrity of a file in another way (e.g. some packed/zipped files), it is still helpful to take advantage of the inode structure and the possibility to put together fragmented files from the pointers inside the inode.

4.5 Forensic Tools supporting QNX6 filesystems

The Linux kernel includes a read-only driver for QNX6 (and QNX4) file systems. Also, some mobile forensic tools like UFED physical analyzer support this file system to a certain degree. Until today, those tools just support volumes formatted with the standard values shown in Table 4.1. Lately, there have been some projects in the Autopsy / Sleuthkit community to support QNX6, but until today, none of the projects has come to an end.

Part II
Mobile File Formats

File format analysis examines one specific file. An App or a program typically interprets the data contained in a file. Files can contain user data as well as configuration data, caches or any data. One aim of file format analysis is to recover corrupted files or restore deleted entries from files that only mark entries as deleted but do not overwrite the deleted data.

In this part of the book, the general design of five common file formats in mobile devices is described, and different analysis techniques are presented. This part abstractly approaches the topic and is not limited to how a specific tool analyzes a file format.

File formats are used by Apps or programs and provide mechanisms to store data in a structured way. File formats can organize metadata as well as and data such that the specific App can use this. The described file formats in this part are typically used in mobile devices.

Chapter 5
SQLite

Dirk Pawlaszczyk

Abstract SQLite is, without doubt, the most widely used database system worldwide at the moment. The single file database system is used, among other things, in operating systems for cell phones, such as Android, iOS or Symbian OS. On a typical smartphone, we usually find several hundred SQLite databases used by a wide variety of apps. Due to its widespread use, the database format is of particular importance in mobile forensics. It is not uncommon for the suspect to try to cover his tracks by deleting database content. Recovering deleted records from a database presents a special challenge. In this chapter, the on-disk database format of the SQLite database system is highlighted. Therefore, we take a closer look at the database header as well as record structure on a binary level. We first examine the structure of the data. Recovery options for erased records are discussed as well. Special attention is paid to the slack areas within the database: unallocated space, Freelist as well as free blocks. In this context, we discuss basic techniques for carving and acquisition of deleted data artefacts. Despite the main database format and recovery options, temporary file types like write-ahead logs and rollback journals are analyzed as well.

5.1 Introduction

A large amount of data is being stored and processed in relational databases. The most widely used database system in the world is undoubtedly SQLite since it is the default solution for the Android and iOS operating systems. So it is not surprising, that web browsers, messenger services and mobile applications employ the free and serverless database solution as their storage format of choice [61],[60]. At the moment, there are more than a trillion SQLite instances in active use [81]. In the vast majority of criminal investigations involving information technology, one task is to make information stored in such databases accessible. Evidence acquisition for

University of Applied Sciences (Hochschule Mittweida), Technikumplatz 17, 09648 Mittweida, Germany, e-mail: pawlaszc@hs-mittweida.de

© The Author(s) 2022
C. Hummert, D. Pawlaszczyk (eds.), *Mobile Forensics – The File Format Handbook*,
https://doi.org/10.1007/978-3-030-98467-0_5

databases is traditionally made with SQL, a powerful query language. Also, SQLite supports most of the SQL language commands. In this way, the data can be accessed with one of the freely available viewers. Unfortunately, this form of analysis usually does not allow access to deleted records or temporary data content such as recently added but not committed entries. This creates the need for alternative ways to analyze such databases forensically.

5.2 The SQLite File Structure

SQLite is a single-file database engine, i.e., all tables are managed in only one file on disk. There is no intermediary server process; an application has to communicate with first, for storing data. It does not work this way. Instead, the database can be integrated directly into an application. Therefore, it provides a library and an easy to use programming interface. This fact has significantly contributed to the current spread and popularity of the program. We will discuss the basic structure of a database before turning to the details of carving for data records.

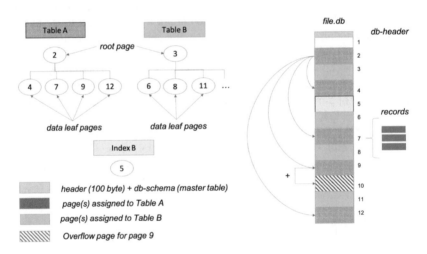

Fig. 5.1: Schematic structure of a SQLite database

Like most structured binary formats, the database file starts with a header part [80]. Its size is exactly 100 bytes. Beyond this, the database file is divided into pages of equal size. The file size is thus always a multiple of the page size. A page number uniquely identifies a single page, whereas the first page has the number one. The default page size usually is 4096 bytes. However, it can be adjusted if necessary to a minimum of 512 bytes and a maximum of 64KB [32]. Of course, the header is part of the first page. In a relational database system, all data is stored in tables. This is also the case with SQLite. In turn, a table is distributed over one or more pages of the database on the binary level (see Fig. 5.1). Each data page again contains one or more records, for precisely one table. To access and acquire all records of a particular table, we must first determine which pages of the database are associated with this table. This information can again be taken from the first page of the database. Besides the header string, this page contains one more piece of information - the database schema. Necessary information such as the root page numbers, column names, and column types of the tables are stored here, in a data structure called *SQLite_Master Table*. We will discuss the details of this table in sect. 5.2.3. To represent a table and its pages, SQLite uses a balanced tree data structure (B+tree) under the hood. In a B+tree, the raw data elements are stored exclusively in the leaf nodes, while the inner nodes contain only links. Since the maximum size of a page is limited from above, we can gain more space for links or branches in the inner nodes by moving the leaves' data records. Moreover, this limits the height of the tree. Since data elements are normally accessed via the tree's root, a lower height reduces the number of nodes to be traversed. Many relational database systems manage their records in this way.

Table 5.1: SQLite page types and byte flags

Page Type	1st Byte in Page
table b-tree interior page	0x05
table b-tree leaf page	0x0d
index b-tree interior page	0x02
index b-tree leaf page	0x0a
overflow page	0x00 (for db-size < 64GB)
freelist page	0x00 (first 8 bytes filled with zero-bytes)
pointer map	0x01 or 0x02 or 0x03 or 0x04 or 0x05
locking page	0x00 (only, if db-size > 1 GB)

A page with links to other pages only is called a *b-tree interior* page [80]. The record nodes are saved in *table b-tree leaf pages*. Beyond this, a table can have multiple indexes. An index contains links to normal table records to speed up searching and sorting by specific fields. Whenever we create an index, SQLite creates a B-tree structure to hold the index data as well. Similar to normal tables we can distinguish between *index b-tree interior pages* as well as *index b-tree leaf pages*. When a data record is too large for a single data leaf page, the excessive bytes are spilt onto so-called *overflow pages*. Several overflow pages are filled at once to store large amounts of data such as Binary Large OBjects (BLOBs). Together all overflow pages for one record form a linked list. To capture all the data associated with a record, we need to read all the pages. The payload for an record and the preceding pointer are combined to form a cell.

Despite the five data page types, SQLite knows three more page classes. A database file might contain one or more pages that are not in active use. Whenever the last record is deleted from a page, this page is released. The freed page will be reused when new pages are required and filled with new table contents. In the meantime, all unallocated pages are stored in a so-called freelist (sect. 5.3). These freelist pages are of particular forensic value since most of the removed content can be found here.

A further not yet discussed page type are so-called *pointer maps*. A pointer map has the function of not losing track when pages are moved from one position in the database file to another. This page type is created whenever the database is reorganized or cleaned up. A pointer map provides a lookup table to quickly determine page types and their parents. However, this page type exists only in auto-vacuum databases. The *locking page* is the last page type in SQLite. The first page of this page class starts at byte offset 2^{30} (1,073,741,824) and always remains unused. Conversely, this means that a locking page only appears when the database size is more extensive the 1 GB. Since it is empty, it has only a technical, but no forensic value and is therefore not considered further.

We can usually determine the type of page by looking at the page's first byte. The flag-byte at offset 0 indicates the page class. Table 5.4 lists all the page types discussed so far. However, not every database will include all of these types. With the page size and type information at hand, an investigator can walk through the database and identify all areas of interest.

5.2.1 The Database Header

Every forensic investigation starts with analysing the file header. The header contains important information that will help us to carve for deleted records. The fields of the header have a precisely defined size and position (see Fig. 5.2). The individual (multi-byte) fields are encoded as big endian (BE) values.

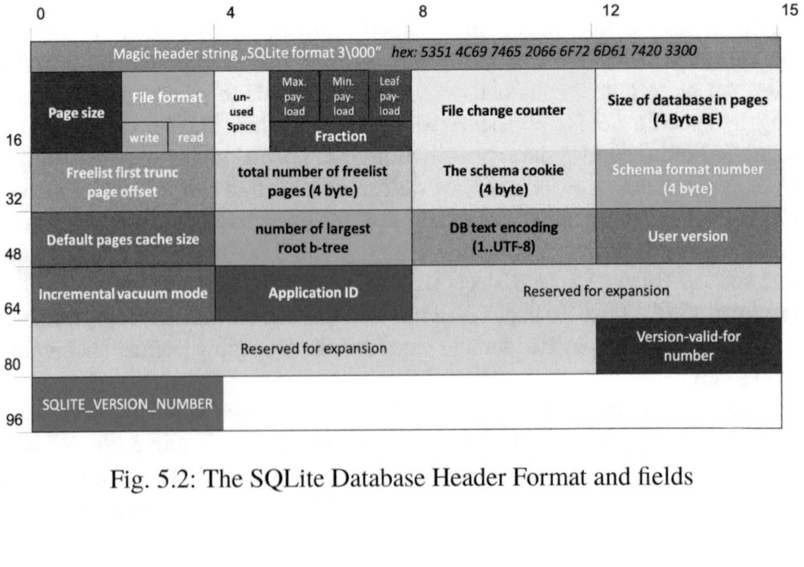

Fig. 5.2: The SQLite Database Header Format and fields

We will discuss the fields below and evaluate them in terms of their respective value for a forensic investigation [80]:

- Each database starts with the header string. The magic header value is always set to "SQLite format 3". We can use the header information to carve the beginning of a database file on the binary level. Offset 15 marks the end of the magic header string. It holds a special character, the null terminator (0x00).
- At offset 16, we can find a two-byte big-endian integer value representing the database's page size. The value in this field must be a power of two. The range of values is between 512 and 32768. There is one exception: The value 0x0001 is viewed as a big-endian 1. It represents the value 65,536 - the largest possible page size - since this number will not fit in a two-byte usually.
- The two flag bytes at offset 18 and 19 control the read and write permission for the database. The values should typically always be either a 1 or a 2. For the rollback journalling mode (sect. 5.4.2), both values are set to 1. In contrast, number 2 in both fields indicates a WAL journalling mode (sect. 5.4.3). If the write version has a value greater than 2, this database file must be accessed as read-only. These two fields' value can indicate whether other files (WAL file or journal file) are present.
- The 1-byte integer value at offset 20 of the header is used to apply for certain SQLite extensions. The number of bytes specified here reduces the usable area within the page. In this way, for example, special salt or nonce values can be stored for each page when using the cryptographic extension. This value is usually 0. The value can be odd.
- The bytes on offset 21 to 23 have fixed values per definition. Maximum and minimum payload fraction must be 64, 32. The byte for the leaf payload fraction always holds the value 32.
- With each transaction carried out on the database, the 4-byte big-endian integer at offset 24 is usually incremented by one. A process that wants to read data from the database can determine whether there has been a change since the last access.
- With the 4-byte integer on offset 28 stores the size of the in-header database in pages. However, this value may differ from the file's actual size when accessing a database before version 3.7.0. Alternatively, you can determine the actual file size and divide by the page size to infer this value.
- At offset 32, we can find a 4-byte big-endian integer which indicates the beginning of the so-called freelist. As already pointed out, unused pages in the database file are stored within this data structure. This field has a significant meaning, as it allows us to access pages of the database that are no longer visible. It holds the offset of the first page of the list. If the value is zero, the list is empty.
- At offset 36 represents the total number of entries on the freelist. Together with the start address, one can thus automatically iterate over the released pages.
- Each change to the database schema, such as adding or deleting a table or creating an index, automatically leads to an increment of the value at offset 40.

- The 4-byte value at offset 44 represents the format number. This field has a value between 1 and 4. For a SQLite database created with the latest version of the database, the value is always 4 and thus supports the more SQL commands. Databases created before November 2005 usually have a value of 3 or less.
- The value default pages cache size at offset 48 queries or sets the suggested maximum number of pages of disk cache for a database file.
- The 4-byte big-endian integer value at offset 52 is only used to manage pointer-maps for auto vacuum-databases. A non-zero value means that this database file contains pointer map-pages.
- All strings in the database are encoded with the same encoding. There are only 3 valid encodings: UFT8 (value 1), UTF16LE (value 2), UTF16BE (value 3). For the analysis of the database, this field value must always be read first.
- The integer at offset 64 is true for incremental_vacuum and false for auto_vacuum mode. A value is larger than 0 means that the database reclaims space after data has been deleted. An autovacuum database thus contains few deleted artefacts - if any. It is defragmented automatically.
- The Application ID at offset 68 can be set by the Application programmer. It is not used by SQLite.
- Offset 92 covers the value of the change counter. The integer at offset 92 indicates which transaction the version number is valid for.
- The 4-byte integer at offset 96 stores the SQLITE_VERSION_NUMBER value. The version number of the database library with which changes were last made to the database is noted here.

All remaining header bytes are reserved for future expansion. Consequently, we can ignore them.

> **Important**

As can be seen from what has been said, various header fields must be read and analyzed as the first step of every examination. Thus, the page size (offset 16) and the number of pages (offset 28) must always be determined, since we need to know the structure and size of the database. In order to interpret the strings correctly, the encoding must also be examined (offset 58). A look at the freelist entries at offset 32 and 36 tells us whether unused pages in the database exist. If we do not find any references to free pages, it may be an auto vacuum database (offset 64). Using the flags for transaction management at offset 18 or 19, we can also find out which additional SQLite files may exist. This is of particular interest because these files can also contain records of former transactions. Thus, old states of the database have been overwritten in the meantime could be made visible again. The header's remaining information is more technical and is, therefore, less interesting for the investigator.

5.2.2 Storage Classes, Serial Types and Varint-Encoding

In order to understand the binary format of records we first need to clarify what data types SQLite knows at the binary level and how they are encoded. Like most other databases, SQLite uses strict typing. Therefore, each value stored is mapped to one of the five storage classes (Table 5.2). The word storage class is just another term for a data type. However, the latter is more commonly used in connection with programming languages. SQLite supports storage classes for integers (INTEGER), floating-point numbers (REAL), strings (TEXT), binary objects (BLOB), and other numeric data such as dates (NUMERIC). The storage class thus determines how the binary data is to be interpreted. Conceptually, each column of a table is assigned with a specific affinity. The affinity denotes the preferred storage class for a column. The data type of a column defines what value the column can hold. However, the SQL standard knows several data type names for one SQLite storage class. For example, there exist more than ten different integer data types in SQL. For texts, there exist seven different types. Accordingly, each data type is mapped to exactly one storage class.

A second essential aspect is a length occupied by a cell value. An integer, for example, will consume a length between zero and a maximum of 8 Bytes. A floating-point number is mapped to a 64-bit field. A text can have an arbitrary length. SQLite uses the so-called serial types to map storage class and length. In simplified terms, this type is a number. The concrete value of the number provides information about the length of a cell value. At the same time, the storage class can be derived from the numerical value. Table 5.3 lists all possible serial types. For serial types 0, 8, 9, the value is zero bytes in length. The serial type is used whenever the type and length of a cell must be determined. Usually, each table row has a corresponding header that summarizes the serial bytes for each column. As a rule, a serial type occupies exactly one byte. Especially with texts or BLOBs, this principle is sometimes deviated from as soon as the numerical value's length exceeds 127. In this case, additional bytes may be added to map the serial type.

Table 5.2: Mapping from SQL types to SQLite storage classes [80]

SQL Data Type	Storage Class
INT, INTEGER, INTUNSIGNED, LONG, TINYINT, SMALLINT, MEDIUMINT, BIGINT, INT2, INT8	INTEGER
TEXT, CHARACTER, CLOB, VARCHAR, NCHAR, NATIVE CHARACTER, VARYINGCHARACTER	TEXT
REAL, DOUBLE, DOUBLEPRESICION, FLOAT	REAL
NUMERIC, DEZIMAL, BOOLEAN, DATE, DTIME	NUMERIC
BLOB (no datatype specified)	BLOB

SQLite uses a particular encoding for storing serial types. The representation form used is a variable-length integer (varint). SQLite version 3 uses this simple byte-oriented encoding where each byte contains 7 bits of the integer being encoded. The most significant bit (MSB) is a flag bit, indicating more bytes to follow. Since most integers in a database have relatively small values, we can keep memory consumption low this way. Storing with a fixed-length integer will mostly generate unnecessarily many null bytes. Instead, SQLite uses a static Huffman encoding of 64-bit twos-complement integers that needs less space for small positive values. The serial type varints for large strings and BLOBs might extend up to nine-byte varints. The following illustration should once again make clear the storage principle of varint-values:

```
1 Byte      0XXXXXXX                                        ..127
2 Bytes     1XXXXXXX 0XXXXXXX                               ..16384
3 Bytes     1XXXXXXX 1XXXXXXX 0XXXXXXX                      ..2097152
4 Bytes     1XXXXXXX 1XXXXXXX 1XXXXXXX 0XXXXXXX ..268435456
```

Since texts have a variable size, and the length calculation is performed by a formula. A numerical value above 12 or 13 can only occur with texts or BLOBs. An odd value will be correspondingly for texts. On the other hand, if the value is even, then it is the BLOB storage class. For example, to store the word *Test*, the value 21(0x15) - 2 * text length + 13 - is stored as the length specification. A JPEG file with, let us say, the length of 109 Bytes would be encoded with the serial type number 230 since $N * 2 + 12$ is what we need to calculate for a binary object. However, since we cannot map this value with 7 bits, we have to add a second byte for the varint:

```
decimal: 230 = 128 + 64 + 32 + 4 + 2
binary:  1110 0110
varint: 1000 0001 and 0110 0110 (2-Byte: 1X.. 0X..)
```

Thus, we must first calculate the respective length specification each time we need to know the exact length of a table cell. The serial values 8 and 9 are noteworthy features. They can be used to map the two values 0 or 1. An extra content byte is not necessary in this case. With the information presented, we are now able to decode the cells of a table row.

5.2.3 Decoding The SQLite_Master Table

A database schema is a set of data definitions that define the structural design of a database. As already explained, the schema, or the master table, resides on the database's first page, just behind the header. Technically, it is a regular table [85]. Table 5.4 shows all columns and their meaning for the master table. The schema table contains all database objects in the database and the statement used to create each object. With the schema table's help, all table names, the corresponding column names and data types can be determined. Each table entry is opened by two additional fields: the *rowid* and the payload (see Fig. 5.3). Both values are only visible on the

Table 5.3: Serial Type Codes Of The Record Format [80]

Serial Type	Size	Meaning
0	0	Value is a NULL.
1	1	A 8-bit twos-complement integer.
2	2	A big-endian 16-bit twos-compl. integer.
3	3	A big-endian 24-bit twos-compl. integer.
4	4	A big-endian 32-bit twos-compl. integer.
5	6	A big-endian 48-bit twos-compl. integer.
6	8	A big-endian 64-bit twos-compl. integer.
7	8	A big-endian 64-bit floating point number.
8	0	integer 0 (schema format $\geq$ 4).
9	0	integer 1 (schema format $\geq$ 4).
10,11	variable	Reserved for internal use. Variable size.
$N \geq 12$, even	(N-12)/2	Value is a BLOB with (N-12)/2 bytes length.
$N \geq 13$, odd	(N-13)/2	Value is a string in the text encoding and (N-13)/2 bytes in length. The nul terminator is not stored.

binary level. Any row of the master table and therefore every database object is assigned to a unique, non-NULL, signed 64-bit integer - the *rowid*. This value is used as the access key for the data in the underlying B-tree. On the binary level, each table row starts with a rowid number greater than null. Most tables in a typical SQLite database schema are rowid tables. A *rowid table* is defined as any table in an SQLite schema that is not a virtual table and is not a WITHOUT ROWID table. The rowid is not part of the table definition. A payload field that stores the length of the record follows directly after the rowid.

Table 5.4: Structure of the sqlite_master table [85]

Column Name	Description
type	type of database object (table, index etc.)
name	name of the database object
tblname	table that the database object is connected to
rootpage	root page
sql	SQL statement used to create the database object.

Interestingly, we can find descriptions for tables that have already been removed. If an object in the database is erased, the schema table's corresponding record is marked as removed. If a table is dropped, the rowid value for the line in question is set to 0x0000. The entry that is no longer needed is only overwritten when a new database object is added. In the meantime, the entry is still accessible. Figure 5.3 shows an example of a deleted entry for a table in hex mode. The table header and all columns of the record are intact. Only the rowid value at Offset 3935 has been wiped with zero bytes.

In the example below, the signature 0x7461626C65 represents the object type of a table. The table name, i.e. "users", directly follows the type column. However, we must parse and analyse the corresponding SQL statement from the fifth column to get all column names and the corresponding type information.

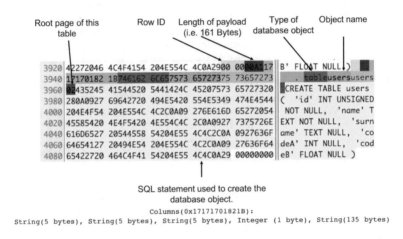

Fig. 5.3: Record of a dropped table from the sqlite_master (example)

By analyzing the SQL statement, a storage class can be derived for each table column. For the five columns of the table <users>, the following columns can be identified: INT, TEXT, TEXT, INT, REAL. This type of vector can be considered as a kind of fingerprint. Sometimes, a found record could be recovered, but it is not clear to which table it belongs. With the help of the table's signature derived in this way, an assignment can still be made, even for a deleted record. Of course, this rule is not always 100% accurate. It is not excluded that two tables have the same signature. However, it can help us make an educated guess, which will be correct in most cases.

5.2.4 Page Structure

All records are stored on pages. Approaching the data of a table requires a leaf page scan. To access the data, we must understand the structure of a page. Each page starts with a header, with a total size of 8 bytes in the case of a data leaf page (see Fig. 5.4). All header bytes are big-endian values. The header starts with the page type at offset 0. In the case of a leaf page, the page starts with the value 0x0D. It can be classified from the other pages by reading this value. The 2-byte value at offset 1 marks the beginning of the first free block on the page. A free block is created whenever a record is deleted from the database. All free blocks are organized as a linked list, whereas the first two bytes of the free block point to the offset of the following free block within the list. If the free block is the last on the chain, this value is zero. If we want to identify deleted records, our search should start right here in the free block list [80].

page header (8 bytes)

page type (1 byte)	first free block on page (2 bytes)	number of cells on page (2 bytes)	start-offset of cell content area (2 bytes)	fragmented bytes (1 byte)

Fig. 5.4: Fields of a b-tree leaf page header

Another essential value is located directly behind the free block field at offset 3. The 16-bit twos-complement integer field is called *number of cells*. Its value indicates how many active cells exist within the current page. In SQLite, the serial type header and the values of a particular table row are combined into a structure called "cell". So if we want to access a record, we need to locate the matching cell. Fortunately, all cell offsets are stored in an array directly after the page header. Hence, to read a regular record of a table, we need to iterate through the cell pointer field.

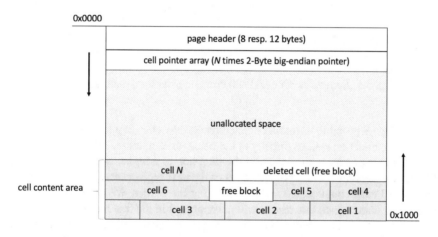

Fig. 5.5: Structure of a regular data leaf page (permanent and temporary)

The next header field at offset 5 provides the start-offset of the content area. A b-tree leaf page is divided into regions (see Fig. 5.5). The cell content area is always located at the bottom of the page. The header and the cell pointer array are always located at the beginning of the page. Between them resides the unallocated space. As the content area grows from the highest memory address towards the lower address, overlapping the two mentioned regions is prevented. The concept is thus similar to the management of heap and stack areas within memory management. The last value in the header denotes the number of fragmented bytes. A free block requires at least 4 bytes of space. Areas between 1 to 3 bytes form a fragment and thus cannot hold any data records.

Figure 5.6 shows an example of the header of a page on a binary level. In addition to 15 cells, we can also find at least one free block of offset 3620(0x0E24). The content area in this example starts at 0x0DEC. The cell pointer array is highlighted in yellow. Interestingly, we can find five more cell pointers shown in red. The value of the surplus cell offsets corresponds to the start offset of the cell content area. From this, we can conclude that apparently, five other records must have existed on the page in the past. Nevertheless, they have been deleted in the meantime. Thus, in addition to the 15 regular records, there should be five more deleted records on the page. However, the deletion turned the cells into free blocks. So, to find and restore them, we need to examine each element of the free block list.

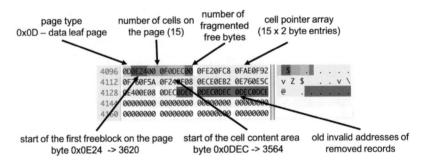

Fig. 5.6: Sample header and cell content array for a data leaf page

It is not always possible to find all deleted records by checking the free blocks. If a record is deleted that resides directly at the unallocated area, the offset value for the cell content area start is moved up in the direction to a higher address. Of course, this address denotes the cell pointer offset of the next regular record. The data set is thus moved to the unallocated area by changing the border. We must consider this case in our search since this record will never appear in the free block list.

However, it gets even worse. If a complete page is deleted, SQLite typically wipes the first 4 Bytes of the header with zeros. So, in this case, the offset for the first free block is erased. Thus, we do not know where precisely the list begins. What does this, in turn, mean for our search for hidden records? The best way to approach our search for slack areas is to use the exclusion principle. *Slack space* is the leftover storage that exists on a page when records do not need all the space which has been allocated. Slack areas are always created when records are deleted. Hence, the total amount of slack space can thus be calculated as shown in the equation below.

```
slack space with (possible) deleted content = page content
                        - header (8 bytes)
                        - N times 2-Byte cell pointer
                        - fragmented bytes
                        - N times cell
```

If we exclude the regular, well-known areas of the page, we automatically access the slack areas. Only the areas determined in this way can contain deleted data artefacts. In any case, we must always consider the unallocated space and the free block list when searching within the page. Fortunately, leaf pages are always structured the same. However, there is a second type of leaf page, the index leaf page. In its structure, this page corresponds to a regular data leaf page, except for one difference. The index leaf page starts with the value 0x0A at offset 0. However, what has been said so far also remains valid for the second type of page.

5.2.5 Recovering Data Records

Now that we know the location of the records, we can start reading them. This information can be derived from the cell offset array (see the last section). Every cell has the same structure (see Fig. 5.7). The cell header opens with a payload value. It indicates the total size of the cell in bytes. This value does not include the cell header itself. Normally, the payload field is followed by the rowid (see sect. 5.2.3). As already explained, the pseudo-column is usually generated automatically by SQLite. It is used to enable efficient access via the table tree. However, not all records have a rowid. For example, index records are created without this field. If the option "WITHOUT ROWID" is part of the CREATE TABLE statement, this field is also missing. Thus, the cell header has a minimum size of 1 byte for a mandatory payload value. The values in the cell header and all other header fields are varint values without a fixed size. So to read a record, we always have to read value by value. Skipping or omitting bytes is not possible because the fields do not have a fixed offset. The actual cell starts again with a header. This time, it is the header of the data record.

The *header size* field indicates how many bytes the header contains. Its value includes the actual header size byte. The individual serial types follow immediately. Column by column, we must first determine the storage class and space for each table cell. The header is followed directly by the actual data record. Since we operate on a binary level, the exact length of each field to be read and the data types can only be determined via the serial bytes in the header. However, it might be challenging to determine the exact beginning or end of the column cell values without this information. An intact header is, therefore, an essential prerequisite for successful data recovery.

The recovery of deleted data depends on the data management policy used. This, of course, differs from application to application. We can distinguish three cases:

1. **Wipe with zeros.** The free block is completely overwritten with zero-bytes. Recovery of data is impossible even if the removed area is identified.
2. **Truncate or remove deleted area.** The second policy is made on a small size of data. It deletes the record itself, and there is no way even to trace the occurrence of deletion. Some iPhone system files are handled this way.
3. **Add to a free list.** The last policy is to mark the record or page as free. The data itself remains in the database. This procedure generates the least I/O-traffic compared to the other two strategies. It is therefore used as the default behaviour of SQLite.

In the case of a data record that has been deleted, it sometimes happens that the cell header and parts of the record header are replaced with new information [59]. These new data fields cover the free block's length in bytes and the address of the following free block. Since both pieces of information are mapped to a 16-bit fixed-length integer, a total of four bytes of the respective cell are overwritten. In total, we can discern six situations when dealing with a deleted record (see Table 5.5).

Many records are deleted without being marked or overwritten. As explained earlier, some records are deleted by merely moving the cell content area's border upwards. Thus, the records slip into the unallocated area of the page. When clearing the browser cache, for example, almost all entries are removed from a caching table. Instead of first marking each record as deleted, the links to the affected pages are deleted from the table tree. Anything else would be a time-consuming process. Instead, the page as a whole is skipped. In both cases, however, the deleted records remain intact. Complete reconstruction is, therefore, possible. Sometimes a record is removed from the middle of the content area of an active page. In this case, the record

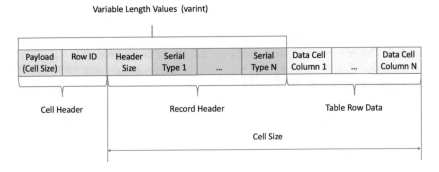

Fig. 5.7: Schematic structure of a data leaf cell

Table 5.5: Recovery Situations

Wiped Data	Recoverability
cell is intact (no wiped bytes)	yes
payload bytes	yes
payload bytes + rowid	yes
payload bytes + rowid + header length	yes
payload bytes + rowid + header length + 1st serial	partly
two or more serial type are wiped	no

is converted to a free block. Thus, the beginning is overwritten, at least partially. The previously occupied space will be released for reallocation. This, in turn, can result in different cases that influence the recoverability of the data record. Sometimes only the payload got wiped. In another case, the payload field, together with rowid, may be overwritten. We can mostly do without this field information. As long as the rest of the cell record remains intact, we can read the required column lengths and types and correctly interpret the data. Even a wiped header length field should not be a big problem. This field only holds the total length of the header. It can be reconstructed by summing the individual serial lengths. It gets tricky when columns are also overwritten. Without a valid column type and length specification for our first column, we cannot reconstruct the remaining columns correctly. However, the first column of a table is often an ID column with a numerical value. Knowing the length of the first column of a regular record on the same page can indirectly infer the first column's length for our destroyed record. Unfortunately, this rule does not work in every case. For example, if the first column contains a text with variable length, we will most likely not restore the record correctly. If more than one serial type has been overwritten, reconstruction seems unlikely. We then have too many possible lengths to consider. Strictly speaking, the number of possible lengths for a column grows exponentially with the number of overwritten length or type information in the header.

Figure 5.8 shows the content area of a data leaf page. There are a total of three records on the page. The cells are located at the end of the page. Remember, the cell content area always grows from higher towards the lower address. The record in the middle is deleted. The records before and after it are intact. Cell header, record header and all data are unaltered. Even without knowledge of the table, it can be deduced from the serial types alone that it is a table with apparently two columns. The first column can store integers (serial types $0x02$ resp. $0x03$). The second column is a string since the value is odd and greater than 13 (see sect. 5.2.2).

We can see that the second of the three data cells have been deleted because the first 4 bytes of the data set have been overwritten with the free block identifier. The identifier is $0x0000000C$. The first two bytes have the value $0x0000$. From this, we can conclude that it is the last free block within the page. The second half of the identifier tells us something about the length of the free block. It is exactly 12 bytes ($0x000C$). The free block is outlined in red in the illustration. As we can see, the actual

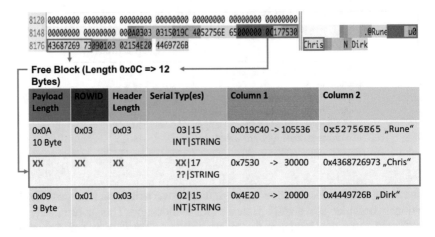

Fig. 5.8: Example data page with three records (one is wiped)

data fields of the deleted record are still intact. However, the PPL-field, ROWID, header length byte, and the first column's serial type are no longer accessible. The serial type of the second column is not wiped. From the length specification of the free block and the knowledge about the length of the second column, we can infer the length of the first column in this case. Accordingly, the first column of our data set can only be 2 bytes in size:

```
length of the first column field =
        12 byte (total free block length)
      - 5 (0x15 -13 / 2) (length of text column)
      - 4 (free block identifier)
      - 1 (serial type byte for 2nd column)
```

Thus, we can recover deleted content in many cases, even when parts of the header have been overwritten.

5.3 Accessing The Freelist

As soon as the last record on a page is deleted, it is transferred to the free list. At the same time, the link within the table tree is removed. From now, the page cannot be accessed from an active table. However, it can be assigned to a new table at any time. Meanwhile, the content of the page is still accessible. Usually, it is not wiped or replaced with random values. The pages are just sitting on the free list, waiting to be used again. Like the slack areas in the standard database pages, these unused pages may contain forensically exciting values such as chat protocols, short messages, or web pages visited [61].

The freelist is a simple linked list consisting of *trunk pages* 5.9. Each trunk page initially contains a 4-byte integer pointer referencing to the next trunk page in the list

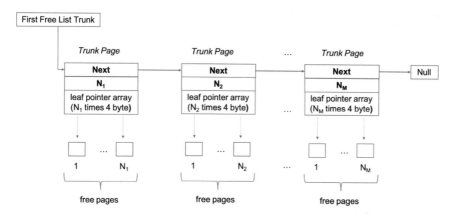

Fig. 5.9: Schematic principle of a freepage trunk list

[80]. A zero-byte value means that this is the last trunk page in the list, and the list ends here. The second 4-byte value in a trunk page contains the number of leaf page offsets. To analyse all the list pages, we must first visit each trunk page and query the offsets stored. Nevertheless, where do we have to start our search for freelist treasures?

The starting address for the freelist can be calculated very easily [59]. We must first determine the start offset of the first trunk page from the header at offset 32 of the database. Second, we need the page size. The latter can also be determined from the header. From these two values, we can calculate the actual offset of the first trunk page:

```
offset of 1st trunk page = (trunk page number - 1) * page size.
```

A trunk page consists of an array of 4-byte big-endian integers. As pointed out, the first 4 bytes of the trunk page header references the next trunk page within the list. The next, a four-byte big-endian integer holds the length of the leaf pointer array of the current page. With these two pieces of information at hand, we can quickly iterate over the array's entries.

The basic algorithm is shown in Listing 1. An example of a trunk page will illustrate what has been said so far (see Fig. 5.10). In addition to the reference to the next trunk page at offset 0, the number of page pointers to follow is visible (offset 4). The offset of the first free page can be found directly behind the two header integers at Offset 8. The second pointer is exactly 4 bytes behind. In the example, there are a total of 555 entries on the TrunkList page. The data size is therefore 8 + 555 * 4 = 2228 bytes. Thus, all unused pages can be found and accessed with linear time complexity with the described algorithm.

Algorithm 1 Freelist Page Recovery

▷ Input: SQLITE *db* filepointer

1: **read** *pagesize* ← 4 byte BE on byte *0x10*
2: **read** *trunk* ← for the first freelist trunk on byte *0x20*
3: **while** *trunk* ≠ null **do**
4:     *start* = (4 Byte BE in offset - 1) * *pagesize.*
5:     *db*.seek(*start*)   ▷ go to start of the trunk page
6:     **read** *trunk* ← for the next freelist trunk page (4 Byte BE)
7:     **read** *length* ← number of cell entries (4 Byte BE)
8:     **for** *j* = 0, 1, . . . , *length* − 1 **do**   ▷ iterate over trunk page array
9:         *db*.seek(*start* + 8 + (4 * *j*))
10:        **read** *freepage* ← next free page number
11:        *fpstart* = (*freepage* - 1) * *pagesize.*
12:        *db*.seek(fpstart)   ▷ go to start of next free page
13:        readPage()   ▷ start analyzing the hidden page
14:    **end for**
15: **end while**

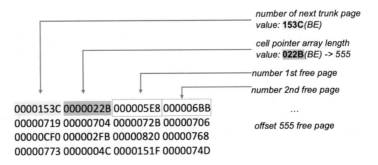

Fig. 5.10: start of a freelist trunk page (example)

5.4 More Artefacts

As explained earlier, SQLite manages all records in a single database file. However, access management, transaction handling, and integrity protection are performed with the help of primarily additional temporary files [84]. Despite the main database file, SQLite uses nine distinct types of temporary files (see Fig. 5.11). Below we will take a look at the other file types of SQLite. The focus is on searching for records no longer in the regular database but can still be found in one of those files.

5.4.1 Temporary File Types

SQLite creates several temporary files when managing the database. A *transient database*, for example, is a temporarily created file when the database is reorganized.

Data pages that are no longer required are removed. The whole process is comparable to the defragmentation of a hard disk. Pages are joined together, and gaps are closed. Then, the temporary file's content is copied back into the original database file, and the temporary file is deleted. However, this file type is generated only for databases for which the VACUUM property is activated. Since the database copy is deleted immediately afterwards, it is not easy to locate it on the disk. However, it might be possible to find old page versions of the database on the medium through carving. From time to time, SQLite makes use of *transient indices*. Each index is therefore stored in a separate temporary file. For example, if the ORDER-BY or GROUP-BY clause is used in an SQL statement, a corresponding index file is created to manage the intermediate results. The index is automatically deleted at the end of the statement that uses it.

In the case of complex SQL statements, partial queries are sometimes stored in a temporary file. In SQLite, this method is called "materializing" the subquery. This is the case, for example, with large SQL INNER JOIN statements. The query optimizer decides for which query a separate swap file is created.

Database users can create a temporary table using the "CREATE TEMP TABLE" command. Since this unique table is created only for a particular database connection and is not visible to other database users, it is swapped out to a separate file. Again, the temporary database file used to store temporary tables is removed automatically when the database connection is closed. When SQLite performs a transaction with multiple statements, a *Statement Journal File* can be used to undo individual steps. Assume that by executing a statement, 100 rows of a table are modified. After half of the records have been modified, the execution must be aborted due to an error. The rows of the database that have been modified so far are written back with the statement journal's help. All five of the temporary file formats discussed can contain data or temporary results of the database transactions. However, these data are highly volatile. In most cases, the temporarily stored results are already deleted when the statement is finished. Thus, it is not very likely for an investigator to come into contact with such artefacts. We will, therefore, not consider them further.

There are four remaining file types in SQLite. Unlike the formats discussed so far, these are files that are often encountered when examining a database. These files are *Rollback Journals*, *Write-ahead Logs*, *Shared-Memory Files* as well as *Super Journals*. They can usually be found in the same directory as the actual database file. Admittedly, the data stored in it is also classified only temporary within the official documentation of SQLite. However, the data stored in them is updated or overwritten much less frequently. We almost always find one of these file types. For this reason, these are also listed under the heading *other permanent files* in Fig. 5.11. Thus, the chance to acquire data from these files is much more likely. However, in some cases, the use of one file format excludes the use of the second. For example, the shared memory file and write-ahead log are usually found together. In contrast, the rollback journal is only found in a directory if the first-mentioned files are absent. Of the file formats mentioned above, super journals are relatively rare. The files are created only in transactions where multiple databases are updated simultaneously in an atomic transaction. Accordingly, without a super-journal in place, transaction commit on

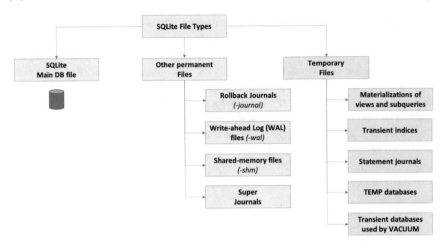

Fig. 5.11: The SQLite file types (permanent and temporary)

a multi-database transaction would be atomic for each database individually, but it would not be atomic across all databases. Due to the relatively low usage level, we will not take a closer look at this file format. Instead, we will focus on the two remaining journal formats. Besides availability and confidentiality, data integrity forms a central goal of every database system. SQLite is no exception. SQLite maintains its integrity by using journals and transactions. Below we will examine the two integrity protection techniques offered by SQLite in more detail: Write-ahead logs and Rollback Journals [80],[32].

5.4.2 Rollback Journals

The idea behind the rollbacks is simple: If a database gets into an inconsistent state due to write access, it is reset to the last valid state. To implement atomic commit and rollback capabilities, SQLite offers a file called *rollback journal*. Rollback refers to resetting the individual processing steps of a database transaction [79]. The system is thus wholly returned to the state before the start of the transaction. In the case of SQLite, a copy is first created for all database pages possibly affected by the transaction and stored in the rollback journal. If something goes wrong during transaction processing, the database can always be reset to the last valid state if required. Note: SQLite permanently stores the entire page in the journal file, even if the transaction modifies only a single record.

A journal file is usually created when a new transaction is started and deleted after the transaction is completed. Although this is the default behaviour, in many cases, there is a deviation from this approach. For example, if the application developer activates the *exclusive locking mode* for a database, then the rollback journal is not immediately deleted. An application can enable the exclusive locking mode by using the following pragma-statement:

```
PRAGMA locking_mode=EXCLUSIVE;
```

In this case, the journal file may be truncated, or the file's header may be wiped with zero bytes. Which behaviour of this occurs depends on the SQLite version used. However, the file is preserved in any case as long as the locking mode is activated. Fortunately, many applications that use rollback journals for transaction safety operate in this mode, reducing unnecessary IO operations. The same behaviour as is seen in EXCLUSIVE locking mode can also be reached by setting the *journal mode pragma* to PERSIST instead of DELETE which is the default behaviour in SQLite:

```
PRAGMA journal_mode=PERSIST;
```

No matter which of the two modes is activated, an investigator can restore the old execution states of the database. In this way, data records that may have been deleted in the meantime can be made visible again.

> **❗ Attention**
>
> The rollback journal file is always located in the same directory as the actual database. One can quickly identify the journal by the file name: It has the same name as the database but with the extension **"-journal"**. Thus, the name of a journal file is precisely eight characters longer than the original name of the database [84].

A rollback journal is a binary format. Just like the main database file, it contains a small header. The header has a fixed size of a maximum of 28 bytes. The individual header fields and their meanings are shown in Table 5.6. Next to the Magic Header String, information about the total number of database pages stored in the journal. The header also records the original size of the database file. So if a change causes the database file to grow, we will still know the original size of the database. Unfortunately, the fields carried in the header are usually automatically overwritten after a COMMIT and wiped with null bytes. Thus, we will rarely be able to recover useful information from it. However, the header is usually preserved if a transaction cannot be completed due to a power down.

The journal file has a preset page size. The value can be determined via the offset 20 in the header. Even if this value can no longer be determined due to wiping, there is a way out. The default value of the first sector is 512. The remaining space of the first journal page is filled with zero bytes. Since the default page size is 512 bytes, the header is thus always followed by a padding area of zero bytes. After the header and padding area, zero or more page records will follow. Such a record contains a copy of precisely one database page. Additionally, each record is introduced by a one-field header. Only with this value, SQLite can reset the correct page in the database in case of a rollback. On offset four, the original content of the database

Table 5.6: Rollback Journal Header Format

Offset	Size	Description
0	8	Header string: 0xd9, 0xd5, 0x05, 0xf9, 0x20, 0xa1, 0x63, 0xd7
8	4	The "Page Count" - The number of pages in the next segment of the journal
12	4	A random nonce for the checksum
16	4	Initial size of the database in pages
20	4	Size of a disk sector.
24	4	Size of pages in this journal.

page follows. The journal page record ends again with a 4-byte big-endian value. It holds the checksum for this page. The value is used to guard against incomplete write operations.

Table 5.7: Rollback Journal Page Record Format [80]

Offset	Size	Description
0	4	The page number in the database file
4	N	Original content of the page prior to the start of the transaction
N+4	4	Checksum

Since the header is always reset for each new transaction, the page records directly following the header are always the most current. However, journal records of past transactions can still be stored in the same journal. For example, suppose a transaction changed ten database pages. The following transaction only rewrote five pages. In that case, the database subsequently contains the database's state before the last transaction plus five more pages from the previous. The following example shows the beginning of the second journal page of a rollback file:

```
|0x1200|61746506 BAC4E54E 0000000B 0D000000 |ate....N........|
|0x1210|0B0E2C00 0F620F35 0FC20F96 0F0E0EFD |..,..b.5........|
|0x1220|0ED10EB8 0E9A0E5A 0E2C0000 00000000 |.......Z.,......|

0xBAC4E54E  -> Checksum of the 1st journal records
0x0000000B  -> page 11 in the database (start of the 2nd journal)
0x0D000000  -> start of a data leaf page (snapshot)
```

The start of 2nd journal record can be calculated as follows:

```
    0x0200   1st sector (header + padding area) - 512 byte
  + 0x0004   page record page number (record start) - 4 byte
  + 0x1000   1st page in journal - 4096 byte
  + 0x0004   checksum of 1st journal page (record end) - 4 byte
  -------
    0x1208   start offset of the 2nd journal record
```

The example shows the end of the first journal page and the beginning of the second journal frame. While the green highlighted value at offset 0x1204 still belongs to the first journal page, the value at offset 0x1208 already initiates the next journal record. Generically, the address of each journal could be determined as follows:

$$\text{Record}_{start}(N+1) = \text{size of 1st sector} + N \times (\text{page size} + 8)$$

However, how can we determine whether the database's journal page belongs to the last transaction or is not perhaps older? A different random nonce is used each time a transaction is started to minimize the risk that unwritten sectors might by chance contain data from the same page that was a part of prior journals. The last nonce is a 4 Byte integer value and can be found at offset 12 in the journal header. By changing the nonce for each transaction, stale data will still generate an incorrect checksum. Since the entire page is always saved from the database, we can restore the actual data described in section 5.2.5.

5.4.3 Write-Ahead Logs

As pointed out in the last section, a copy of the data page to be changed is first created before writing directly into the database file in a classic rollback journal [86]. Version 3.7.0 of the SQLite database engine introduced an alternative concept for transaction management [84]. With *write-ahead logs (WAL)*, this procedure is reversed. The content of the original database file is not changed. Instead, every change is appended into a separate WAL file. It works like a roll-forward journal. All changes are first written to the WAL file. Even a COMMIT does not automatically update the database file [79]. If, for example, other reading database connections exist simultaneously, they can operate as usual on the original unaltered data. Meanwhile, a concurrently running write process stores its changes into the WAL file. Moving the WAL file transactions back into the database is called a *checkpoint*. Usually, SQLite does a checkpoint automatically. If the WAL size reaches a threshold size of 1000 pages, a checkpoint is triggered by default. As soon as we examine a database that works in WAL mode, we must also analyse the included WAL archive. Simultaneously, this also means that we may have different versions of the same database page in the main database and the WAL file. As long as no checkpoint has been carried out, the WAL file exclusively contains the latest changes. The database is, therefore, still in an old state. If we look at both files together, we can get a consistent view [86].

To access the content of a WAL file, all we have to do is open the corresponding database file. When opening a WAL mode database, the WAL file's content is automatically transferred back to the database. In other words, a checkpoint is executed. However, this procedure is usually not recommended for various reasons. With this approach, old artefacts that are evidentially valuable to the investigator could be overwritten and thus lost. Moreover, we would be violating a fundamental rule of any forensic investigation: Never change the evidence.

> **Important**

It is best not to work with a standard database viewer when evaluating a database in WAL mode. Even by opening the database, one risks losing old data due to checkpointing.

But how should we proceed then? One possibility is the use of a special forensic database browser. An example would be the FQLite[1] browser. This program reads the database and the WAL file separately. Since access is read-only, all data is preserved.

! Attention

A particular database will use either a rollback journal or a write-ahead log. It is not possible to use both at the same time. The write-ahead log is always located in the same directory as the actual database. One can quickly identify the journal by the file name: It has the same name as the database but with the extension **"-wal"**.

Let us now turn to the actual structure of the file. The WAL file starts with a header. Zero or more so-called WAL-frames follow it. Just as with the rollback journal, a frame represents the altered content of exactly one page of the database. The file header has a size of exactly 32 bytes. It starts with a 4 byte long Magic Number (see Table 5.8). At offset 4 follows the file format version. Again, this is a 4-byte unsigned integer value. The size of one page of the database is stored at offset 8. Using the field *checkpoint sequence number* at offset 12, we can again determine how many checkpoints have already been executed since their creation.

Table 5.8: WAL Header Format [86]

Offset	Size	Description
0	4	Magic number. 0x377f0682 or 0x377f0683
4	4	File format version. For example 3007000.
8	4	Database page size. Example: 1024
12	4	Checkpoint sequence number
16	4	Salt-1: random integer incremented with each checkpoint
20	4	Salt-2: a different random number for each checkpoint
24	4	Checksum-1: First part of a checksum on the first 24 bytes of header
28	4	Checksum-2: Second part of the checksum on the first 24 bytes of header

The last fields of the header form two salt values and two checksum values. Using these fields, we can determine which frames belong to the current checkpoint and

---

[1] https://github.com/pawlaszczyk/fqlite

have not yet been transferred to the database. Figure 5.12 shows an example of the header of a WAL archive in FQLite.

Each WAL frame also starts with a header [84]. The structure of the header with its fields is shown in Table 5.8. The header consists of exactly six big-endian values, each with a size of 4 bytes. The first object is the page number this frame is assigned. Using the page number, we can identify the place in the database where the change takes effect. The value at offset four can be used to determine whether a COMMIT was performed. A value other than 0 is a so-called *commit frame*. Let us remember that a COMMIT does not automatically update the database. Like the header of the WAL file, each frame header ends with two salt values and two checksums. The four big-endian 32-bit unsigned integer values are located from Offset 8 to 24.

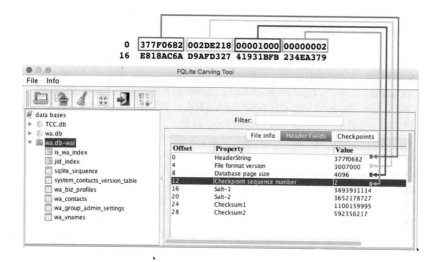

Fig. 5.12: View on a WhatsApp-DB WAL-Header with FQLite Carving Tool

A WAL archive always grows from the beginning. It can cause frames from different checkpoints to appear in the same file, whereas current ones are always at the file's beginning. Fortunately, we can use the mentioned salt values to determine relatively quickly whether the frame under consideration is valid or whether it belongs to an older state already transferred to the database. Whether a frame is valid can be determined as follows [86]:

1. The Salt-1 and Salt-2 values from the header must both match the values in the respective frame.
2. The 8-byte checksum in the frame must match the cumulative checksum over the first 24 bytes of the WAL header plus the first 8 bytes and the contents of all previous frames.

If a checkpoint was executed successfully, the WAL file is reset afterwards. In this case, the salt values are overwritten. The value of salt-1 is incremented, while a

Table 5.9: WAL Frame Header Format [86]

Offset	Size	Description
0	4	Page number
4	4	For commit records, the size of the database file in pages after the commit. For all other records, zero.
8	4	Salt-1 copied from the WAL header
12	4	Salt-2 copied from the WAL header
16	4	Checksum-1: Cumulative checksum up through and including this page
20	4	Checksum-2: Second half of the cumulative checksum.

new random value is assigned to salt-2. Previously valid frames are automatically discarded due to this procedure. However, the previous frames usually remain in the archive due to the I/O- operations when the file is truncated. Thus, there is an excellent chance to make past states of database pages visible again with the help of the WAL file.

Let us take a look at how write-ahead logs work. Figure 5.13 shows the frames list of a WAL file. Below the header field for the Salt-1 value, several frames are shown. All frames with matching salt values belong to the same checkpoint. The first seven frames thus form a unit. The remaining frames are part of an older checkpoint. As we can see, the salt in the header matches the salt in the first unit. Accordingly, the pages have not yet been transferred to the database. In other words, the WAL file contains the latest version of page 2,4,6,18. The pages within the database are out of date. The next checkpoint is usually executed when opening the database, and these data records are transferred to the database. Since WAL files always work at a page level, the complete database page is updated. Remember, the salt value changes for each checkpoint. Thus the Salt-1 field in the header is discarded afterwards.

Interestingly, page 6 has been updated three times. When a checkpoint occurs, each page will be written back to the database in the same order written to the WAL file. Pages are written from the start of the WAL file. Accordingly, the update order would be 2,6,4,12,6,18,6. This allows a timeline to be created, starting with the first to the last update step.

5.5 Conclusions

The SQLite database format has great importance in the field of mobile forensics. In this chapter, we have therefore tried to take a look behind the scenes. As quickly became apparent, the file format of SQLite has some similarities to a classic file system, where files are usually stored in blocks. Instead of blocks or clusters, data content in SQLite is managed in pages. As has been shown, even records are often recoverable after they have been deleted. Analogous to a file system, these are usually

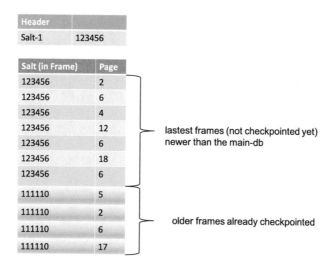

Fig. 5.13: Frame list of a WAL file (example)

not wiped but merely marked as deleted. However, we do not manage files but data sets.

We further identified different slack spaces of an SQLite database. Besides free blocks and the unallocated space, we can find deleted records, especially in the freelist area of the database. The carving techniques discussed within this chapter can help make these data sets visible again in many cases.

Of the temporary file-formats considered, rollback journals and the WAL files are of particular interest to the investigator, as they may contain old or previously altered data. However, special care must be taken when acquiring data from these files. Thus, the data stored in a WAL file can be reconstructed manually or with specialized forensic tools. Using an ordinary SQLite reader, on the other hand, can lead to the loss of data.

Chapter 6
Property Lists

Christian Hummert and Georgina Louise Humphries

Abstract Property List files (*.plist) are a widely used data storage format used by Apple software. Most of the system properties are stored in plists, but also, many apps store their configuration in plist-files. The data held within Property is regularly of high evidential value for forensic analysts, so understanding the format is essential for the forensic investigation of Apple mobile devices and computers. Not all of today's digital forensics tools recover plists properly. Especially for carved or damaged plists, the support is insufficient. So the forensic examiner must understand the principles of this file format. This chapter gives an overview of the plist structure to give the examiner the knowledge to get the most information out of the evidence possible.

6.1 Introduction

Property List files (*.plist) are one of the widely used data storage formats used by Apple software . Most of the system properties are stored in plists (many of them are located in /Library/Preferences/), but many apps store their configuration in plist-files. Therefore, property lists can be found in various places on Apple systems. They sometimes can even be found on devices other than Apple operating systems (especially if other Apple software like Safari or iTunes is installed). The data held within Property is regularly of high evidential value for forensic analysts, so understanding the format is essential for the forensic investigation of Apple mobile devices and computers.

Christian Hummert

Agentur für Innvation in der Cybersicherheit, Halle, Germany, e-mail: hummert@cyberagentur.de

Georgina Louise Humphries

Politihøgskolen - Norwegian Police University College Department of Postgraduate Studies, Oslo, Norway, e-mail: georgina.louise.humphries@phs.no

C. Hummert, D. Pawlaszczyk (eds.), *Mobile Forensics – The File Format Handbook*,
https://doi.org/10.1007/978-3-030-98467-0_6

Property lists offer a structured and efficient way to represent and persist hierarchies of objects to disk. They are the standard way to save and load data between the internal representation within objects in Objective-C or Swift programs and disk files. The standard objects of the Cocoa framework have built-in methods to deal with plist files.

The first plists were developed with the NeXTSTEP operating system. NeXT-STEP is a discontinued operating system that merges the Mach kernel and the BSD kernel. It was developed by NeXT, a company founded by Steve Jobs in 1985, and released in 1989. NeXTSTEP had a text-based, human-readable format for plists, serialized to ASCII in a syntax somewhat like a programming language. Apple replaced the format with an XML-based format and also introduced the binary plist format. Since Mac OS X 10.7, in addition, JSON notation can be read and written. So, there are four different property list formats[9]:

- NeXTSTEP property lists (deprecated since OS X 10.0)
- XML property lists (introduced with OS X 10.0)
- Binary property lists (introduced with OS X 10.2)
- JSON property lists (introduced with OS X 10.7, but not 100% compatible)

The formats except the binary plist have the advantage of being human-readable. In contrast, the binary plist offers the most efficient representation on disk and fast serialization/deserialization. OS X offers the plutil utility (introduced in OS X 10.2) to check the syntax of property lists or convert a property list file from one format to another. It also supports converting plists to Objective-C or Swift object literals. Another tool that comes with OS X is PlistBuddy (it can be found at /usr/libexec). PlistBuddy allows to merge plists or edit their content.

Property Lists in XML or JSON notation can be easily edited and evaluated in any desired text editor. Apples IDE Xcode also contains a hierarchical viewer and editor for binary and XML plists. In addition, Apple offers an Apple Script interface to create, edit and write property lists (since OS X 10.5). Due to the human-readable notation of NeXTSTEP, XML and JSON property lists, they are not an obstacle for forensic investigates. Therefore, this chapter concentrates on the binary plists (bplist) format and will afterwards describe some of the interfaces to plist files.

6.2 Binary plist Structure

Apple disclosed the structure of the binary property list format; it is documented in the comments of the Apple-provided open-source CFBinaryPList.c[1] and declarations of the ForFoundationOnly.h[2]. Every binary plist file comprises four sections: a header, an object table, an offset table and a trailer (compare table 6.1).

Each bplist file begins with an 6-byte header, containing the magic bplist (Hex: 0x62706C697374). The header is followed by a 2-bye version. The most common

---

[1] https://opensource.apple.com/source/CF/CF-550/CFBinaryPList.c

[2] https://opensource.apple.com/source/CF/CF-550/ForFoundationOnly.h

Table 6.1: Structure of a bplist file.

Offset	Size	Description
0x00	6	bplist header (0x62706C697374)
0x06	2	format version
0x08	LEN1	object table
0x08 + LEN1	LEN2	offset table
0x08 + LEN1 + LEN2	32	trailer

version on Apple devices is 00, but there are at least two other versions of binary property lists, too; bplist15 or bplist16 occur. Unlike for bplist00, there is no documentation for either format. The bplist15 format appears to be internal to CoreFoundation. The bplist16 format is internal to Foundation, too, and is used almost exclusively in Objective-C remoting over XPC. The format of bplist16 is similar, but not compatible with bplist00, noting the following differences: Files in format version 16 do not have a trailer, and the items start directly at the head of the property list, right after the bplist16 magic, and are packed (not aligned). In addition, in bplist16 there are more data types available.[47]

The bplist file ends with a 32-byte long trailer. The structure of the trailer is shown in table 6.2. The bytes 0 to 4 of the trailer are unused. Byte 5 contains the sort version. Byte 6 stores the information of the size in byte of each offset entry in the offset table. Similarly, byte 7 stores the information of the size of each object reference in a container. At offset 0x8, there is an 8-byte entry that saves the number of objects that are encoded inside the object table. The following 8 bytes save the offset of the first offset in the offset table (usually zero). The last 8 bytes of the trailer denotes the start of the offset table, counting from the start of the bplist.

Table 6.2: Structure of the bplist trailer.

Offset	Length	Description
0x0	5	unused
0x5	1	sort version
0x6	1	size per offset in offset table in bytes
0x7	1	size per object reference in a container
0x8	8	number of objects in object table (big endian)
0x10	8	offset of the first offset in the offset table (big endian)
0x18	8	offset of the offset table (big endian)

The second section in every bplist file is the object table. The object table contains all the data objects of the plist. All object types are identified by a single byte, also called a marker (compare Table 6.3). This byte encodes the type of an object and the size of the data.

Table 6.3: Format of object types.

Object	Marker	(Additional Info)	Description
null	0000 0000		
bool	0000 1000		false
bool	0000 1001		true
fill	0000 1111		fill byte
int	0001 nnnn ...		2^{nnnn} bytes (big endian)
real	0010 nnnn ...		2^{nnnn} bytes (big endian)
date	0011 0011 ...		8 byte float (big endian)
data	0100 nnnn [int] ...		nnnn bytes unless 1111 then [int] count followed by bytes
string	0101 nnnn [int] ...		nnnn chars unless 1111 then [int] count followed by bytes
string	0110 nnnn [int] ...		Unicode string, nnnn chars unless 1111 then [int] count followed by bytes
	0111 xxxx		unused
uid	1000 nnnn ...		nnnn+1 bytes
	1001 xxxx		unused
array	1010 nnnn [int] objref*		nnnn entries unless 1111 then [int] count followed by entries
	1011 xxxx		unused
set	1100 nnnn [int] objref*		unused
dict	1101 nnnn [int] keyref*		nnnn entries unless 1111 then [int] count followed by entries
	1110 xxxx		unused
	1111 xxxx		unused

The marker is the binary representation of a single byte. All other objects can be uniquely identified by the marker byte's 4 most significant bits (MSB). At the same time, the least significant bits (LSB) of the marker byte denotes sizing information. If the object size is small enough, the size is encoded immediately in the 4 right-most bits, and then the actual data values follow. If the object size is larger, the LSB matches 0xF (1111), denoting that the next bytes encode size information before the actual value bytes.

The size is encoded as follows: The MSB equals 0x1 (0001), and the LSB contains a value x. The size will be stored in the following 2^x bytes in big-endian.

For example: let us assume the object table contains the sequence 0x5F 10 19. The first 0x5F is converted into its binary representation 0101 1111. The MSB is 0101, so the object denotes a string. The LSB matches 1111, so the size is encoded in the next byte. The next byte is 0x10 = 0001 0000. The MSB equals 0x1, and the LSB shows that $2^0 = 1$ byte follows, which stores the size of the string. The next byte is 0x19 resulting in a 25-byte long string.

Markers corresponding to objects such as ints, real numbers, strings are immediately followed by a multibyte sequence representing their actual values. This is not always the case, though. In the case of object containers, such as arrays and dictionaries, the marker byte is followed by object references that are simply offset to the offset table. The length of this offsets is determined in the bplist trailer, and are counted from the beginning of the offset table. Therefore, a container element is just a reference that points back to a position in the offset table, which points back to the object table and specifically to a marker corresponding to the individual object. This technique flat-maps the actual multi-level hierarchy and allows all objects to have fixed sizes.

The third section in bplists contains offsets to the object table and guides to the actual values of objects. The size of each offset is defined in the file trailer. All offsets are calculated from the beginning of the file (not the end of the header). The number of offsets stored in the offset table is also given in the trailer.[40]

6.3 Example

Given is the following plist (Table 6.4) from a MacBook Pro:

Table 6.4: Example plist (object table colored in blue, offset table colored in red, trailer colored in yellow).

```
62 70 6C 69 73 74 30 30 D2 01 02 03 04 5E 42 61 b p l i s t 0 0 "        ^ B a
74 74 65 72 79 48 69 73 74 6F 72 79 5F 10 13 54 t t e r y H i s t o r y _       T
6F 74 61 6C 4E 75 6D 62 65 72 6F 66 45 76 65 6E o t a l N u m b e r O f E v e n
74 73 09 10 0A 08 0D 1C 32 33 00 00 00 00 00 00 t s _    2 3
01 01 00 00 00 00 00 00 00 05 00 00 00 00 00 00
00 00 00 00 00 00 00 00 35                              5
```

The given bplist is version 00 as the header states. To analyze the bplist in a first step the trailer is marked (here yellow) the trailer comprises the last 32 bytes of the file. Now the trailer can be decoded (result in Table 6.5):

Table 6.5: Decoded example bplist trailer.

Content	Offset	Length	Description
0x00	0x5	1	sort version
0x01	0x6	1	size per offset in offset table
0x01	0x7	1	size per object reference
0x0000000000000005	0x8	8	number of objects in object table
0x0000000000000000	0x10	8	offset of the first offset in offset table
0x0000000000000035	0x18	8	offset of the offset table

Now, it is clear that the bplist contains five objects in the object table, and the offset table starts at 0x35, whereas the first object-offset starts at 0x35 + 0x00, and each offset has the size of one single byte. In consequence, the offsets from the offset table are 0x08, 0x0D, 0x1C, 0x32 and 0x33, which leads to the following four objects from the object table:

1. 0xD2 01 02 03 04
2. 0x5E 42 61 74 74 65 ...
3. 0x5F 10 13 54 6F 74 ...
4. 0x09
5. 0x10 0A

The first object starts with 0xD2, which is 1101 0010 in binary. The MSB (1101) shows that the object-type is a dictionary. The LSB (0010 = 2) shows that the dictionary has two entries. The data 0x01 02 03 04 has to be interpreted as object references that are simply offsets to the offset table. Before interpreting the dictionary as an object container, the other four entries should be decoded.

The second object starts with 0x5E, which is 0101 1110 in binary. The MSB (0101) shows that the object type is a string. The LSB (1110 = 14) shows that the string is 14 chars long. The content of the string is "BatteryHistory".

The third object starts with 0x5F, which is 0101 1111 in binary. The MSAB (0101) shows that the object is another string. The LSB (1111) shows that the string is longer than 14 chars, and the size is encoded in the following bytes. The next byte is 0x10, which is 0001 0000 in binary. The MSB (0001) is defined as 0001, and the LSB (0000) shows that the following $2^0 = 1$ bytes encode the length of the string size. So the next byte has to be decoded. It is 0x13, which states that the string has a length of 0x13 = 19 chars. The content of the string is "TotalNumberOfEvents".

The fourth object starts with 0x09, which is 0000 1001 in binary. The MSB (0000) indicates the object as bool, and the LSB (1001) indicates the content as "true".

The fifth object starts with 0x10, which is 0001 0000 in binary. The MSB (0001) indicates the object as an integer. The LSB indicates that the integer is $2^0 = 1$ byte long. The content of the integer is 0x0A which is 10. Now the dictionary (the first object) can be decoded. The dictionary has two entries: the objects at offset 0x01 and 0x02 in the offset table, which are the two strings. The first entry is connected to the object on offset 0x03, which is the boolean. The second entry is connected to the object on offset 0x04, which is the integer. That gives the following result (Table 6.6):

Table 6.6: Decoded example bplist.

dictionary (2 entries)		
	BatteryHistory	TRUE
	TotalNumberOfEvents	10

Fig. 6.1 shows the same plist file decoded with Apples XCode IDE and confirms the correct decoding.

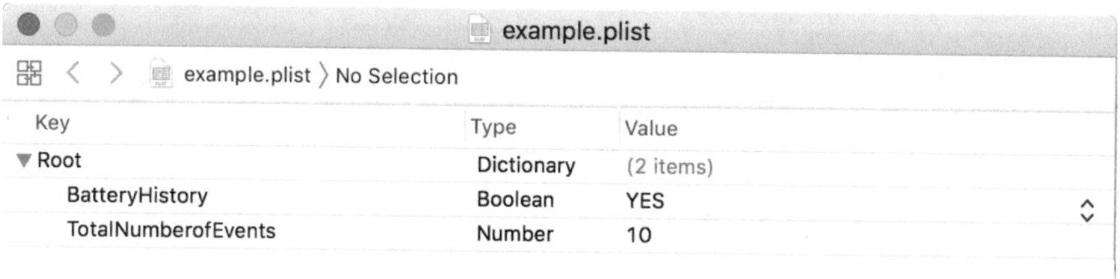

Key	Type	Value
▼ Root	Dictionary	(2 items)
BatteryHistory	Boolean	YES
TotalNumberofEvents	Number	10

Fig. 6.1: Illustration of the elements of a block group.

6.4 Forensic Tools Supporting plists

There is quite a bunch of tools supporting the decoding of plist files. Most of the tools support binary plists as well as XML property lists. As the property lists are in an Apple format, the macOS universe gives the best support. If the given property list file is in XML format, it can be edited in any text editor. On the other hand, if the given property list file is in the binary format, it can be converted to XML first by running on the macOS shell:

```
plutil -convert xml1 file.plist
```

If an XML property list should be converted back this is possible with:

```
plutil -convert binary1 file.plist
```

A more convenient way to edit and browse plist files is to install the Apple development platform Xcode. The suite includes a graphical editor which is easy to use (compare Fig. 6.2).

For old versions (Xcode 4.2 and earlier) there was a separate application for editing property lists (/Developer/Applications/Utilities/Property List Editor.app/).

Nevertheless, despite the Apple world, there are plenty of alternatives. One free plist parser for binary property lists is binplist [3] a parser module written in Python. For forensic use, it is possible to create an instance of the BinaryPlist class and then call the Parse() method, with a file-like object as an argument.

```
with open("myfile.plist", "rb") as fd:
    bplist = BinaryPlist(fd)
    top_level_object = bplist.Parse(fd)
```

The *Parse()* method returns the top-level object, just as readPlist. Once parsed, BinaryPlist. is_corrupt can be checked to recognize whether the plist had corrupt data. This allows to maybe decode the corrupted data manually and gather the maximum information on the plist even when they are corrupt.

---

[3] https://github.com/google/binplist

Key	Type	Value
● ● ● com.apple.SoftwareUpdate.plist		
com.apple.SoftwareUpdate.plist ⟩ No Selection		
Key	Type	Value
∨ Root	Dictionary	(17 items)
LastSuccessfulDate	Date	2021-05-14T12:48:29Z
AutomaticCheckEnabled	Boolean	0
LastAttemptSystemVersion	String	11.2.2 (20D80)
LastBackgroundCCDSuccessfulDate	Date	2016-09-30T13:05:07Z
AutomaticallyInstallMacOSUpdates	Boolean	0
LastUpdatesAvailable	Number	1
SkipLocalCDN	Boolean	0
LastRecommendedUpdatesAvailable	Number	1
LastAttemptBuildVersion	String	11.2.2 (20D80)
AutomaticDownload	Boolean	0
∨ RecommendedUpdates	Array	(1 item)
∨ Item 0	Dictionary	(5 items)
Identifier	String	MSU_UPDATE_20E241_patch_11.3.1
MobileSoftwareUpdate	Boolean	1
Display Name	String	macOS Big Sur 11.3.1
Product Key	String	MSU_UPDATE_20E241_patch_11.3.1
Display Version	String	11.3.1
LastFullSuccessfulDate	Date	2021-05-14T12:48:29Z
LastRecommendedMajorOSBundleIdentifier	String	
∨ PrimaryLanguages	Array	(2 items)
Item 0	String	de
Item 1	String	de-DE
LastSessionSuccessful	Boolean	1
LastBackgroundSuccessfulDate	Date	2017-07-20T19:07:32Z
LastResultCode	Number	2

Fig. 6.2: View of an example plist in the Xcode editor.

Another Python module dealing with binary property lists is ccl-bplist[4]. A C-library to handle plists is libplist[5].

Forensic Suites on Windows create a different picture. The MSAB Forensic suite[6] offers property list decoding as well as the Cellebrite[7] suite. Oxygen Forensics[8] offers the Oxygen Forensic Plist Viewer that automatically unpacks one plist file and displays its content as a folder tree (compare Fig. 6.3). The entries can be converted to different encodings. In addition, the binary content of cells, such as images, video and sound, can be decoded and visualized. The Forensic Toolkit (FTK)[9] does support plist decoding, whereas the Encase Forensic Software[10] offers a plugin script to decode these files.

---

[4] https://code.google.com/archive/p/ccl-bplist/

[5] https://github.com/JonathanBeck/libplist

[6] https://www.msab.com/

[7] https://www.cellebrite.com/

[8] www.oxygen-forensic.com

[9] https://accessdata.com/products-services/forensic-toolkit-ftk

[10] https://security.opentext.com/encase-forensic

Fig. 6.3: View of an example plist in the Oxygen Forensic Plist Viewer.

6.5 Conclusions

Property Lists have great importance in the field of mobile forensics. In this chapter, a look behind the scenes was given. There are four different types of property lists. The chapter concentrated on the binary property list format because it is not intuitive to decode and has a certain prevalence. The binary property list format contains a header, a trailer and an object table. The type of the single objects can be found in a look-up table.

There are plenty of tools that support the decoding of plist files. But in a forensic manner, information from corrupted files (especially parts of files carved from the unallocated space) must be revealed. To fulfill this challenge, deep knowledge about file structures is crucial.

Chapter 7
Java Serialization

Dirk Pawlaszczyk

Abstract Java Serialization is a popular technique for storing object states in the Java programming language. In the field of mobile forensics, we come across such artefacts. App developers very often resort to this technique to make their application state persistent. Serialization is also used when transferring data over a network between two Java applications using Remote Method Invocation(RMI). In the past, there have been recurring security issues associated with this technology. Despite its importance for forensic casework, one can hardly find any literature on this topic. In this chapter, we give an insight into the binary format. For this purpose, special features of the format are presented using an example. In addition to the actual protocol structure, basic steps for acquiring such data and analyzing it will be discussed. Practical hints for searching serials are given. Finally, the security issues are addressed.

7.1 Introduction

Among app developers, the Java programming language has been the first choice for many years. The popularity of the language can be attributed to its simple syntax and compelling framework. As with any object-oriented language, the execution state of the program is managed through objects. From time to time, an application needs to back up its current state to disk. Of course, it is possible to store important data in a database such as SQLite. However, this usually requires object-relational mapping to be performed first. From the beginning, Java offers an alternative for persistent writing of objects: the so-called Java Object Serialization (JOS) [93]. Java's standard serialization seems to be a good choice, especially for app developers who want to store objects' current execution state. By serialization, we understand the ability to

Faculty for Applied Computer Science
University of Applied Sciences (Hochschule Mittweida), Technikumplatz 17, 09648 Mittweida, Germany, e-mail: pawlaszc@hs-mittweida.de

© The Author(s) 2022
C. Hummert, D. Pawlaszczyk (eds.), *Mobile Forensics – The File Format Handbook*,
https://doi.org/10.1007/978-3-030-98467-0_7

convert an object in the application's main memory into a format that allows the object to be written to a file or transported over a network connection.

Since many apps rely on this format by default to store their program data, investigators are of particular interest. This chapter will take a closer look behind the scenes at the Standard Serialization concept in Java. We pay special attention to the binary format and explore how to analyze this file type.

7.2 Object Serialization in Java

7.2.1 Serialization Techniques in Java

Under Java SE, objects can be automatically mapped and stored persistently using various approaches [91], [54]:

- **Standard serialization:** The object structure and states are saved in a binary format. As already mentioned, this procedure is also called Java Object Serialization (JOS). Standard serialization is very important for remote method calls and storing things over time and then retrieving them from the closet at some point.
- **XML serialization via JavaBeans Persistence:** JavaBeans - and only such - can be saved in an XML format. One solution is JavaBeans Persistence (JBP), which was originally intended for Swing. When the state of a graphical user interface is binary persisted with JOS, changes to the Swing API's internals are not easily possible since the binary format of JOS is very tightly coupled with the object model. That is, objects sometimes cannot be reconstructed from the binary document. JBP decouples this by communicating only through setters/getters and not on internal references, which are an implementation detail, which can change at any time. Nowadays, JBP hardly plays a role in practice.
- **XML mapping via JAXB:** With JAXB, a second API is available for mapping the object structure to XML documents. The eXtensible Markup Language (XML) supports a text-based data format based on markups. The platform-independent exchange format is part of the standard library from version 6. It is a fundamental technology, especially for Web service calls.

All three options are already built into Java by default. The standard object serialization creates a binary format and is very strongly oriented towards Java. Other systems cannot do much with the data. XML is convenient as a format because other systems can process it. Another compact binary format that also allows interoperability is Protocol Buffers [1] from Google. The company uses it internally when different applications are to exchange data.

Finally, objects can also be stored in relational databases called object-relational mapping (OR mapping). This technique is very sophisticated because the object

---

[1] http://code.google.com/p/protobuf/

models and tables are quite different. The Java SE does not offer any support for OR mapping, but it can be done with additional frameworks, such as the JPA (Java Persistence API).

7.2.2 Serialization by Example

The traditional way from an object to persistent storage is via Java's serialization mechanism [57][54]. JOS is the technology we want to deal with in the following. The standard serialization offers a simple possibility to make objects persistent and to reconstruct them later. The object state (no static ones!) is written into a byte stream (serialization). From this, it can be reconstructed to an object again later (deserialization). The object state is written into a serial data stream of 0 and 1. Java provides two special classes for this purpose: *ObjectOutputStream* and *ObjectInputStream* with a *writeObject()* respectively *readObject()*-method. Both classes can be found in the *java.io* package of the Java standard class library [2]. To save an object's state, we must pass the object reference as a parameter to the writeObject()-method. In the Java ecosystem, the applications programmers are encouraged to use serialization almost everywhere.

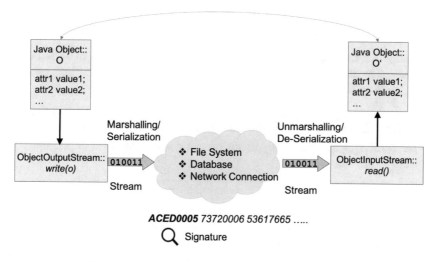

Fig. 7.1: Java Object Serialization (JOS) - Concept

Serialization concept can show its strengths, especially in communication between different Java processes distributed over a network. We serialize some of the objects, send them to another process for processing, serialize the transformed object and send

---

[2] https://docs.oracle.com/javase/7/docs/api/java/io/ObjectOutputStream.html

---

it back. To illustrate this, we will discuss a small example program. In the following, we want to make a class *SaveMe* serializable. For this, we need the following code:

Listing 7.1: Class definition of a class to serialize

```java
import java.io.Serializable;

public class SaveMe implements Serializable {

        private static final long serialVersionUID = 1L;
        private int x;
        private double d;
        private String s;

        public SaveMe() {
                this(100, 3.14, "hello");
        }

        public SaveMe(int x, double d, String s) {
                this.x = x;
                this.d = d;
                this.s = s;
        }

        public String toString() {
                return s + " " + x + " " + d;
        }
    }
}
```

In Listing 1.1, the class *SaveMe* is defined first. In order for objects to be Serialized, the classes must implement the *Serializable* interface. This interface thus serves as a marker to indicate that the class can be Serialized.

❗ Attention

When serializing an object, only its attributes are stored. Methods or program code remains in the *.class* file.

Java is assigning a serial number to each object of the class it writes to a stream. This serial number is then used to re-create the class when it is reread. If two variables contain references to the same object and we write the objects to a file and later read them from the file, then the two objects that are read will again be references to the same object. All attributes of an object can be made persistent in this way. However, there are two exceptions. Attributes defined with the prefixed key *transient* are not Serialized. This identifier was explicitly introduced to exclude an attribute from Serialization. It can be helpful, for example, if confidential or volatile data should not be saved. The second exception is class attributes preceded by the keyword *static*. With one exception, such attributes shared by all objects of a class are not Serialized. In our example, there are no transient attributes and only one static class attribute. Since the serialVersionUID property is defined as static and thus should not be stored. In this case, however, an exception is made. In Java, serialVersionUID is like version control, ensuring that both Serialized and deSerialized objects use the compatible class. For example, if an object is saved into a stream with serialVersionUID=1L, when we convert the stream back to an object, we must use the same serialVersionUID=1L. Otherwise, an InvalidClassException is thrown.

If we create a *SaveMe* object *o*1 and call *writeObject(o*1), the ObjectOutputStream pushes the variable assignments (here *x*, *d* and *s*) into the data stream. An example is shown in the next listing:

Listing 7.2: Output Class 'Serializer'

```
import java.io.*;

public class Serializer {

public static void main(String[] args) throws IOExectpion {
            ObjectOutputStream o =
                new ObjectOutputStream(
                        new FileOutputStream("saved.ser"));
            SaveMe o1 = new SaveMe();
            o.writeObject(o1);
            o.close();
}}
```

This routine creates a file, *saved.bin*, on the disk that contains the serialized object. With a few lines, the state of our object *o*1 can be saved to a file. In the example shown, the serialized object is written to a file. To send the object over the network, we have to create an object of the Socket class and start writing to the output stream of this class:

Listing 7.3: Output to a socket connection instead of a file

```
...
Socket connection = new Socket(hostName, portNumber);
OjbectOutputStream oos =  new
        ObjectOutputStream(connection.getOutputStream(), true);
oos.writeObject(o1);
```

We only need to adjust two lines in our program, and we are ready to go. It could not be simpler. However, this form of serialization also has disadvantages. Standard serialization works according to the principle: Everything reached from the object graph enters the data stream serialized. Suppose the object graph is extensive, the time for serialization and the data volume increase. Unlike other persistence concepts, it is not possible to write only the changes. For example, if only one attribute value has changed in an extended object list, the entire list must be rewritten. This is not efficient. However, let us focus on analyzing the binary format.

The output file <saved.ser> from the above example has a size of 80 bytes. The content of the file can be seen in Fig. 7.2. In addition to the actual attribute values, information about data type and class type is also stored in the file. Fig. 7.3 offers a high-level look at the serialization algorithm for this example. In the next section,

```
00  AC ED 00 05 73 72 00 06 53 61 76 65 4D 65 00 00 00    ....sr..SaveMe...
11  00 00 00 00 01 02 00 03 44 00 01 64 49 00 01 78 4C    ........D..dI..xL
22  00 01 73 74 00 12 4C 6A 61 76 61 2F 6C 61 6E 67 2F    ..st..Ljava/lang/
33  53 74 72 69 6E 67 3B 78 70 40 09 1E B8 51 EB 85 1F    String;xp@...Q...
44  00 00 00 64 74 00 05 68 65 6C 6C 6F                   ...dt..hello
```

Fig. 7.2: Hex view of the serialized object *o*1

we will take a closer look a the serialized format of the object and see what each byte represents.

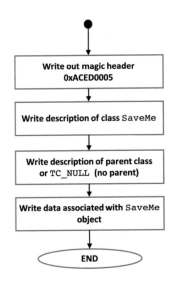

Fig. 7.3: Outline of the Serialization steps for class *SaveMe*

7.3 Java Object Serialization Protocol Revealed

As already discussed, Java's object Serialization creates a binary stream. Unlike JavaBeans persistence, for example, it is not readable by humans. Fortunately, the format is well documented. Oracle provides corresponding documentation on its website in which details of the *Object Serialization Stream Protocol* are presented [56]. The specification defines context-free grammar for the stream format. It gives a good insight into the Serialization process. The stream rules formulated in it are used directly in the Serialization of an object. In addition, a look at the source code of the *ObjectOutputStream* class reveals a lot about concrete implementation. Fig. 7.4 shows the first part of the grammar using a syntax diagram. It defines a set of production rules (<R_n>). These rules can then be used directly to generate an object data stream.

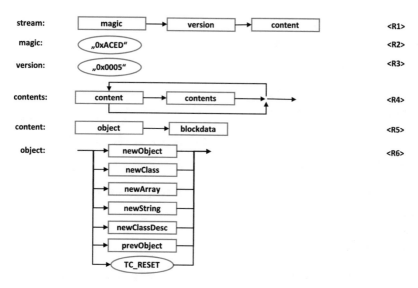

Fig. 7.4: Syntax-diagram for the Java Object Serialization Protocol (Header Detail)

The syntax diagram for this is thus as follows: Definitions of symbols are followed by a ":". We first distinguish between the terminal and non-terminal symbols. The latter can be recognised by the fact that they consist of a literal enclosed in double quotes. Constant values are enclosed in an oval. A rectangle marks non-terminals. A sequence of values is represented as a series of symbols on the same line. The individual values can be found precisely in this order in the stream. A definition consists of zero or more alternative values. Alternatives are indicated by a branch (exclusive OR).

Let us now turn to the concrete meaning of the rules. Each object stream initially consists of a magic number, the version number and the actual content specification (R_1). A magic number opens the data stream. The 2-byte integer value resides on offset 0. On offset two, the stream version field follows. According to the internal specification, this is assigned to value *0x0005* (R_3). Thus, a Java object stream can be detected with the help of the header signature 0XACED0005 ($R_2 + R_3$). This information is beneficial when carving to serial format files on disk. The actual content directly follows the header in the data stream.

The *contents* field is defined recursively (see R_4). Thus it can hold multiple content objects. A *content* object is first divided into an object description and a data block with the concrete attribute values (R_5). Thus, valid values for a content element are *objects, classes, arrays, strings, enumerations, exceptions* (R_6). In this way, all elements of a class and its objects can be described. Within the byte stream, limiter symbols indicate the type, start and end of particular elements. These terminal constants (TC) are shown in Table 7.1.

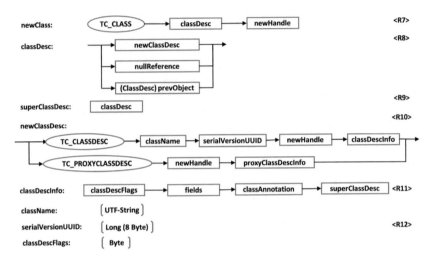

Fig. 7.5: Syntax-diagram for the 'newClass' production rule

Table 7.1: Stream Terminal Constants (TC)

Constant	Value(hex)
TC_NULL	0x70
TC_REFERENCE	0x71
TC_CLASSDESC	0x72
TC_OBJECT	0x73
TC_STRING	0x74
TC_ARRAY	0x75
TC_CLASS	0x76
TC_BLOCKDATA	0x77
TC_ENDBLOCKDATA	0x78
TC_RESET	0x79
TC_BLOCKDATALONG	0x7A
TC_EXCEPTION	0x7B
TC_LONGSTRING	0x7C
TC_PROXYCLASSDESC	0x7D
TC_ENUM	0x7E
baseWireHandle	0x7E0000

Fig. 7.5 describes the syntax definition for a class. Besides the class name, the *SerializationUUID* and *ClassDescInfo* elements are of particular importance (see R_{10}). Note: A corresponding class description must first be placed in the data stream

for each object to be Serialized. It contains information about attribute names and data types. If the class has been derived from a special super-class, the class must, of course, also be Serialized. Since attributes of the super-class are also inherited in the deriving class, we must also capture them. If the super-class, in turn, has a parent class, then this must also be described. Inheritance relationships thus significantly increase the data stream. Fortunately, Java supports only single inheritance.

Particular attention should be paid to the symbol TC_CLASSDEC. It is used to show the start of a new class definition. The byte TC_OBJECT (0x73) represents the start of an object. A data block (TC_BLOCKDATA) is in turn initiated by the byte value 0x77. We need to search the serial stream for these symbols to make the data visible. The constant *baseWireHandle* is of particular importance. Each Serialized element is assigned to such a handle. The first Serialized element contains the handle 0x7E0000, the next object is the trade 0x7E00001 and so on. In this way, for example, an object can reference its class.

Table 7.2: Type Codes / Stream Symbols for Primitive Types

Symbol	Datatype
B	byte
C	char
D	double
F	float
I	integer
J	long
S	short
Z	boolean

Table 7.2 shows the identifiers used in the stream for the eight built-in data types in Java. We can now start decoding the first part of our sample file <saved.ser> with what we have discussed so far (see below). As discussed above, the binary stream is opened by the magic number (0xACED) and the stream version (0x0005). The next byte indicates that this is an object that follows (0x73). The following byte introduces the class identifier (0x72).

> **Important**

Java serialized objects have a specific signature. We can use it to identify an object stream. The binary value is 0xACED0005. It translates to BASE64 as "rO0ABQ==" in a HTTP-Stream for example.

The sub-element is composed of the className. The class name is again composed of a length specification 0x0006 and the actual name string 0x536176654D65.

```
|0x00|ACED0005 73720006 53617665 4D650000 |....sr..SaveMe..|
|0x10|00000000 00010200 03440001 64490001 |.........D..dI..|
|0x20|784C0001 73740012 4C6A6176 612F6C61 |xL..st..Ljava/la|
|0x30|6E672F53 7472696E 673B7870 40091EB8 |ng/String;xp@...|
|0x40|51EB851F 00000064 74000568 656C6C6F |Q......dt..hello|
```

```
STREAM_MAGIC - 0xACED
STREAM_VERSION - 0x0005
Contents
  TC_OBJECT - 0x73
    TC_CLASSDESC - 0x72
      className
        Length - 6 - 0x0006
        Value - SaveMe - 0x536176654d65
      serialVersionUID - 0x0000000000000001
      newHandle 0x007E0000
      classDescFlags - 0x02 - SC_SERIALIZABLE
      fieldCount - 3 - 0x0003
      Fields
        0:  Double - D - 0x44
              field name 'x'
              Length - 1 - 0x00 01
              Value - d - 0x64
        1:  Int - I - 0x49
              field name 'd'
              Length - 1 - 0x00 01
              Value - x - 0x78
        2:  Object - L - 0x4C
              field name 's'
              Length - 1 - 0x00 01
              Value - s - 0x73
              class name
              TC_STRING - 0x74
                newHandle 0x007E0001
                Length - 18 - 0x00 12
                Value - Ljava/lang/String; -
                0x4C6A6176612F6C616E672F537472696E673B
      classAnnotations
        TC_ENDBLOCKDATA - 0x78
      superClassDesc
        TC_NULL - 0x70. <- end of class description
```

integer. The value in the example is 0x0000000000000001. The *SaveMe* class is internally assigned with the handle 0x007e0000. The handle never appears directly in the stream. Only if later, a stream element again refers to the class will be visible in the stream. Various flags typically follow the class name. This flag indicates that this class supports serialization (0x02). Now we have to read out the actual attribute values. They follow directly after the class description. The object we stored in the above example has a total of three more attributes: 'x', 'd' and 's'. Since the serial number attribute is not counted, the property *fieldcount* has the value 0x0003. The individual attribute descriptions with a data type, name and length specification follow directly afterwards (see Fig. 7.6). The string attribute is different here. Since this value itself is an object and not a primitive data type, it is also handled. Again, this is not displayed in binary code. However, Java carries an internal counter. The TC_ENDBLOCKDATA (0x78) value marks the end of the class description. Next, the serialization algorithm checks to see if the current class has any parent classes. If it did, the algorithm would start writing that class. Since we have not specified a superclass, the superClassDesc field remains empty or is assigned the terminal symbol TC_NULL(0x70). Finally, the actual attribute values for our object *o1* are still missing:

```
|0x30|6E672F53 7472696E 673B7870 40091EB8 |ng/String;xp@...|
|0x40|51EB851F 00000064 74000568 656C6C6F |Q......dt..hello|
```

```
newHandle 0x00 7e 00 02
    classdata
      SaveMe
        values
          'd' (double)3.14 - 0x40091EB851EB851F
          'x' (int)100 - 0x00000064
          's' (object) TC_STRING - 0x74
                newHandle 0x007E0003
                Length - 5 - 0x0005
                Value - hello - 0x68656C6C6F
```

As we surely noticed, the object name *o1* is missing. This information is not stored in the stream since it is only an identifier. The programmer decides under which identifier the object can be accessed after deserialization. The value assignment of the ordinal types *d* and *x* follows directly in the stream. The first attribute has 8 bytes in length for the LONG value. The integer value has a length of 4 bytes. Thus, unlike database formats such as SQLite, no compression is used. The memory content is transferred 1:1 into the stream. The string value terminates the stream. A string is not an ordinal type but an object itself. Therefore first, the identifier follows as a string (0x74). The length of a string is dynamic. Therefore the length specification is additionally prefixed to the string value (0x05). The actual value follows last. There is no particular end identifier. Instead, the stream ends [54].

There are some production rules which are not listed so far. Special stream types like enumerations, exceptions or proxy classes are missing. At this point we refer to the protocol description on the oracle website [57][56].

7.4 Pitfalls and Security Issues

In the last years, the serialization protocol of Java was increasingly in the criticism due to different vulnerabilities [76][34]. At this point, we want to shed light on the background and show how these threats can be minimized.

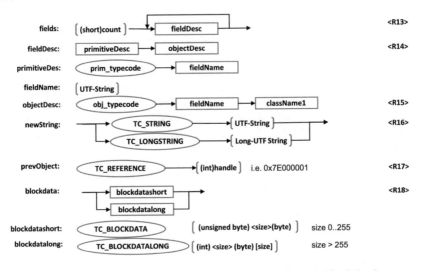

Fig. 7.6: Syntax-diagram for the objects 'fields' and 'blockdata'

7.4.1 Hands on Serialized Objects

With what we already know about serialization, it is easy to find a point of attack. It is not uncommon, although it is not recommended, to transmit or store important confidential information in streams. Assume a user-supplied serialized object we discovered. We can manipulate program logic by tampering with the information stored within the stream. For example, let's take our object *SaveMe*. We can easily modify the string at the end of the stream:

```
0005 68656C6F | ..hello    ->  0007 62656576 696C | ..beevil
```

Since there are no parity bits or checksums, we do not need to adjust anything else within the stream. In our case, that is probably not a big deal. If somebody cheats on a gaming app and overwrite the high score, we can certainly get over it. However, the whole thing changes quickly when confidential data is included in our stream (e.g. user=admin, password=abc123). For example, if the Java object is used as a cookie for access control, we can change the usernames, role names, and ID-token. One can also try tampering with any value in the object that is a file path. We can even alter the program's flow if we override the correct field.

7.4.2 Beware of Gadget Chains

As if that were not enough, we can sometimes even perform remote code execution (RCE) [34][76]. In Java applications, so-called *gadget classes* can be found in the libraries loaded by the application. Using gadgets that are in-scope of the application, we can create a chain of method invocations that eventually lead to RCE. This chain can be bumped during or after the deserialization process.

Listing 7.4: Possible Vulnerable Class

```
public class Vulnerable{
    public Object invoke(SaveMe o) {
        return Runtime.exec("echo \"I just want to say\"" + o.s);
    }
}
```

An example class is shown in the listing above. The *invoke()* method in this example uses the string attribute we modified earlier. If we set the string *s* to "hello | mkdir somedirectory", the second part of the statement causes the creation of a new directory on the target system. This sort of attack is called *Command injection*. Alternatively, we can, of course, execute any command we like. The goal is to execute arbitrary commands on the host operating system via a vulnerable process. Web servers are very prone to this form of attack.

All we need to find is an appropriate hooking point. Therefore, we should look for gadgets in commonly available libraries to maximize the chances that this gadget is in-scope of the application. To date, exploits utilizing gadgets are already known and published. Those classes are mostly part of popular libraries such as the Apache Commons-Fileupload, Apache Commons-Collections, or Groovy. A collection with the gadget chains for Java can be found in the *ysoserial* project from Chris Frohoff [3]. The repository offers a collection of utilities and gadget chains discovered in shared Java libraries. Due to unsafe serialization, a gadget chain may automatically be invoked and cause the command to be executed on the host system. The creation of an unsafe serial object with *ysoserial* is straightforward:

```
$ java -jar ysoserial.jar [gadget chain] '[command to execute]'
```

The dangerous thing about this is that it does not depend on what classes we use in our application. It is sufficient that the class in question is accessible via the local classpath. To honour the rescue of Java developers, however, it must be said that this is not only a particular problem of Java Runtime Environment. Such security issues can also be found in languages like Python, PHP, or Ruby [92],[87].

However, how can we prevent such attacks now? One measure is to blocklist or allowlist object classes before deserializing them. Most suitable for this is the *resolve()* method of the ObjectInputStream class (see Fig. 7.7). If we would validate the object directly after *readObject()* has finished its work, it may already be too late. However, if serialization is performed by a framework class working in the background, we do not even have to notice it.

---

[3] https://github.com/frohoff/ysoserial

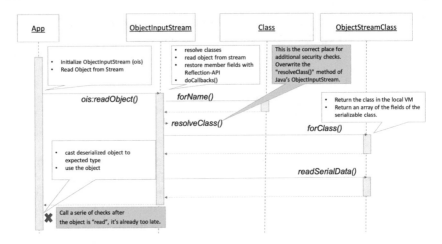

Fig. 7.7: Sequence Diagram of Object De-Serialization

7.5 Conclusions

In this chapter, insight into the standard Serialization format of Java was given. Serialized objects are used in many places in Java. Despite the security problems mentioned earlier and the relatively modest performance, the format enjoys unbroken popularity. Forensically, the file format is exciting because it is not uncommon for confidential or sensitive data to be stored in a stream. However, it should not be a problem to restore attribute assignments with the appropriate tools, even for unknown classes.

Chapter 8
Realm

Phil Cobley and Ginger Geneste

Abstract In this chapter, we explore some of the fundamentals of the Realm database (sometimes referred to as RealmDB or simply Realm). It is widely known within the Digital Forensics discipline that SQLite is the most commonly found database format within any mobile device application and even some desktop applications. Realm is a relatively new database format built as a potential replacement for SQLite, as technology and applications continue to develop and evolve. At the time of writing, it is clear that the database is not as commonly found as some might have expected, but that is not to say the database format will not eventually find its way into many modern apps over the coming years. To that end, we decided to research the database to try and provide some of the details of interest relating to the fundamentals behind the new format. We hope this chapter will help digital forensic examiners and investigators learn and grasp some of the basic concepts of Realm, hoping that any new knowledge and understanding might support and assist in future research into the topic.

8.1 Organisation of this Chapter

You will find a chapter dedicated to the SQLite file format within this book. We shall be covering some of the basics behind SQLite for ease of readability and not assume prior knowledge. We look at some of the differences between SQLite and Realm before looking at Realm in more depth. We want to highlight that the Realm code is under constant development and is still in the early stages of that development,

Phil Cobley

MSAB, 2nd Floor East, Central Point, 25-31 London Street, Reading, RG1 4PS, UK e-mail: phil.cobley@msab.com

Ginger Geneste

Netherlands Forensic Institute, Laan van Ypenburg 6, 2497 GB Den Haag e-mail: g.geneste@nfi.nl

C. Hummert, D. Pawlaszczyk (eds.), *Mobile Forensics – The File Format Handbook*,
https://doi.org/10.1007/978-3-030-98467-0_8

meaning there are some limitations as to what can be confirmed both in the short and long term.

We have broken the chapter down into sections to help readers navigate through a journey of discovery, starting with some high-level and generic concepts, eventually drilling down into more detail later on. Each section builds on the last, but we have tried to write this chapter so that you can easily use the content as reference material if needed.

We start by looking at some of the similarities and differences with SQLite, exploring the concept of object-oriented database design and development over traditional relational tables and SQL queries. We then move into looking at how Realm works and how data is structured similar to a table-like format, but without actually creating any tables. We detail some object-oriented concepts before exploring the Realm files and their data structures in far greater detail. We discuss the concept of data and reference arrays and how these play an important part in Realm databases and break down the various file and array headers at the byte level.

We use example files in the chapter that can be created or downloaded, with the links available within the text itself, if you wish to either create those files or download them yourself. We use those files to break down a Realm array, looking at the offset pointers, the header, and how we can examine the data to identify the size of the payload and the type of data each array contains.

8.2 Introduction

In Digital Forensics, we are often interested in collecting and reviewing data held in databases. Most applications and operating systems rely on databases to store, organise and manage their data instead of swathes of unconnected files and unsorted data blocks. Databases make storage and retrieval simple and provide standardised mechanisms and schemas that modern applications can easily harness.

Within mobile device forensics the most commonly found database type used by applications is SQLite [78], which is a cross-platform, serverless database type, that has become a valuable tool for mobile app and operating system (OS) developers over recent years. The SQLite database was designed to be simple to use, easy to connect to applications across any platform, and could be installed and run upon the client device without the need for a bulky, backend server [83].

However, as devices, applications, and our usage needs of mobile devices evolve, so do the databases harnessed by applications. SQLite is a powerful database format, but it has its limitations. Often, modern-day developers are forced to generate and write additional code to enable their applications to do what they need them to do due to the emerging limitations present within SQLite. This additional code often involves implementing workarounds to enable natively unsupported data values stored within the SQLite tables.

This chapter seeks to explore the Realm database format [71], which has emerged over recent years as a possible successor to the now ageing SQLite format, looking at how this database format plugs those emerging gaps. Understanding how this database structure differs from SQLite should enable forensic examiners to understand better the types of data they are likely to encounter and appreciate how the format works in practice. For example, Realm databases do not use relational tables, a core feature within SQLite databases, but instead, work with linked objects. How does this impact forensic analysis? In this chapter, we shall look at what artefacts we can expect to find when a Realm database has been used and clarify what data may be found within.

> **⚠ Attention**
>
> It is worth noting that research into this subject is still ongoing, and so, while this chapter seeks to explore how Realm databases work, it is not a comprehensive deep-dive into the full workings and data structures. This chapter may expand and evolve in future revisions of this book. However, we have ultimately tried to incorporate as many confirmed findings and factual content as possible at the time of writing. You will see that we have included enough for researchers to understand the fundamentals of these data structures and for forensic examiners to decode various headers and attributes, and we hope that this is the strong starting point to encourage and support examiners in taking this research further.

8.3 SQLite, It is Not!

While Realm might be replacing SQLite in some applications, the way they are coded and operate differ greatly. In order to understand how the object-oriented approach of the Realm database structure works, we will first go through an introduction to the more common relational database structure. We will then explore the concepts of an object-oriented approach for database structures, comparing its features with that of a relational database.

8.3.1 Relational Databases

There are many ways to define what a relational database is. However, in essence, it is a method of organising data into tables, which are linked together through common criteria or data components [38]. Data is typically organised into rows and columns, with each row being assigned a unique identifier. Tables can then reference data in other tables through the use of these unique identifiers, which is the "relational" aspect of the relational database concept.

As a simple example of how this might work, imagine we wish to use this concept when looking at grocery shopping. When grocery shopping, we may wish to search for the items we need by searching under specific categories, such as fruit, vegetables, meats, bakery, and so on. In a relational database setup, it may be that these are each represented as different tables, each containing the various items that you might find under that category (see Table 8.1).

Table 8.1: Example Grocery Tables

Fruit	Price	Vegetables	Price	Bakery	Price
Apple	0.2	Carrots	0.11	Bread	0.8
Orange	0.3	Potatoes	0.15	Rolls	0.4
Pear	0.15	Cabbage	0.2	Wraps	0.95
Banana	0.25	Cauliflower	0.3	Bagels	1.6

Structured Query Language (SQL) [39] is often used as a standardised language to both write data to and query data from such databases that support it. It has enabled developers to quickly and easily write and format queries and code to edit and pull data from relational databases through a global standard. Tables are connected to one another through functions known as "Joins" with search queries generating combined results sets in newly created tables containing various record (row) content, depending on the query made.

When carrying out searches across data sets, such as those found in our grocery example, SQL may be used in the background of a website or application to run queries across the tables, utilising search terms input by the user. This may include filters we commonly see on websites to narrow down the search. For example, we may be looking for a loaf of bread and therefore click on a "Bakery" filter and search for the term "bread" Fig. 8.1. SQL may then be used in the background to search for row items containing the keyword "bread", but only within the "Bakery" table. Equally, applying no filters may conduct the search across all tables, thus conducting a wider search.

When searching such as this, there may also be an empty table either created or already available, that is used to hold copies of the search results. The column structure would likely be very similar to have compatibility with the existing data sets from the other tables but may have additional columns specific to a search. You could think of this table as possible where a typical search results page on a website may be drawing data from.

There are obviously countless ways to develop and programme these structures, and so this is just one (very simplistic) possible example of how data may be held, linked, and manipulated within a relational database. However, you will often have tables of fixed data content that are used as a reference point for the application. You will also have other tables populated and edited through user interaction or system processes, containing live or deleted content.

If we use our grocery example from a forensic standpoint, it might be that the grocery item tables are of little interest to us. However, the search table, or possibly

Fig. 8.1: Background Table Searches

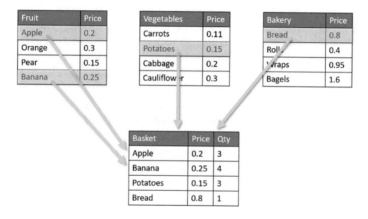

Fig. 8.2: Relational Table Results Collated in a New Table

a "Basket" table that is populated by the user when they add items to their basket might be of forensic interest as it would help identify user activity.

8.3.2 SQLite as a Relational Database

SQLite uses a relational database structure, storing all of the data tables and links within a single file, usually with a file extension similar to *.sqlite or *.db, although this can vary depending on the intended software platform and how the developers decide to build their applications (in mobile devices you will often find them with no file extension at all). This use of a simple, single, self-managing file, is what has helped make SQLite so popular with mobile developers, as there is no need to rely on additional backend servers, and the data becomes self-contained and very portable. These days we see mobile devices with huge storage capacities, but back when smartphones were first coming onto the market storage was still at a premium. SQLite databases enabled developers to build database storage into their mobile applications without taking up very much space on a user's device, and without the need to install additional software or depend on addition software or services running in the background, taking up valuable processing capacity, memory, or network bandwidth.

SQLite is also a cross-platform file format, which means it can be run and used on any common or major operating system, reducing the need for developers to concern themselves with huge changes in their application architecture when developing for multiple platforms, such as Android and iOS.

Given that SQLite utilises SQL as a query language, and given both SQL and SQLite are platform agnostic, it means that a software developer building an application in Swift for iOS will most likely utilise the same or similar SQL queries to a software developer building the same application in Java or Kotlin for the Android operating system. This, in turn, means that the structure, layout, and logic of the backend database does not have to change very much from one system to the next, allowing app developers to focus on only having to adapt the code that surrounds the database when building for different systems, rather than having to also be concerned with what database to use and how to update, edit, and retrieve data from within it.

In digital forensics this is great news for examiners and investigators, as most of the time we only need to concern ourselves with the content of the database – and for a standardised database format such as SQLite that is found on both iOS and Android, it means we only need to learn how to interrogate one database format, regardless of what type of device that data resides within.

8.3.3 SQLite Schema

A schema is essentially a specification confirming and defining the structure of a database, usually written or presented within the appropriate language or format for that database type. SQL developers define their database schema using what is known as Data Definition Language [77] which is used to create tables and define the types of data that each column should hold, such as integers, dates in specific formats, strings, and so on, as well as stating what columns can or cannot contain NULL values (see Fig. 8.3).

8.3.4 Temporary SQLite Files

Something that we commonly find alongside SQLite databases are the shared-memory (SHM) and write-ahead log (WAL) files, that we may find located in the

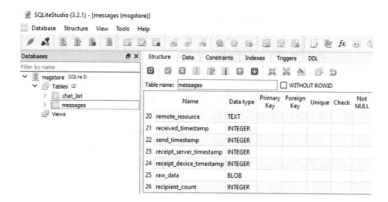

Fig. 8.3: SQLite Studio Displaying SQL Schema

same directory location as the SQLite database file [86]. There are actually several more additional temporary files that are sometimes found as well, but we will not go into detail of how these work here as they are explained in more depth within the SQLite chapter. However, we will touch on what the commonly found WAL and SHM files do and why they (sometimes) exist, for our later comparison.

Name	Type	Size
sqlite-example.db	SQLite database	8 KB
sqlite-example.db-shm	DB-SHM File	32 KB
sqlite-example.db-wal	DB-WAL File	9 KB

Fig. 8.4: SQLite Files, including SHM and WAL

The WAL file is a form of journal that stores updates and changes to the SQLite database file. Rather than writing changes directly to the database file itself, which could cause complications and problems in numerous possible implementations of the database, those changes are written to the WAL first. Multiple changes and amendments can be made (resulting in duplicate entries within the WAL), pending the appropriate trigger to "Commit" those changes in the WAL. This committed content only gets written to the database itself once a "checkpoint" is triggered, where the most recent versions of all the changes and amendments are then transferred across to the database itself. Those triggers vary depending on the version and implementation of SQLite, but occasionally the commit does not take place during a single session, and may only be triggered when the database is reopened and accessed later on. This means that the WAL file can persist in a file system even after a connected application is closed, and it is not actually uncommon to find the WAL file to be even larger in size than the database itself.

The SHM is a file created to help manage concurrent connections to the database and allows the WAL to use a specified area of memory for indexing and managing the various changes and commits being made to the database. In essence, if you have multiple system services or process threads access the SQLite database file at the same time (which is very common) then an SHM file will be created to help service those connections. If one is created then it will typically persist on disk with the WAL file until the WAL file is deleted.

Why are these files important? Well, it is not uncommon for forensic analysts to find evidence and vital data buried within these temporary files, rather than the data being within the main database file itself. We shall see how this differs within Realm databases later on.

8.3.5 SQLite File Format

SQLite is an open-source file format with a very distinct and well documented structure. A lot of digital forensic training and education programmes will teach examiners about the specific layout and structure of the SQLite database header, as understanding the various attributes and byte values can be invaluable, particularly when dealing with more complex and challenging forensic scenarios where the database cannot be automatically parsed and decoded, albeit these instances are rare due to the wide range of comprehensive forensic software tools available. The header information can be found at: `https://www.sqlite.org/fileformat.html`, (see Fig. 8.5) [82]).

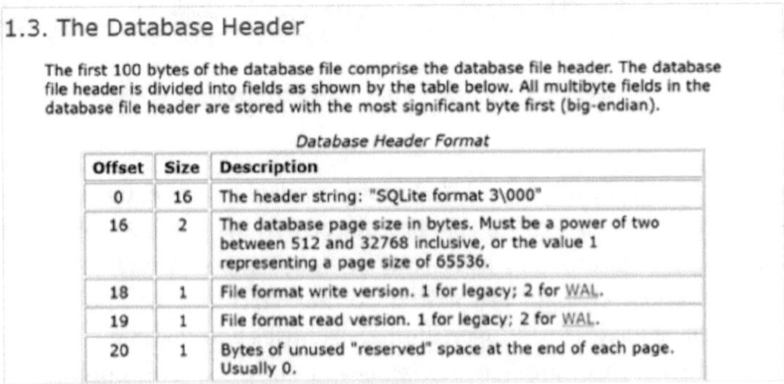

1.3. The Database Header

The first 100 bytes of the database file comprise the database file header. The database file header is divided into fields as shown by the table below. All multibyte fields in the database file header are stored with the most significant byte first (big-endian).

Database Header Format

Offset	Size	Description
0	16	The header string: "SQLite format 3\000"
16	2	The database page size in bytes. Must be a power of two between 512 and 32768 inclusive, or the value 1 representing a page size of 65536.
18	1	File format write version. 1 for legacy; 2 for WAL.
19	1	File format read version. 1 for legacy; 2 for WAL.
20	1	Bytes of unused "reserved" space at the end of each page. Usually 0.

Fig. 8.5: Screenshot from sqlite.org File Format Webpage

You can visit the referenced website to find the full database header format content, along with explanations and documentation around each offset specification.

8.4 How Realm Works

8.4.1 Realm Database Fundamentals

Realm is described on the realm.io website as:

> *"... an open source, developer-friendly alternative to CoreData and SQLite. Start in minutes, port your app in hours, and save yourself weeks of work."* [71]

The database itself is an object database as opposed to a relational database, harnessing the principles of object-oriented programming over traditional database models such as SQLite. This approach allows the database to benefit in ways that are not possible in SQLite, such as having a zero-copy architecture and a near endless possibility to handle, store, and manipulate almost any file format or data type with ease.

As we already know, relational databases, such as SQLite, consist of tables that join and work together to reference various data sets, locating and identifying records and data by navigating rows and columns. Sometimes the table connections (joins) can become incredibly complex, often requiring tables built specifically to hold unique reference variables to help tables navigate to and reference one another. Any queries that are run have their results copied into another table, duplicating data content for the purposes of generating query results. This can be time consuming, memory and processor intensive, and take up considerable data storage as databases grow and expand. The sheer act of copying data out of tables to represent the same content within another table could also be seen as being inefficient and unnecessary.

In their paper "Evolution of Object-Oriented Database Systems" [2] Alzahran compares traditional relational data models with object-oriented models, discussing the future of database structures and a shift in the current paradigm. An example of an object-oriented model (such as Realm) and relational data model (such as SQLite) is given in Fig. 8.6.

In the example presented in Fig. 8.6, we can see how data tables in a relational model are replaced with object instances of different classes, with a new object instance being created instead of a new row being added to a table. The columns in a table are now represented through object attributes, meaning that in order to locate data the object instance is queried and asked to return the attribute values, rather than tables being queried through SQL expressions.

8.4.2 Common Concepts and Terminology

Here we shall define and provide an overview for some common concepts and terminology used within Realm database architecture.

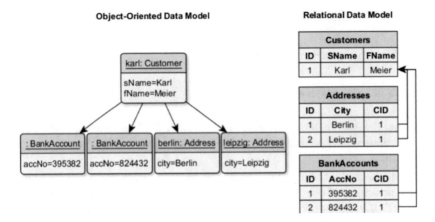

Fig. 8.6: Screenshot from sqlite.org File Format Webpage

Basic Object-Oriented Programming Concepts

In object-oriented programming, used in languages such as Java and Python, there are a number of concepts and principles that are considered as very important when it comes to software design and development [16]. One of these concepts is known as "low coupling, high cohesion" and another being the concept of having small, well-defined objects that do specific jobs, rather than large, bulky objects that carry out multiple tasks.

The reason behind these concepts helps promote code design that is flexible and dynamic as well as being easily maintainable and adaptable. By having small, single function objects, you can build code where any other objects requiring that function simply call those specific object instances, rather than running the risk of duplicating the function within many larger objects. While singular, self-sufficient objects may seem like a good idea, it makes the code more difficult to maintain and manage. For example, say a specific function requires updating; if it is duplicated within multiple object types then they all require updating to ensure no objects are running with legacy code. However, if you have a single object for that function that other objects call upon to use, then simply updating that one object function will update the capability for all connected objects with minimal updates being required. This concept is sometimes referred to in other industries as "single-source" and relates to many different practices, not just software development.

The concept of low-coupling and high cohesion links into this through design principles in software development that suggest objects should work well together (high cohesion) but remain independent so that changes to one do not negatively impact the other (low-coupling). This allows developers to design code that is more easily maintainable and resilient to change. If objects can work well together and have a means to communicate without being dependant on exactly "how" the code has been implemented, then when that code needs changing or updating, so long as the communication methods remain in place, other objects remain unaffected.

Realm databases are able to leverage these benefits through an object-oriented approach to the database design, where the application creates and maintains lightweight, connected object instances as opposed to bulky, rigid, relational table structures. In SQLite, complex systems and database designs often rely upon queries that fully understand and recognise exactly what they're looking for, where, and how. The benefit this brings forensic examiners is that those queries and table structures are relatively straight-forward to reverse engineer and piece together, given how explicit the calls and queries often have to be. In Realm, this is not necessarily the case, as the database queries and calls are highly dependent upon how the developer has decided to implement the Realm database objects and instances, how they have coded the various communication methods and object attributes, and how complex the communication structure ends up becoming. The way this often happens is through objects communicating in a chain, from one to the next, making singular queries to one another, rather than a single, large, complex query statement across multiple tables (Fig. 8.7).

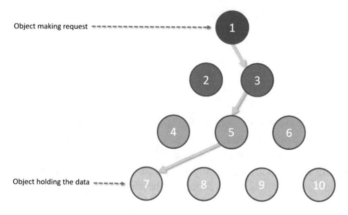

Fig. 8.7: Object Instance Communication

Top-level Objects

Top-level objects could be considered the equivalent of a relational table within an SQLite database. They are typically found to be object classes, such as "Fruit" or "Vegetables", similar to our example earlier in section 8.3.1.

In the following example we use a screenshot from a demo file available for download from the realm.io website [72] viewed within the official free Realm Studio tool [74], used for testing and training purposes to demonstrate some of what Realm can do.

In the screenshot you can see:

- Listed object classes – these are equivalent to a relational table
- A list of object instances – these are equivalent to the rows/records in a table
- The defined object properties/attributes – these are equivalent to table columns

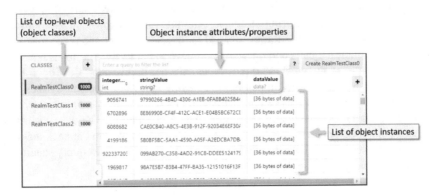

Fig. 8.8: Realm Top-level Object Structure Example

Object Types

It may sound obvious to some, but within Realm databases, an Object Type is a term used to help define exactly what any given object is recognised to be by the database. Object Types link to the database schema, which is defined in code by the database developer and works in a similar way to that of a database schema within SQLite. However, this is one area where Realm goes beyond the capabilities of SQLite in its capabilities.

In SQLite schemas column values are restricted to predetermined values, such as string or integer values, with a finite list of available types that are coded into the SQLite codebase. Anything that does not fit within this predefined list is typically managed through the use of BLOB data, which stands for Binary Large Object [49]. BLOB data can be almost anything that a developer wishes to include, but the data management can sometimes be complicated, and sometimes requires encoding. Furthermore, the database itself will usually not be able to determine exactly what the BLOB data represents, as this has to sometimes be managed through additional software components or tools outside of the database environment.

Within Realm , as the entire schema can be developed alongside the object code, the "type" values can be absolutely anything that the developer wishes to include or use, so long as the type represents a coded object class. This means that proprietary data objects can be built within the Realm code, teaching the database how to handle, manage, store, and manipulate that data natively, regardless of what it is or how it is constructed.

This can be potentially very powerful for database and application developers, but prove to be a huge challenge to forensic examiners and investigators, as it may require reverse engineering the original code in order to understand any proprietary or custom object types or formats. The MongoDB documentation for Realm has an example schema which shows possible schema code for storing data about books in libraries, where "Library" and "Book" are object types [49]:

```
[
  {
    "type": "Library",
    "properties": {
        "address": "string",
        "books": "Book[]"
    }
  },
  {
    "type": "Book",
    "primaryKey": "isbn",
    "properties": {
        "isbn": "string",
        "title": "string",
        "author": "string",
        "numberOwned": { "type": "int?", "default": 0 },
        "numberLoaned": { "type": "int?", "default": 0 }
    }
  }
]
```

Every object within a Realm database must be of a type that is validated by the schema and properly defined. It is worth noting, given Realm is based on the concept of everything being an object instance, that the Realm database itself is an object of type "realm". When a Realm database file is opened and accessed an instance of the Realm database is initialised, with the relevant attributes and properties loaded into that instance from the stored data.

Group

When a Realm database is accessed or opened, the schema is read and interpreted to begin validating and initialising the appropriate object instances. Groups are collections of top-level objects (so, the equivalent of a collection of tables in SQLite) which together help identify and clarify the schema requirements.

Essentially, whenever a Realm database file is accessed through one of the Realm database SDK's, the file is verified and loaded into a Realm object by calling the Realm Group [73].

Arrays

Realm databases predominantly store their data within data arrays, and so first we shall take a quick look at what an array actually is.

It is probably fair to say that almost every programming language can implement arrays in some form, and whilst their implementation may differ depending on the language, the concepts behind them remain fundamentally unchanged. They are simply a data structure that can be used to store an ordered collection of data within a single programmable component. What does that mean, exactly? Let us use an example to explore the answer to that question. Imagine you are programming a simple application and have decided you want to assign variables to hold the names of people who are attending an event. Now, there would be hundreds of different way to do this, and some more efficient than others, but this is just a simplified example to help with our understanding.

You may decide to programme individual variables, maybe something similar to the following:

$$attendee1 = \texttt{"John"}$$
$$attendee2 = \texttt{"Sarah"}$$
$$attendee3 = \texttt{"Sam"}$$

This might work really well for the first few attendees, but when you expand your system to a thousand, it may begin to get tedious and time consuming, not to mention a huge amount of code. Instead, you may consider an array. This component allows you to define a certain number of elements which are automatically numbered sequentially as the values are added to the component, so it is similar to a table that has two columns and a finite number of rows. The first column is automatically determined by the array and grows sequentially from 0 upwards, and the second column is for the data you wish to assign to each row. This allows you to forget about needing to code variables for each user, and instead lets you simply add the names directly to the array, so the array might be conceptualised similar to Table 8.2.

Table 8.2: Conceptual Array

index	value
0	"John"
1	"Sarah"
2	"Sam"
...	...
1000	"Yvette"

The order of adding values is very important with an array, as the indexes are filled sequentially to ensure efficiency, so no gaps are purposefully left. Arrays make it very easy for the software to locate specific data values as the index can be used to locate the data quickly. However, arrays do not care about the order in which they store their data, which differentiates them from other similar data structures where ordering and sorting is an important part of their function.

Another way of looking at arrays is like the chapters in a book. The chapters in a book are fixed and will not change, and the book provides a way for the reader to use the chapters to locate the information of interest to them. In this example, the book is the array and the chapters are the indexes and their data values (Fig. 8.9).

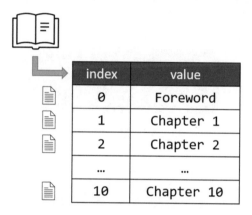

Fig. 8.9: Array Book Analogy

A Realm database file consists of a file header and is followed almost exclusively by 'Realm Arrays'. If the database is not encrypted then these arrays can be located and identified with a hex viewer and parsed out either manually or with appropriate scripting. There are two types of arrays found within Realm databases that we found through testing:

1. Arrays containing references to other arrays (referred to as a **Reference Array**)
2. Arrays containing data (referred to as a **Data Array**)

Essentially, a Realm database utilises what is known as a B+-Tree structure, where the tree can be recreated and mapped by following the pointers of the headers and reference arrays (the branches), until you reach the data arrays (the leaves). These arrays are all essentially nodes within that structure.

In the next section we shall begin exploring the structure behind some of these arrays, along with details of the Realm header and associated files that may be found with the *.realm database file.

8.5 File Storage and Structures

8.5.1 Realm Files and Folders

Here we are going to have a quick look at the files you may encounter when examining realm databases, including some of the temporary files that may be created, similar to how we sometimes find SHM and WAL files accompanying SQLite databases. Two core files will be commonly found with a Realm database, along with a folder that may be empty when recovered [48].

Fig. 8.10: Realm Files

❗ Attention

We will not be covering Realm encryption in this book chapter, but it is worth being aware that they can be encrypted at source.

8.5.2 The Realm File

The most obvious file is the Realm database itself. The Realm database is referred to in documentation simply as a "**Realm**" which is a term that encapsulates the database and all associated files and data. The Realm is a single file that has a *.realm file extension, and contains all the generated data and associated objects. Developers are encouraged to initialise the Realm instance (create a Realm file) the first time an application is opened and run on a device, which means it may be possible to have realm-based applications that have been installed, but where no database is yet present if the application has not been run since installation. Realms can be encrypted by the developers, which would mean that static analysis may not be possible through standard tools without initial decryption taking place.

Fig. 8.11: The *realm File

The Lock File

The Lock file is created when the first connection is made, then recreated and reinitialised at the beginning of every session. This means that the file does not need to be present when the database is initially opened. The purpose of the file is to enable "synchronization between writes" [48] and even if deleted, will be recreated when the database is reopened.

Fig. 8.12: The Lock File

A session is initiated and closed with the opening and closing of a Realm file via database objects. However, it also includes any sequence of temporarily overlapping openings of a particular Realm file via multiple database objects. For example, if there are two database objects, A and B, and the file is first opened via A, then opened via B, then closed via A, and finally closed via B, then the session stretches from the opening via A to the closing via B, rather than two individual sessions. This might be two different application instances opening the same Realm database file simultaneously, for example (like a multi-user session).

The Management Directory

This folder appears, like the lock file, when the database is opened and a connection established. Through testing we have yet to come across any files within the folder itself, but it is reported by MongoDB to "[contain] internal state management files" [48] which are likely to be of little interest within a forensic investigation.

Stateless Realm Instances

It is possible to create and run a Realm entirely within memory, resulting in no actual files being saved to persistent storage. In these instances no trace of any realm

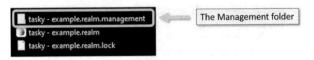

Fig. 8.13: The Management Directory

data will be located within extracted data storage but the data may be present within extractions of any volatile memory from an active device.

8.5.3 Creating Realm Test Instance

We are going to explore two different databases through this chapter. One is a demo file provided by Realm.io, which can be downloaded directly from their website or via a link within the Realm Studio software package:

- Realm Studio can be downloaded from the following URL:
  https://docs.mongodb.com/realm-legacy/products/realm-studio.html
- The Realm demo file can be downloaded from the following URL:
  https://static.realm.io/downloads/realm-studio/demo-v20.realm

The second database we are going to look at is a simple realm database created using Java within Android Studio [22] designed as a simple tasking app.

> **Important**

When writing this chapter we considered including a step-by-step guide on how to create a simple Realm database within Android Studio. However, we found, through our research, that constant changes to Android Studio, Java, Realm, and associated libraries and dependencies, meant that the guides would be out of date by the time they were published, with errata being required almost immediately. We stumbled upon a well-documented guide as written by developer Joyce Echessa, published in a blog article on behalf of auth0 [12] which we have used to build the Task app referenced within this section. This has been done so that you can follow the referenced web page and create your own database, if you wish. We found we had to update a number of referenced versions and dependencies, but overall the guide was still valid at the time of writing, and we were kindly given permission to include a reference to it within this book.

Upon creating our Task application within Android Studio we now need to run our task app for the first time to initialise the database and create a Realm instance. We then need to access our emulated device via the ADB (Android Debug Bridge) [21] to pull the newly created files out.

> **! Attention**
>
> If you are not familiar with ADB then then we encourage you to visit the android-studio documentation [1] to learn more about it and download the relevant software and tool packages. This walkthrough is completed using Windows 10, but you can achieve the same results on other operating systems.

Step 1: Launch the Task Application

From Android Studio, open up your emulated Android environment with your Task app present and load the operating system. Navigate to the applications list and you should see your Task app present (Fig. 8.14):

Fig. 8.14: ADB Walkthrough - Find Application

Now launch the application by clicking on the icon (Fig. 8.15) and then close it down:

---

[1] https://developer.android.com/studio/command-line/adb

Fig. 8.15: ADB Walkthrough - Launch Task App

Step 2: Open a CMD Window

Open a CMD Command Prompt (or Powershell if you prefer), which can be done simply by opening your Start menu and typing "cmd", which will present the option to open a Command Prompt window similar to Fig. 8.16.

Fig. 8.16: ADB Walkthrough - Open CMD Window

Step 3: Create an Output Folder

Create an output folder where your Android files will be placed. For this example we have created a folder called "Android" at the root of the Windows C:\ drive as this will keep the commands in later steps, much smaller and easier to manage, but you can choose any location you like.

Step 4: Start ADB

In your CMD window type the command:

adb devices

> **Important**

This is assuming you have added ADB to your PATH. If not, we suggest you do this before proceeding.

What you should see is a list of devices attached to your computer via ADB (Fig. 8.17). Your emulated Android may have a different reference number or name, but you should see something similar to:

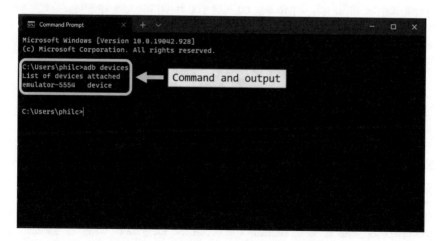

Fig. 8.17: ADB Walkthrough - "adb devices" Command

This has confirmed that your emulated device is visible to your computer via ADB, and we can proceed with pulling the data from the device.

Step 5: Get ADB Root

This is only really going to work as we are emulating our Android device and simply using the content for research purposes. However, usually you would have to use additional steps to pull the application data from a modern Android handset due to permission restrictions and device security settings. However, in the interests of speed and simplicity, type in the following command to your CMD window:

```
adb root
```

This will provide you with root access to the device via ADB, meaning we can bypass a lot of the existing security and protections.

Step 6: Find the Application Data

Here we shall navigate through the device to confirm the location of the application data. We would expect the find the app package and associated directories, located within the file path:

```
/data/data/<package ID>
```

In this example I have named the app "Tasky" and it has a package ID of:

```
com.tutorial.tasky
```

Yours may be different, depending on how you build the app and what name you gave it, so just bear this in mind when looking for the package. First, in your CMD window type the following commands in order and press enter/return at the end of each one:

```
adb shell
```

Then type:

```
ls
```

Next type the command:

```
cd /data/data
```

This takes us to the data folder where all of the packages are located. We could have done two separate steps of running the command cd /data twice in succession as there are two directories called "data", one nested within another. However, the command we used combined both into a single command. Next, use the ls command to locate your application package:

```
ls
```

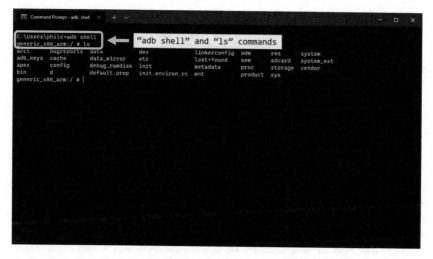

Fig. 8.18: ADB Walkthrough - "adb shell" and "ls" Commands

The list of packages will be displayed, and you can look through the list to find your application. In this example, the app we have created is located near the end of the list (Fig. 8.19):

Fig. 8.19: ADB Walkthrough - Locate Package ID

We have now confirmed that our app package directory is located at:

/data/data/com.tutorial.tasky

Now, exit the adb shell using this command:

```
exit
```

Step 7: Use the "pull" Command

In this final step we use the "pull" command to pull a copy of the package directory out from the device and place the copy into a location of our choice on our computer. In your CMD window type the following command:

adb pull "/data/data/com.tutorial.tasky" "C:\Android"

Here we have specified the command adb pull, and provided what are known as parameters. The pull command can recognise several parameters, and we have provided both a target for our pull action, as well as a destination of where to place the copied content.

You should now be able to open the destination location on your computer and find the exported copies of the package folders. Within these folders you will find your initialised Realm database file.

Fig. 8.20: ADB Walkthrough - Output Files

8.5.4 The Realm Database File Structure

As digital forensic examiners and investigators it is usually helpful to understand the inner workings of the artefacts that we analyse and decode. It is not always possible for us to fully reverse engineer these artefacts, but with research and testing we can often, as a community, begin to figure out some of the key and important hex strings and data blocks that reside within. With Realm this is no exception, and as the source code is publicly available, we have the benefit of being able to use this code to help identify how the database is structured at a byte level for some of those important components.

So far in this chapter we have discussed how Realm compares to traditional SQLite databases, how it differs, and have provided a brief overview of what to expect from a Realm database. We shall now take that understanding and dive deeper into the inner-workings of the files themselves, highlighting and identifying some key structures. We include this in the hopes that it can both direct examiners to relevant documentation to continue this research, as well as assist those who wish to begin creating scripts and other tools to begin parsing these databases themselves.

This section will guide you through the basic concepts of the Realm database file structure based on the implementation of the 'Realm Core' . The source code of the Realm Core implementation is available on Github at https://github.com/realm/realm-core [62]. At the time of writing, the source code referenced with this chapter relates to 'realm-java-v10.4.0'. The Realm Core is actively being developed which does mean that any static analysis of the source code may change over time.

Navigating to the Github repository directory /src/realm/ we find many C++ source code files (*.cpp). We have analysed and researched some of these files to help identify some of the content for this section, identifying some structures and confirming some byte references and offsets. However, remember that this code is under active development, and therefore we advise examiners and investigators to validate and verify these findings, as is good practice, for all future versions of the source code.

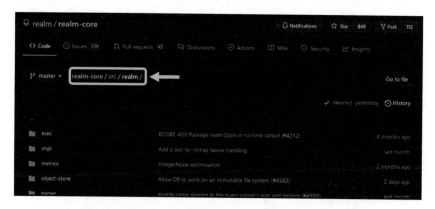

Fig. 8.21: Screenshot of the realm-core/src/realm/ directory

8.5.5 Realm File Header

Each Realm database contains a 24-byte header that can be broken down into component parts. We found the header to be defined within the file `alloc_slab.hpp` which is a form of header file, and can be found at https://github.com/realm/realm-core/blob/master/src/realm/alloc_slab.hpp [65]. The code relates to the definition of what is known as a struct, which is a C++ data structure where the term literally stands for "structure". It is used to store different elements of different data types within a fixed, structured environment, which is perfect for building a header of a set size and design. At the time of writing, the code was located at line 520 and reads as follows:

// 24 bytes

```
struct Header {

    uint64_t m_top_ref[2]; // 2 * 8 bytes

    // Info-block 8 bytes

    uint8_t m_mnemonic[4]; // "T-DB"

    uint8_t m_file_format[2]; // See 'library_file_format'

    uint8_t m_reserved;

    // bit 0 m_flags is used to select between the two top
        refs.

    uint8_t m_flags;
};
```

Based on this declared Header struct, the 24-byte header contains a reference to a 'top ref', the 'mnemonic', a 'file format', 'reserved' and 'flags'. Each of these elements will be described below. However, in essence, the byte allocations are as follows:

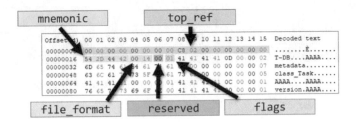

Fig. 8.22: Realm Header Structure

- **16 bytes**: 2 x 8 byte references to the 'top_ref'
- **4 bytes**: mnemonic / 'magic value'
- **2 bytes**: file_format
- **1 byte**: reserved
- **1 byte**: flags - bit 0 is used to select between the two top_ref pointers

"Top Ref" - Bytes 0x00 to 0x0F (d0–d15)

The top_ref element stands for "Top reference" and relates to the root of the database. The element is sixteen bytes in length, using the first sixteen bytes of the database file, but is actually made up of two eight byte components (see Fig. 8.23). Both components are a top_ref but each eight byte string references an offset within the file, with the first referencing the start of the first top_ref, and the next eight byte string referencing the second top_ref.

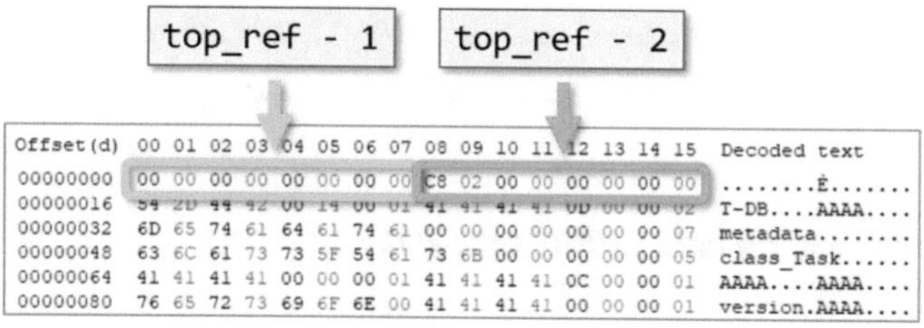

Fig. 8.23: Realm Header - top_ref

These references point to two separate arrays that act as the root nodes. These, in turn, point to two distinct branches that each link to a series of arrays, both branches seemingly mirrored (or almost mirrored). At the time of writing, our understanding based on testing suggests that the database utilises multiple branches through the top_ref mechanism as a form of journaling, alternating writes and commits between the two different root nodes. Starting at one of the two top_ref arrays, one can follow the references to other reference arrays to build up a tree. The current, most up to date state of the database is represented by rebuilding the Tree from the root node of the 'current top ref'. The database identifies the current top_ref through the flag byte, and writes new data to the other top_ref, preserving the current branch of arrays. This could be thought of as a form of WAL, where the "current" top_ref is like an SQLite database file and remains untouched, but the other referenced root node is used to write changes prior to any commits.

However, similar to an SQLite database where WAL checkpoint rules do not always appear to be followed by the database itself, the rules governing changes with Realm arrays also appear to be fairly flexible and not always consistent.

"Mnemonic" - Bytes 0x10 to 0x13 (d16–d19)

These four bytes contain the ASCII value 'T-DB' which is called the 'mnemonic' of the Realm file. In other words, bytes 0x10 to 0x14 contain the magic value of the Realm file.

At the time of writing the mnemonic values are static and always equate to the ASCII "T-DB". This may change with future iterations of the database code, but currently this is a very good way of being able to immediately identify the file as a Realm database, and enables examiners to utilise the hex string 0x542D4442 in searches when seeking to find Realm database amongst datasets.

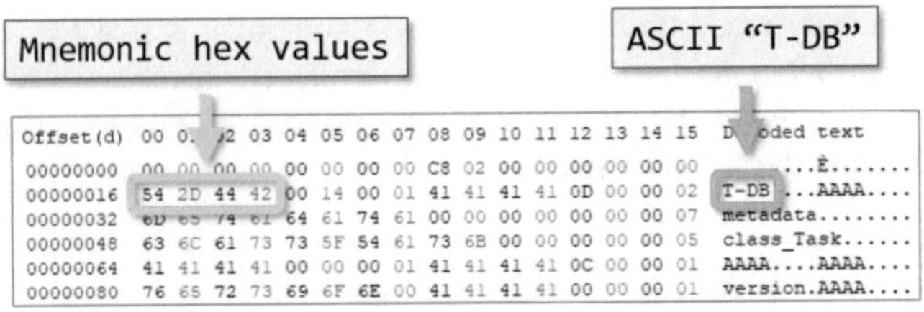

Fig. 8.24: Realm Header - mnemonic

"File Format" - Bytes 0x14 to 0x15 (d20–d21)

These two bytes are described in the Realm core source code as the 'file format'. Both bytes form an integer value and represent the version number.

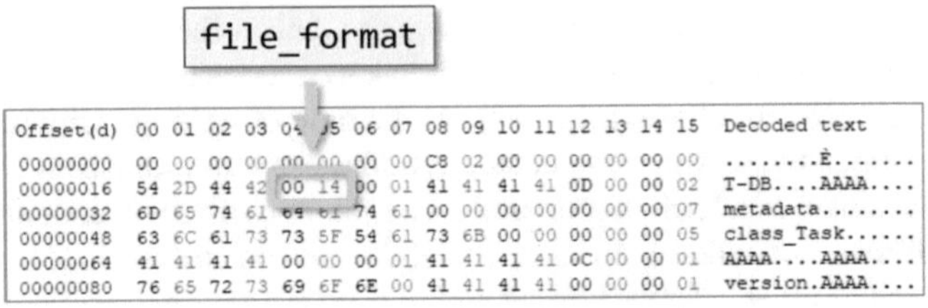

Fig. 8.25: Realm Header - file_format

In the documentation the file format is actually also referred to as the "version", and in the alloc_slab.cpp file [63] there is actually reference to the variable file_format_version variable, along with an object method of get_committed_file_format_version() get_committed_file_format_version(). In this method, it was observed that the file format may be updated to 0x14 (d20) whenever the process (called 'session' in the Realm Core source code) accessing the Realm database requires so. This functionality is likely built in to provide compatibility with processes that handle newer/future file formats. For example, in the group.cpp file, the object method read_only_version_check() requires a file format upgrade if the file_format_version is lower than 0x14 (d20) when the database needs to be opened in read only mode. At the time of writing the maximum value for the file format was 0x14 (d20) but may be subject to change in the future.

The file group.cpp of the source code contains an object method called void-Group::open(). In this method, the target_file_format_version is assigned to a value determined by get_target_file_format_version_for_session(), suggesting the desired file format version of the file itself is determined by the current process which calls open(). The open() object method only returns without errors if the target_file_format_version is 0 or equal to the file format version.

The file format version is assigned to 0 upon the creation of an empty database file where the Realm file header needs to be initialised. The initialisation of an empty header is defined in `alloc_slab.cpp` as follows:

```
const SlabAlloc::Header SlabAlloc::empty_file_header = {
    {0, 0},  // top-refs
    {'T', '-', 'D', 'B'},
    {0, 0},  // undecided file format
    0,       // reserved
    0        // flags (lsb is select bit)
};
```

"Reserved" - Byte 0x16 (d22)

The reserved byte, at the time of writing, is always set to zero, and has never changed throughout testing. This byte currently appears to be unused, as the name suggests, but may be utilised.

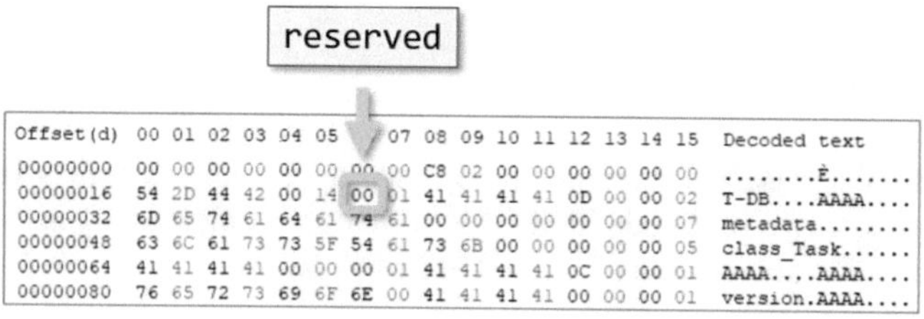

Fig. 8.26: Realm Header - reserved

"Flags" - Byte 0x17 (d23)

The final byte value of the header represents flags. The first bit (the least significant bit) of the last byte indicates which top reference is currently active. If this bit is set to 0, the first top reference is currently active and when this bit is set to 1, the second top reference is active. The other seven bits of the last byte are at the time of writing unused.

In Fig. 8.27 we can see that the byte value is 0x01, meaning that the last bit must be a 1 (the binary breakdown of 0x01 being b0000001), indicating that in this example the current referenced array branch is top_ref 2 (Fig. 8.28).

flags

Offset(d)	00	01	02	03	04	05	06	07	08	09	10	11	12	13	14	15	Decoded text
00000000	00	00	00	00	00	00	00	00	C8	02	00	00	00	00	00	00	........È.......
00000016	54	2D	44	42	00	14	00	01	41	41	41	41	0D	00	00	02	T-DB....AAAA....
00000032	6D	65	74	61	64	61	74	61	00	00	00	00	00	00	00	07	metadata........
00000048	63	6C	61	73	73	5F	54	61	73	6B	00	00	00	00	00	05	class_Task......
00000064	41	41	41	41	00	00	00	01	41	41	41	41	0C	00	00	01	AAAA....AAAA....
00000080	76	65	72	73	69	6F	6E	00	41	41	41	41	00	00	00	01	version.AAAA....

Fig. 8.27: Realm Header - flags

top_ref - 2

Offset(d)	00	01	02	03	04	05	06	07	08	09	10	11	12	13	14	15	Decoded text
00000000	00	00	00	00	00	00	00	00	C8	02	00	00	00	00	00	00	........È.......
00000016	54	2D	44	42	00	14	00	01	41	41	41	41	0D	00	00	02	T-DB....AAAA....
00000032	6D	65	74	61	64	61	74	61	00	00	00	00	00	00	00	07	metadata........
00000048	63	6C	61	73	73	5F	54	61	73	6B	00	00	00	00	00	05	class_Task......
00000064	41	41	41	41	00	00	00	01	41	41	41	41	0C	00	00	01	AAAA....AAAA....
00000080	76	65	72	73	69	6F	6E	00	41	41	41	41	00	00	00	01	version.AAAA....

Fig. 8.28: Realm Header - top_ref 2 example from flag value of 0x01

8.5.6 Realm File Arrays

After the Realm header a *.realm file is made-up entirely of arrays in a B+tree format, with a single root node, inner nodes that act as sign posts, and leaf nodes that generally contain the data of interest to investigators.

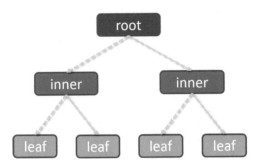

Fig. 8.29: Example Node Structure

The top_ref header information points to offsets within the file where you will find (typically) "reference arrays". These reference arrays point to other nodes and arrays within the database, some of which will be other reference arrays, and some will be what are known as "data arrays". These data arrays are where the actual core object data is stored.

Opening up a copy of the downloadable "demo.realm" file, available from realm.io, we will use the first array found after the Realm header, as an example of how arrays are structured and can be broken down (see Fig. 8.30).

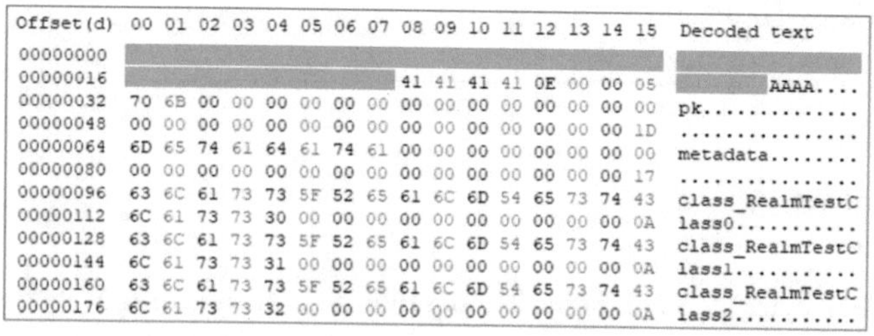
Offset(d) 00 01 02 03 04 05 06 07 08 09 10 11 12 13 14 15 Decoded text
00000000
00000016 41 41 41 41 0E 00 00 05 AAAA....
00000032 70 6B 00 00 00 00 00 00 00 00 00 00 00 00 00 00 pk..............
00000048 00 00 00 00 00 00 00 00 00 00 00 00 00 00 00 1D ....
00000064 6D 65 74 61 64 61 74 61 00 00 00 00 00 00 00 00 metadata........
00000080 00 00 00 00 00 00 00 00 00 00 00 00 00 00 00 17 ....
00000096 63 6C 61 73 73 5F 52 65 61 6C 6D 54 65 73 74 43 class_RealmTestC
00000112 6C 61 73 73 30 00 00 00 00 00 00 00 00 00 00 0A lass0...........
00000128 63 6C 61 73 73 5F 52 65 61 6C 6D 54 65 73 74 43 class_RealmTestC
00000144 6C 61 73 73 31 00 00 00 00 00 00 00 00 00 00 0A lass1...........
00000160 63 6C 61 73 73 5F 52 65 61 6C 6D 54 65 73 74 43 class_RealmTestC
00000176 6C 61 73 73 32 00 00 00 00 00 00 00 00 00 00 0A lass2...........

Fig. 8.30: Example Node Structure

8.5.7 Realm Array Header

Every array within Realm starts with an 8-byte header broken into two distinct parts:

1. Checksum value (4 bytes)
2. Array characteristics (4 bytes)

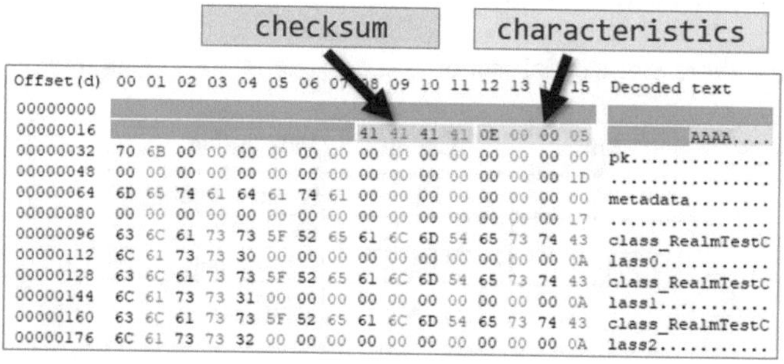
checksum
characteristics
Offset(d) 00 01 02 03 04 05 06 07 08 09 10 11 12 13 14 15 Decoded text
00000000
00000016 41 41 41 41 0E 00 00 05 AAAA....
00000032 70 6B 00 00 00 00 00 00 00 00 00 00 00 00 00 00 pk..............
00000048 00 00 00 00 00 00 00 00 00 00 00 00 00 00 00 1D ....
00000064 6D 65 74 61 64 61 74 61 00 00 00 00 00 00 00 00 metadata........
00000080 00 00 00 00 00 00 00 00 00 00 00 00 00 00 00 17 ....
00000096 63 6C 61 73 73 5F 52 65 61 6C 6D 54 65 73 74 43 class_RealmTestC
00000112 6C 61 73 73 30 00 00 00 00 00 00 00 00 00 00 0A lass0...........
00000128 63 6C 61 73 73 5F 52 65 61 6C 6D 54 65 73 74 43 class_RealmTestC
00000144 6C 61 73 73 31 00 00 00 00 00 00 00 00 00 00 0A lass1...........
00000160 63 6C 61 73 73 5F 52 65 61 6C 6D 54 65 73 74 43 class_RealmTestC
00000176 6C 61 73 73 32 00 00 00 00 00 00 00 00 00 00 0A lass2...........

Fig. 8.31: Realm Array Header Example

This can actually be broken down further into the following components:

Table 8.3: Table of Realm Array Header Components

Header Section	Offset	Size	Description
Checksum	0x00 (0)	4 bytes	Checksum (dummy) ("AAAA" in ASCII)
Characteristics	0x04 (4)	1 byte	Flags
Characteristics	0x05 (5)	3 bytes	Size

8.5.8 Checksum

The first four bytes contain a checksum value that, at the time of writing, is only considered a "Dummy Checksum" within documentation, suggesting that this component may change in future iterations of the code. The checksum consists of four matching byte values, namely 0x41414141, which reads as "AAAA" in ASCII. The source code shows us that these four ASCII characters are used when scanning for arrays within the database [69].

8.5.9 Flags

The fifth byte of the array header represents flags and utilises several bit groupings to denote different configurations for the array [66]. This means that to read or parse the bit groupings we need to breakdown the byte into 8-bits and identify which bits represent which groups. The breakdown is as follows:

Table 8.4: Breakdown of "Flags" byte into bit groupings

Bit	Group	Description
1	1	is_inner_bptree_node
2	2	has_refs
3	3	context_flag
4	4	width_scheme
5		
6	5	width_ndx
7		
8		

Bit Group 1: is_inner_bptree_node

The first bit of the flags byte indicates whether a Realm array is an 'inner node'. A value of 1 would indicate that the node is an inner node, which would mean that the array must be a reference array, as opposed to a data array. While analysing several Realm database files, none of the Realm arrays had the `is_inner_bptree_node` flag set. One reason for not using the `is_inner_bptree_node` flag in the Realm array header could be that the tree structure of the Realm database can still be constructed without checking this flag: starting from the root node (the top_ref array), and following all references of the tree until all identified references have been exhausted and pursued, allows a researcher to build the tree manually. Take a look at the code snippet below, which comes from the file `array.cpp`:

```
void Array::set_type(Type type)
{
    REALM_ASSERT(is_attached());

    copy_on_write();  // Throws

    bool init_is_inner_bptree_node = false, init_has_refs =
        false;
    switch (type) {
        case type_Normal:
            break;
        case type_InnerBptreeNode:
            init_is_inner_bptree_node = true;
            init_has_refs = true;
            break;
        case type_HasRefs:
            init_has_refs = true;
            break;
    }
    m_is_inner_bptree_node = init_is_inner_bptree_node;
    m_has_refs = init_has_refs;

    char* header = get_header();
    set_is_inner_bptree_node_in_header(init_is_inner_bptree_node,
        header);
    set_hasrefs_in_header(init_has_refs, header);
}
```

It appears an array with the `is_inner_bptree_node` flag set, also sets the bit flag for `has_refs`. Therefore, it is concluded that any array that is considered an `inner_bptree_node`, also contains references to other arrays.

Bit Group 2: has_refs

A Realm Array header where the second bit of the flags byte is set to 1, indicates the Realm Array contains references to other Realm Arrays in its payload, making it a "reference array". This, in turn, makes the array the parent of any other arrays that it directly references. The payload of any reference array will typically consist of elements that store pointers to the child arrays. These pointers will be integer values that directly correspond to an offset in the file. These offsets always consist of 8-byte strings.

Bit Group 3: context_flag

The third bit within the flags byte is known as the "context_flag". However, rarely set to 1, and the full purpose of the flag remains unclear. Code from the `array.hpp` file [66] enables us to deduce that the context flag can be used to tell what type of leaf node the given array is. Unfortunately, there is not much more information currently shared regarding the 'context flag' in the Realm Core source code at the time of writing.

Bit Group 4: width_scheme

The array header contains information that enables us to calculate the total size, in bytes, of the payload held within the array. This calculation is done by using both the `width_scheme` and `width_ndx` bit groupings. We can therefore calculate the total size of the array by identifying the values held within these two bit groups.

The `width_scheme` consists of two bits which are added together to create a integer value. This type of calculation, therefore, allows for three possible value outcomes: 0, 1, or 2. Depending on the value, the payload is calculated in a certain way, as defined in `node_header.hpp` [67]. The following code snippet outlines the calculations and intentions:

```
static void set_wtype_in_header(WidthType value, char* header)
    noexcept
    {
        // Indicates how to calculate size in bytes based on
           width
        // 0: bits        (width/8) * size
        // 1: multiply    width * size
        // 2: ignore      1 * size

        typedef unsigned char uchar;
        uchar* h = reintercept_cast<uchar*>(header);
        h[4] = uchar((int(h[4]) & ~0x18) | int(value) << 3);
    }
```

Therefore, the `width_scheme` could be translated as per Table 8.5. The 'size' in the calculation is the value represented in the last three bytes of the Realm Array header. The value of 'width' in the calculation is represented in bit group 5, after applying the width translation table (see Table 8.6 below).

Table 8.5: Calculations Required for width_scheme Values

Value of width_scheme	Meaning	Calculation for array payload
0	Calculate size with number of bits	Cell(width*size/8)
1	Calculate size with number of bytes	Width*size
2	Ignore width in size calculation	size

Bit Group 5: width_ndx

Bits 6, 7, and 8 of the flags byte form 'bit group 5', referred to as width_ndx. These three bits collectively are used to represent the values 0 to 7 (7 being when all three bits are set to 1), and are used to indicate the value of 'width'. With the translation table below, the translation from width_ndx to the actual value of 'width' can be found. The value "width" represents the number of elements that are contained within the Realm Array payload.

Table 8.6: Translation table for width_ndx

width_ndx calculated value	0	1	2	3	4	5	6	7
Value of 'width'	0	1	2	4	8	16	32	64

8.5.10 Size

The size of the Realm Array payload is described in the last 3 bytes of the Realm Array Header. The size represents the amount of bits or bytes of one element in a Realm array. The value of width_scheme determines how the size value is used to calculate the overall payload. Since the amount of elements is represented in width_ndx, the size of each element can be calculated by using the knowledge found in the width_scheme along with the value of size, one can calculate the complete size of a payload, and thus calculate the total size of the array. So to summarise:

Table 8.7: Calculations Required for width_scheme Values

WIDTH_SCHEME	The method used to calculate the overall size of the payload
WIDTH_NDX	The number of elements present within the payload
Size	The size of each element within the payload

8.5.11 Realm Array Payload

After the 8-byte header, the remainder of the Realm Array is followed by multiples of 8-bytes, which makes up the "payload". The amount of bytes that follow after the Realm Array Header (so, the total size of the payload) can be calculated by taking the width_ndx, width_scheme and size as explained in the section above.

This is outlined within the node_header.hpp file found within the Realm-core documentation [67] where you will find the following code:

```
static size_t calc_byte_size(WidthType wtype, size_t size,
    uint_least8_t width) noexcept
    {
        size_t num_bytes = 0;
        switch (wtype) {
            case wtype_Bits: {
                // Current assumption is that size is at most
                    2^24 and that width is at most 64.
                // In that case the following will never
                    overflow. (Assuming that size_t is at least
                    32 bits)
                REALM_ASSERT_3(size, <, 0x1000000);
                size_t num_bits = size * width;
                num_bytes = (num_bits + 7) >> 3;
                break;
            }
            case wtype_Multiply: {
                num_bytes = size * width;
                break;
            }
            case wtype_Ignore:
                num_bytes = size;
                break;
        }

        // Ensure 8-byte alignment
        num_bytes = (num_bytes + 7) & ~size_t(7);

        num_bytes += header_size;

        return num_bytes;
    }
```

From this code-snippet we can deduce that if we take the value of size and multiply it with the width value, these are the amount of bits or bytes of the complete Realm Array payload. Whether this value is in bits or bytes depends on the width_scheme (referred to by wtype in the code example). This number is padded until it becomes a multiple of 8. The total size of a Realm Array is the payload size in addition to the Realm Array Header size (which is 8 bytes).

8.5.12 Size Calculation Example

We shall revisit the example content used when introducing the Realm Array Header in 8.5.7 above, to demonstrate how some of these calculations work.

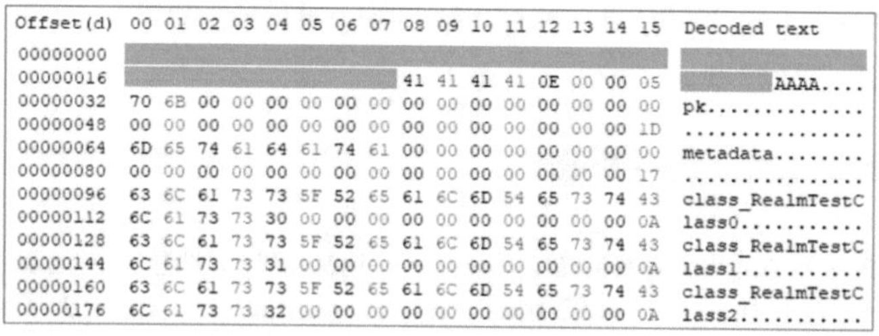

Fig. 8.32: Realm Array Example

This example looks at an Array that is stored immediate after the Realm file header, which we have blanked out to help focus on the Array itself (Fig. 8.32). Remember, our Array Header consists of eight bytes that can be broken down into two distinct elements (Fig. 8.33).

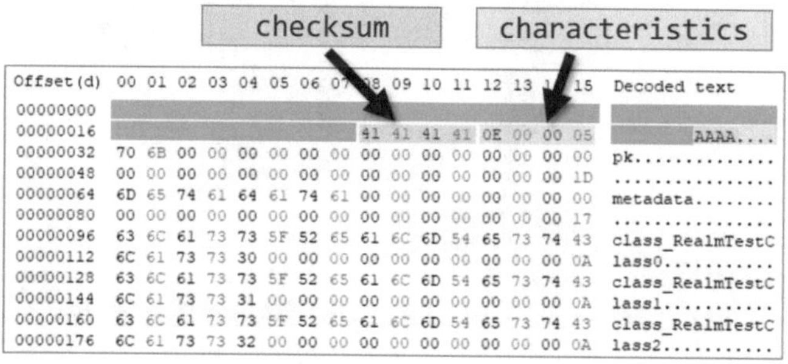

Fig. 8.33: Realm Array Header Example

We can see that the header for our array is made up of the following eight bytes:

Table 8.8: Array Header Bytes

Byte	1	2	3	4	5	6	7	8
Hex Value	41	41	41	41	0E	00	00	05

8.5.13 Array Example - Header

The first four bytes are our checksum, which, at the time of writing, is always 0x41414141 ("AAAA" in ASCII) and then our next set of four bytes are the characteristics values. If you recall from earlier in the chapter, this is further broken down into two different components, namely the flags and size values.

8.5.14 Array Example - Flags

The fifth byte is our flags, which is currently the value 0x0E, which is the binary value of b00001110. If you recall, the flags byte is broken into five "Bit Groups" that represent different things depending on their values. For our example value, we can breakdown the byte as follows:

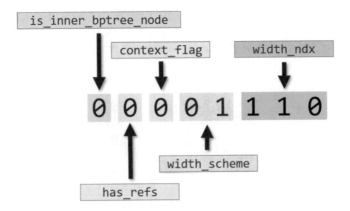

Fig. 8.34: Realm Array Example - Header Breakdown

From this we can identify the following:

- Our array is not an "Inner Node", given our is_inner_bptree_node value is set at 0.
- Our array is likely a "Data Array" as the has_refs value is set at 0.
- Our value of width_scheme is set at 1. Looking back at Table 8.5 in 8.5.9 above, this tells us that the scheme we need to use is calculating with the number of bytes (Width*size).
- The value of width_ndx is 110 in binary, which is the value 6 in decimal, which gives us the width_ndx value of 32 from the translation table provided by Table 8.6 in section 8.5.9 above.

To clarify how we made this conversion, we followed these simple steps:

1. Convert the Binary Value 110 into Decimal

This can be done using a calculator or converter, but to manually do this conversion we can simply look at the base 2 number values:

Table 8.9: Calculations Required for width_scheme Values

Base 2 columns	4	2	1
Binary Value	1	1	0

So our decimal calculation is:

$$1 \times 0 = 0$$
$$2 \times 1 = 2$$
$$4 \times 1 = 4$$
$$0 + 2 + 4 = 6$$

2. Find the Decimal Value on the Translation Table

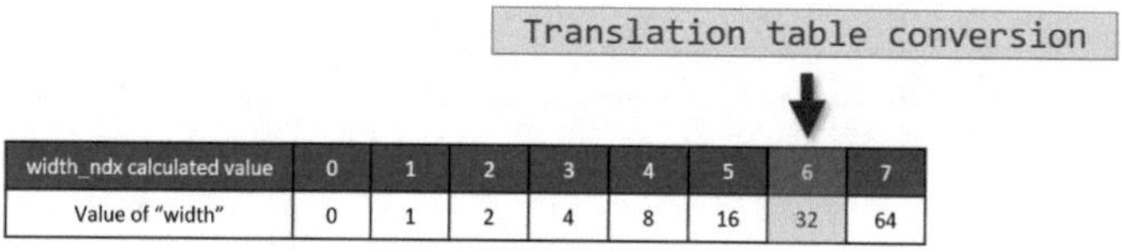

width_ndx calculated value	0	1	2	3	4	5	6	7
Value of "width"	0	1	2	4	8	16	32	64

Fig. 8.35: Annotated Copy of the width_ndx Translation Table

3. Identify the Given Value that the Table Returns

As we can see above, the returned value for "width" is 32.

8.5.15 Array Example - Size

Our final series of bytes within the Array Header denotes the value for size. Given we have a three-byte value of 0x000005, which is the decimal value of 5, we can confirm the value of size to be 5.

Now that we have our values for both "width" and "size" we can use the given width_scheme calculation method to identify the total size of the payload for this array, as follows:

Size x Width = Payload size in bytes
5 x 32 = 160 bytes

Remember that the total size of our array is the header plus the payload size. Our header is always going to be 8 bytes long, and our payload is 160 bytes, so this array should be 168 bytes in total. You can see in the following screenshot of our Realm file viewed through the software tool HxD [36] that our array is, indeed, 168 bytes in length (Fig. 8.36):

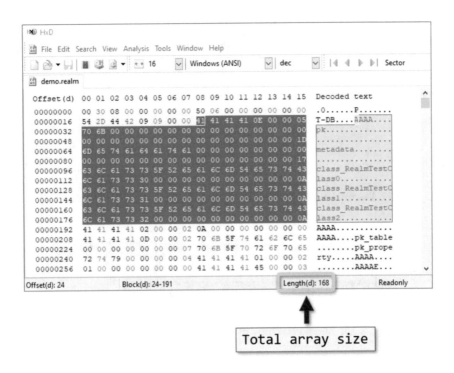

Fig. 8.36: Screenshot of Realm File in HxD showing Total Size of an Array

If you look closely at the end of the array in Fig. 8.36, you will notice that the byte following the end of the highlighted array is the start of another array, with the array header ASCII values "AAAA" clearly visible within the decoded text.

8.6 Conclusion

Realm databases have been considered, by some, to be the new format that will ultimately replace SQLite. While we have seen some evidence of this with some applications, the anticipated change has been far slower than originally believed, and

Realm databases are still not commonly found within the most common applications examined by Digital Forensic examiners. This may change in the future as momentum builds for the database, or the movement may continue to struggle to gain traction as developers find workarounds and clever ways to continue implementing the more widely known and understood SQLite format.

The Realm database format has, at the time of writing, an active developer community with an ever-evolving code-base. The format is still relatively new, with a number of areas of code still using "dummy" or "temporary" values or data structures while the code is developed. The open-source nature of the realm-core code enables forensic examiners to reverse engineer the code in order to discover exactly how these database are structured and operate, which may be vital in digital forensic investigations.

However, the move away from SQL structures and into editable and customisable object-oriented code also adds challenges for forensic examiners, especially when every database could, in theory, be coded to operate and function is very different ways from any other. Understanding the fundamental concepts and structures behind Realm databases should enable examiners to navigate and understand some of the core data structures, even if the object functions remain challenging to decode and decipher.

This chapter has aimed to introduce some of the core fundamentals behind the Realm database, with a view of providing the foundations and tools that could be helpful in continued, further research and analysis. We hope that readers are able to use any knowledge gained from this chapter and referenced materials, to continue to explore and build their understanding of this database format, and we hope that the community continues to explore, share knowledge, and help one another enhance our understanding of new and developing file formats and structures for the benefit of all.

Chapter 9
Protocol Buffers

Chris Currier

Abstract Protocol Buffers (Protobufs) are discussed in this chapter, from creating one to analyzing the data. This particular serialization format, originally developed by Google, is used in various apps. We discuss creating a protocol buffer and adding data through Python step by step. This provides a better understanding of how and why protocol buffers are formed and used. We also clarify how to recognize and decode them during a forensic examination.

9.1 Introduction

I remember being on the edge of my seat as Johan Persson, a developer at MSAB, first introduced me to Protocol Buffers. Why? *Protobufs*, as they are commonly referred to, contain data that we as examiners may find helpful in an investigation. I had no idea how to find them and view the payload they carried. However, that was to change quickly.

9.1.1 What is a Protocol Buffer?

A Protocol Buffer provides a format for taking compiled data (many different languages/platforms supported) and serializing it by turning it into bytes represented in decimal values. This makes the data smaller and faster to send over the wire. We call this *serialization* in computer science.

A protocol buffer is a data format structured in a very efficient binary format. The structure is defined in a *.proto* file, which is in a readable text format. The concept is similar to XML, where the schema description can be done inline or in a separate

Chris Currier
MSAB, Hornsbruksgatan 28 SE-117 34 Stockholm Sweden e-mail: chris.currier@msab.com

© The Author(s) 2022
C. Hummert, D. Pawlaszczyk (eds.), *Mobile Forensics – The File Format Handbook*,
https://doi.org/10.1007/978-3-030-98467-0_9

223

file. The *.proto* file is then used to generate code for reading from and writing data to the protocol buffer. Due to its nature, protocol buffer data is very suitable for transmission over networks. When transmitted over networks, it is often compressed with GZIP to minimize the size of the data. The protocol buffer concept was created and is used extensively by Google. Other users of protocol buffers include Apple and app developers.

So, where do we begin? Of course, the best place to learn about Google's Protocol Buffers is Google (see Fig. 9.1). Google defines how to structure and use Protocol Buffers [24]. The structured or rigid format used by Protocol Buffers is often referred to as a *schema*.

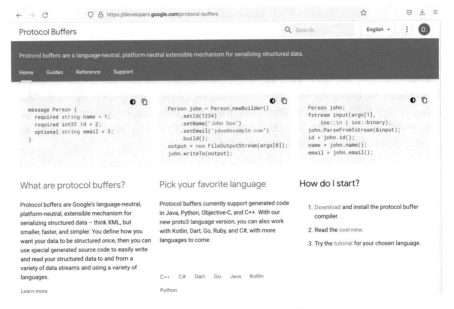

Fig. 9.1: Google's Protocol Buffers

Google itself says about its format in the developer documentation that it is a platform-independent, language-independent and easily extensible serialization format. Of course, other formats allow serialization of data too. Java-Serial is an example of this. Unlike this, Protobuf is a language-independent transmission format. Also, XML would be an option. However, Protobuf is smaller and faster than most of the other formats [24]. A significant advantage of Protobuf is that we only need to define the structure for the data to be transferred once and can then exchange it over a wide variety of data channels. The programming language is secondary since we are language-neutral. The data stream itself (network or file) is also irrelevant. The definition of the protobuf message always remains the same [24].

9.1.2 Why are Protocol Buffers Used?

Now think of a network with data being transmitted through it. How do we get data through the network faster? The smaller the data, the faster it will be. We also do not need it to be human-readable during transmission. This is where Protocol Buffers shine with faster transmission. Figures 9.2 and 9.3 demonstrate the time and size of Protbufs, based on tests performed to consider encoding and decoding benchmarks and common browsers [58, 43].

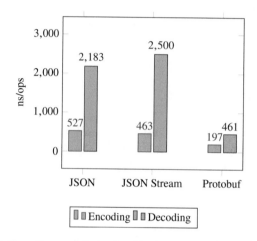

Fig. 9.2: Encoding and Decoding Performance of Protobufs [58]

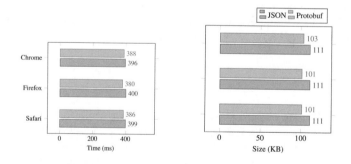

Fig. 9.3: Compression Environment of Protobufs and JSON [43]

The authors of a benchmark study in [43] conclude that ProtoBuf performs significantly better than JSON. The messages are significantly smaller and are transmitted much faster at the same time. However, there is always someone faster, and that brings us to the term FlatBuffers:

"Protocol Buffers is indeed relatively similar to FlatBuffers, with the primary differ-ence being that FlatBuffers does not need a parsing/ unpacking step to a secondary representation before you can access data, often coupled with per-object memory allocation. The code is an order of magnitude bigger, too. Protocol Buffers has neither optional text import/export nor schema language features." [15]

As you can see, it is not just about speed but also the size of the data. The protocol buffer is not only the code but also the key. The data sent is binary and can be converted and looked at. Different languages (code) may be supported and used to enter and view this data.

9.2 Using Protocol Buffers

This section will clarify how ProtoBuf works and what data is needed. For this, the first step is to generate a description of the message types used and the access service:

Messages

To create a ProtoBuf message, we must first create an appropriate template. This template is usually saved in a file with the extension *.proto*. The file is set up and used alongside another programming language such as Python. The data (or user data) can be added using the same scheme (Field assignments: Type, Name, Tag) and then sent internally or externally over the wire. Google set up Protocol Buffers for their internal communication. Data is transmitted as binary. For this reason, we can encounter it in almost every Google app.

Services

Protocol Buffers are not just about messages but also services. For this reason, we need a service description. It describes the interface of the methods offered via the service. If we want to create an RPC service using a proto buffer, then the service must be given a name under which it can later be called once. In this case, the developer documentation recommends formulating both the service name and the access methods in CamelCase (with an initial capital). Here we have a brief example of defining a chat service that provides precisely one access method:

```
service ChatService{
    rpc GetChats(ChatRequest) returns (CharResponse);
}
```

One such service is Google's *gRPC*. These RPC (Remote Procedure Calls) methods accept a request "message" and return a response "message". Protobuf is often used with HTTP and RPCs for local and remote client-server communication. Protobuf is used for the description of the required interfaces and message types. The protocol composition is also summarized under the name gRPC [30]. In this case, the call to the remote method - encapsulated by a service - is provided platform-independently via a service description. The steps for generating a protobuf message and subsequent transmission are briefly summarised again in Fig. 9.4. The message data (message refers to type or object and not to chat or text) is then transmitted over the wire (internal or external). The supported platforms can all have code generated to deserialize the data and make sense of it, regardless of what coding platform created the data.

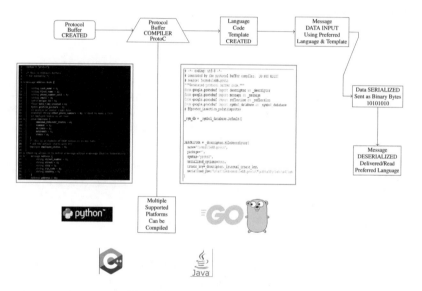

Fig. 9.4: How Protobufs Work

Looking at the data, we may not make sense of it without having the original code to know what the data represents. Unfortunately, we will not find the schema to help us make sense of the fields. So, let us look at the code to start with. That will give us a better understanding of what we see during the examination. Therefore, we will first discuss the design and implementation of a proto buffer using two small examples before turning to the forensic analysis of these special artefacts.

The Proto File

We start by creating a *.proto* file. We like to think of this file as the key or legend to the data we will see on a mobile device. Unfortunately, we will not find this key or legend on the device itself as examiners. The *.proto* file is not included with the binary, with a few exceptions. As we will see, this often leaves some room for interpretation when we deserialize a Protocol Buffer manually. We will walk you through an example of the process. This example (see Fig. 9.5) will be for an Address Book, so we will name it *formobileAB.proto*. The file can be created with any editor.

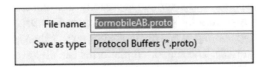

Fig. 9.5: FORMOBILE Protobuf Example

Define the Syntax

Google made Protocol Buffers public in 2008. In 2016 Google published Protocol Buffers 3. Since there is a different version, we have to identify which version of Protocol Buffers will be used. So, the first line of code needs to state this. Version 3 is used in these examples, as shown below.

```
syntax = "proto3";
```

Message Type

Now the message needs to be defined or named. This "message" is a code term that refers to the data and is not confused with terms chat or SMS text messages. The name should reflect the type of message based on content. The term *address book* should define our Protocol Buffer just fine. When using two words they use CamelCase and form one word i.e. *addressBook* or *AddressBook*, as shown below.

```
syntax = "proto3";

message AddressBook {

}
```

Fields

To create the first property, we need to know the type of data [int32], followed by property name [thread] and then identify it as the sequential property [1]. Fields identify these data characteristics through Field Type, Field Name, and a Field Tag (or also called a *Field Number*). This is where we define the class characteristics that will be used. We consider what information would we want to know about, for example, a:

- Person
- Contact
- Web Broswer Search
- Location and a Chat

! Attention

Remember, the idea behind Protocol Buffers is to take code from another language and package it into a smaller container. This starts defining the data by naming it and then following with fields.

The actual data such as: *John Smith 40 1.85 90.71 Brown Blue* will not exist in this proto file, but in another file. This should remind you of how meta data type looks like in a chat message. Fig. 9.6 is an example found in an address book showing the fields and associated data and profile picture.

Scalar Values

A message is normally composed of a number of different scalar values. Each value is assigned to a particular type. Looking at an SQLite database table definition, we will find terms such as Integer, Boolean, Float, and String. These define data types. Protocol Buffers use these as well (see table 9.1). Since we usually want to exchange messages between different applications, the data they contain must be preserved. As we can see in the table below, Protocol Buffers are easily used with other programming languages: C++, Java, Python, and Go. Accordingly, we can easily map the data type of a programming language to a ProtoBuf type and vice versa. For more information about types and unsigned bit integers please refer to [26].

Fig. 9.6: Address Book Profile Example

.proto Type	Notes	C++	Java Type	Python Type	Go Type
double		double	double	float	*float64
float		float	float	float	*float32
int32	Uses variable-length encoding. Inefficient for encoding negative numbers – if your field is likely to have negative values, use sint32 instead.	int32	int	int	*int32
int64	Uses variable-length encoding. Inefficient for encoding negative numbers – if your field is likely to have negative values, use sint64 instead.	int64	long	int/long	*int64
uint32	Uses variable-length encoding.	uint32	int	int/long	*unint32
uint64	Uses variable-length encoding.	uint64	long	int/long	*uint64
sint32	Uses variable-length encoding. Signed int value. These more efficiently encode negative numbers than regular int32s.	int32	int	int	*int32
sint64	Uses variable-length encoding. Signed int value. These more efficiently encode negative numbers than regular int64s.	int64	long	int/long	*int64
sfixed32	Always four bytes.	int32	int	int	*int32
sfixed64	Always eight bytes.	int64	long	int/long	*int64
bool		bool	boolean	bool	*bool
string	A string must always contain UTF-8 encoded or 7-bit ASCII text.	string	String	unicode (Py2) or str (Py3)	*string
bytes	May contain any arbitrary sequence of bytes.	string	ByteString	bytes	[]byte

Table 9.1: Mapping Table for possible Scalar Types (Detail) [26]

In this chapter, we will discuss several examples of Proto Buffers: (1) an address book, (2) a chat message, and (3) an Apple Maps example. You will find most of the files mentioned here: `www.github.com/Xamnr/ProtocolBuffers`. If you like, you can analyze the examples discussed here yourself. Just give it a try.

9.2.1 The Schema Defintion

The Protocol Buffer defines the Object (type of data and position). Not the actual data or user data. The actual data will be coded in Python or another language format. However, the type of data that will go into these fields needs to be defined. Protocol Buffers use fields. There are three types of fields:

- Field Type
- Field Name
- Field Tag (or Number)

Field Type

The field type uses the scalar values to define the type of data like *integer*, *string*, or *bool*. Thinking back to our Apple contact, shown below (Fig. 9.7), we have the following fields and data to consider:

- Name or maybe Last Name and First Name
- Phone Number (Home, Work, Cell)
- Email (Home, Work)
- A Unique Identifier
- A Profile Picture

If not set, specified, or unknown, every field will have a default value. Protocol Buffers do not recognize required fields. Instead, the runtime environment of the programming language is responsible for that, i.e. Java, Python, Go. This means that a field whose assignment corresponds to the default value is not serialized. It is just left out. Since the field is missing in the data stream, the receiver side automatically uses the default value in this case. This property, which may seem confusing at first glance, ensures that no unnecessary values are transmitted. The serialized data on the wire remains small.

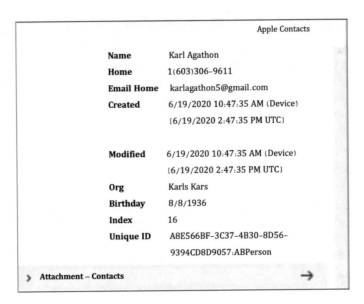

Fig. 9.7: Field Type and Scalar Values (example)

VALUE	DEFAULT
Bool	False
Number	0
String (UTF-8 or 7-bit ASCII)	Empty String
Byte (or byte array)	Empty Bytes (or empty byte array
Enum	First Defined Value 0
Repeated	Empty List

Table 9.2: Field Type Default Values

Field Names

The field name represents one particular element within the message, therefore identifying the data for us. To identify a contact, we may use identifiers such as *last_name, first_name, phone_number_cell, email, unique_id, date_time_created, profile_picture*. When multiple words are used, each word is separated by an underscore "_". Again, we do not add the data such as *Karl Agathon*. This data will be input elsewhere. Now that we have our field names, we need to identify the field type values for each field. We will focus on using Python. See Table 9.3 below.

The field tag is the last element. It works as a place holder. Tags are simply a number ranging from 1 to 536, 870, 911. However, there are some rules that come with these tags:

- The number may only be used once so that it is unique (more on this later).

VALUE	DEFAULT
last_name	String (UTF-8 or 7-bit ASCII)
first_name	String (UTF-8 or 7-bit ASCII)
phone_number_cell	Int (int32)
email	String (UTF-8 or 7-bit ASCII)
unique_id	Int (int32)
date_time_created	float (could be a double in another language)
profile_picture	Bytes

Table 9.3: Field Name Python Example

- Numbers 19000 through 19999 cannot be used. Reserved by Google.

There are also some strategies to speed up the data with these tags:

- Numbers 1 to 15 use only 1 byte, so these are used for fields used most often.
- Numbers 16 – 2047 use 2 bytes

Now we put this together in the code with the Field Type, Field Name, and Field Tag.

Fig. 9.8: Code Structure

A correct schema definition for our address book example could thus look like the following:

```
message AddressBook {
    string last_name = 1;
    string first_name = 2;
    int32  phone_number_cell = 3;
    string email = 4;
    int32  unique_id = 5;
    float  date_time_created = 6;
    bytes  profile_picture = 7;
```

As you can see above the address book has 7 assigned fields. Each field is defined by a Type, Name, and unique Tag. Certain rules still apply to the message fields [27]:

- *singular*: Such fields have the cardinality 1. Thus, a message can only have none or exactly one of this field values. This is the default rule.

- *repeated*: Array or list of values. It can be repeated any number of times - even zero times.

Since the keyword *singular* is the default case, it can be omitted when defining a field. Once we have chosen the field tag number, that number is unique and cannot be reused. However, we could change the *.proto* file by commenting out a field. Field names or field tags can also be reserved for future use. Using a reserved field may cause compiler issues if the data type is not identified correctly.

For example, to define the field other phone numbers as a list, we can use the following assignment:

```
repeated string other_phone_numbers = 8;
```

Enums

An *Enumeration (Enum)* is used when the values for a field are known or fixed. An Enum must start with tag 0 (default value). An example could be a status: Unknown Status (default), Read, Unread, Sent. The Enum values are all capitalized (upper case). See the example below. Here we added the employee's employment status. The default value is the first one tagged with zero:

```
1  syntax = "proto3";
2
3  /* This is Protocol Buffers
4   * for FORMOBILE */
5
6  message AddressBook {
7      string last_name = 1;
8      string first_name = 2;
9      int32  phone_number_cell = 3;
10     string email = 4;
11     int32  unique_id = 5;
12     float  date_time_created = 6;
13     bytes  profile_picture = 7;
14     // profile or avatar (jpg) file
15
16     repeated string other_phone_numbers = 8;
17
18     //Employee Status as an Enum
19     enum EmployeeStatus{
20         UNKNOWN_EMPLOYEE_STATUS = 0;
21         CURRENT = 1;
22         RETIRED = 2;
23         RESIGNED = 3;
24         APPLICANT = 4;
25         FIRED = 5;
26     }
27
```

```
28      /* This is an example of an ENUM notice
29       *it is ALL CAPS and the default starts with zero */
30      EmployeeStatus employee_status = 9;
31 }
```

Nesting

Messages can be added inline into another message. Nesting allows us to have message(s) types within a message type. This functionality is well known in programming languages and is called aggregation. That means some other message type is part of a second message type.

❗ Attention

Here a message refers to code and not a chat message.

In the example shown below, the address entry has been added to include street, city, zip code, and country. Notice the indentation. In this example, the original message refers to the AddressBook, and the nested message refers to the message Address that starts on line30. The enum used tag 9 and the nested message is now assigned tag 10. This is now defined as AddressBook.Address.

```
1 syntax = "proto3";
2
3 import "myproject/timestamp.proto";
4
5 message AddressBook {
6      string last_name = 1;
7      string first_name = 2;
8      int32  phone_number_cell = 3;
9      string email = 4;
10     int32  unique_id = 5;
11
12     //....
13
14     //Nesting allows us to define a message within a
15     //message (notice the indentation)
16     message Address{
17         string street_number = 1;
18         string street = 2;
19         string city = 3;
20         string zip_code = 4;
21         strong country = 5;
22     }
23     Address employee_address = 10;
24 }
```

Importing & Packages

Importing allows us to use other .proto file(s) or package(s) with the code you need
from a different proto file. Below is a timestamp.proto file that has the set up for
an epoch time stamp, which will be shown on the following pages.

When importing, we use *import* followed by the full path where the file is located
ending with a semicolon, as seen below. Code can be compiled and put into a package.
Protocol Buffers are no different, which is helpful for other coding languages. This
also helps to avoid naming conflicts. A package can be created and then imported
into a protocol buffer. Following is the timestamp.proto file. The package name
is google.protobuf.timestamp and save the file to the same directory as the
formobileAB.proto file.

```
syntax = "proto3";

package google.protobuf.timestamp;

option csharp_namespace = "Google.Protobuf.WellKnownTypes";
option cc_enable_arenas = true;
option go_package = "github.com/golang/protobuf/ptypes/timestamp";
option java_package = "com.google.protobuf";
option java_outer_classname = "TimestamProto";
option java_multiple_files = true;
option obj_class_prefix = "GPB";
```

```
message Timestamp {
  // Represents seconds of UTC time since Unix epoch
  // 1970-01-01T00:00:00Z. Must be from 0001-01-01T00:00:00Z to
  // 9999-12-31T23:59:59Z inclusive.
  int64 seconds = 1;
  // Non-negative fractions of a second at nanosecond resolution.
  // Negativebsecond values with fractions must still have
  // non-negative nanos values that count forward in time.
  //Must be from 0 to 999,999,999 inclusive.
  int32 nanos = 2;
}
```

To include the message definition of a Timestamp to our address book, we have
to open formobileAB.proto file and add the imported proto file as well as the
package name. Now we have to change the 'date_create'd field so that the timestamp
epoch time is recognized from the package:

```
1 syntax = "proto3";
2
3 /* This is Protocol Buffers
4  * for FORMOBILE */
5 import "google/protobuf/timestamp.proto";
6
```

```
 7  package google.protobuf.timestamp;
 8
 9  message AddressBook {
10      string  last_name = 1;
11      string  first_name = 2;
12      int32   phone_number_cell = 3;
13      string  email = 4;
14      int32   unique_id = 5;
15      google.protobuf.timestamp.Timestamp date_created = 6;
16      bytes   profile_picture = 7;
17      // profile or avatar (jpg) file
```

Now we have some idea of how a protocol buffer .proto file is created. The .proto file itself does not contain user data but just the schema. We will find such schema definitions in our analysis. However, they may appear like the timestamp.proto file shown in Fig. 9.9. Our analysis tool or a hex viewer may not be the best way to view this file. Here, an ordinary text editor is certainly the better choice.

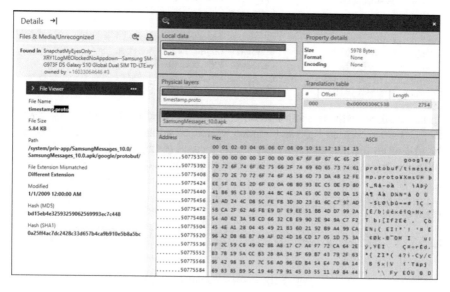

Fig. 9.9: timestamp.proto demonstrated in a Hex Viewer

The above information covers some of the code options for creating the .proto file. More information can be found at [27]. We will now look at the .proto file from a forensic analysis perspective. But first, we have to transfer our newly created message type into a concrete programming language.

9.2.2 Compiling Your Protocol Buffer

Once the custom data structures are defined as desired in the .proto file, generate the classes needed to read and write the protobuf messages. For this purpose, apply the protocol buffers compiler (protoc) to the configuration file. The `protoc.exe` is what we will be using to look at the data that we find. So first, let us see how it is used to serialize or encode the data from a protocol buffer file. The link to obtain ProtoC is `www.github.com/protocolbuffers/protobuf/releases`. ProtoC will generate code from the Proto File to the supported language. A template for coders to follow and use the defined terms.

First, we have to specify the directory to search for imports. It may be specified multiple times; directories will be searched in order. If not given, the current working directory is used. If not found in any of these directories, the `--descriptor_set_in` descriptors will be checked for required `proto` file. Next, we have to define the output language:

```
--cpp_out=OUT_DIR          Generate C++ header and source.
--csharp_out=OUT_DIR       Generate C# source file.
--java_out=OUT_DIR         Generate Java source file.
--js_out=OUT_DIR           Generate JavaScript source.
--objc_out=OUT_DIR         Generate Objective-C source.
--php_out=OUT_DIR          Generate PHP source file.
--python_out=OUT_DIR       Generate Python source file.
--ruby_out=OUT_DIR         Generate Ruby source file.
```

In this case, we will be using Python `--python_out=OUT_DIR`. Other languages like GO are supported and can be found referenced online. Now to take the formobileAB.proto file and compile the code for Python (or another language). We will place the ProtoC executable here and create a python folder.

Fig. 9.10: Python Folder Example

Then open up a command prompt in this location and follow steps 1, 2, 3 or 1, 2, 4.

1 Determine the directory name that your `proto` files are in.
2 Add Output language (Java, Python...).
3 Add Absolute path of your `proto` file with extension.
4 or all `proto` files in that location folder.
'

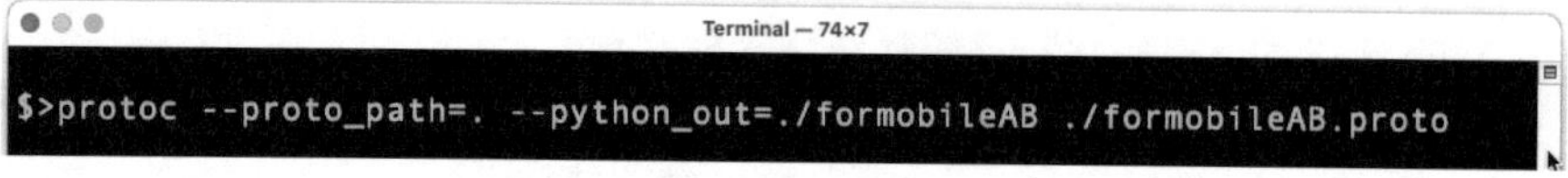

```
  ● ● ●                    Terminal — 74×7
$>protoc --proto_path=. --python_out=./formobileAB ./formobileAB.proto
```

Fig. 9.11: File Path Example

Analysing the Python Protobuf-Code

In our example, we have chosen Python as the target language. We will briefly discuss the file formobileAB_pb2.proto created in the process below. In the first section, we see imports from google.protobuf. One of the imports mentions reflection. This can be observed throughout the following Python example. This means the coder will have to identify the objects in their code. Descriptors are shown as well. A serialized_pb binary buffer could be found.

```python
# -*- coding: utf-8 -*-
# Generated by the protocol buffer compiler.  DO NOT EDIT!
# source: formobileAB.proto
"""Generated protocol buffer code."""
from google.protobuf import descriptor as _descriptor
from google.protobuf import message as _message
from google.protobuf import reflection as _reflection
from google.protobuf import symbol_database as _symbol_database
# @@protoc_insertion_point(imports)

_sym_db = _symbol_database.Default()

DESCRIPTOR = _descriptor.FileDescriptor(
  name='formobileAB.proto',
  package='',  syntax='proto3',
  serialized_options=None,
  create_key=_descriptor._internal_create_key,
  serialized_pb=b'\n\x11\x66ormobileAB.proto\"\xf7\x03\n\x0b\x41
  \x64\x64AressBook\x12\x11\n
  \tlast_name\x18\x01 \x01(\t\x12\x12\n\n
  first_name\x18\x02(\t\x12\x19\n
  \x11phone_number_cell\x18\x03 \x01(\x05\x12\r\n
  \x05\x65mail\x18\x04 \x01(\t\x12\x11\n
  \tunique_id\x18\x05 \x01(\x05\x12\x14\n
  \x0c\x64\x61te_created\x18\x06 \x01(\x02\x12\x17\n
  \x0fprofile_picture\x18\x07 \x01(\x0c\x12\x1b\n
  \x13other_phone_numbers\x18\x08 \x03(\t\x12\x34\n
  \x0f\x65mployee_status\x18\t
  \x01(\x0e\x32\x1b.AddressBook.EmployeeStatus\x12.\n
  \x10\x65mployee_address\x18\n
  \x01(\x0b\x32\x14.AddressBook.Address\x1a\x61\n
  \x07\x41\x64\x64ress\x12\x15\n
  \rstreet_number\x18\x01 \x01(\t\x12\x0e\n
  \x06street\x18\x02 \x01(\t\x12\x0c\n
  \x04\x63ity\x18\x03 \x01(\t\x12\x10\n
```

```
    \x08zip_code\x18\x04 \x01(\t\x12\x0f\n
    \x07\x63ountry\x18\x05 \x01(\t\"o\n
    \x0e\x45mployeeStatus\x12\x1b\n
    \x17UNKNOWN_EMPLOYEE_STATUS\x10\x00\x12\x0b\n
    \x07\x43URRENT\x10\x01\x12\x0b\n\x07RETIRED\x10\x02\x12\x0c\n
    \x08RESIGNED\x10\x03\x12\r\n\tAPPLICANT\x10\x04\x12\t\n
    \x05\x46IRED\x10\x05\x62\x06proto3'
)
```

Scrolling down the page we find the **AddressBook** message descriptors. You should be able to see the Field Names and the Field Tags.

```
    full_name='AddressBook.Address',
    filename=None,
    file=DESCRIPTOR,
    containing_type=None,
    create_key=_descriptor._internal_create_key,
    fields=[
      _descriptor.FieldDescriptor(
        name='street_number',
        full_name='AddressBook.Address.street_number',
        index=0, number=1, type=9, cpp_type=9, label=1,
        has_default_value=False, default_value=b"".decode('utf-8'),
        message_type=None, enum_type=None, containing_type=None,
        is_extension=False, extension_scope=None,
        serialized_options=
        None,file=DESCRIPTOR,c
        reate_key=_descriptor._internal_create_key),
      _descriptor.FieldDescriptor(
        ↩
      name='street', full_name='AddressBook.Address.street', index=1,
        number=2, type=9, cpp_type=9, label=1,
        has_default_value=False, default_value=b"".decode('utf-8'),
        message_type=None, enum_type=None, containing_type=None,
        is_extension=False, extension_scope=None,
        serialized_options=
        None,
        ↩
      file=DESCRIPTOR,    create_key=_descriptor._internal_create_key),
```

A 2nd Example - The FormobileChat message

Having created the first example so easily, let us follow it up with a second example right away. This time it will be about defining a chat message with data fields and then generating a corresponding protobuf message. A second example was generated. The `formobilechat.proto` file has been created. After reading through this material you should have a good idea of what you are looking at. There is a message named *FormobileChat*. Followed by Field Types, Names, and Tags. There are also two **enums**

used for message direction and status. Does this data remind you of something? Chat
message data, maybe?

```
syntax = "proto3";
// Formobile Protocol Buffers
message FormobileChat {
    int32  chat_thread_id = 1;
    string chat_contact = 2;
    string chat_text = 3;
    bytes chat_attachment = 4;
    float chat_latitude = 5;
    float chat_longitude = 6;
    int64  chat_timestamp = 7;
enum Chat_Direction {
    UNKNOWN_DIRECTION = 0;
    OUTGOING = 1;
    INCOMING =2;
}
Chat_Direction chat_direction = 8;
enum Chat_Status {
    UNKNOWN_STATUS = 0;
    UNREAD = 1;
    READ = 2;
}
Chat_Status chat_status = 9;
```

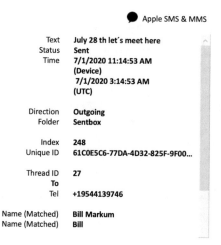

As with our address book example, next, we need to have the schema file compiled
using the compiler protoc. The result, in our case, is again a Python source file. We
could use ProtoC -proto_path and -python_out commands to generate the code
for Python.

! Attention

Note there are two dashes "– " before both proto and python.

```
$> protoc --proto_path=. --python_out=.  ./formobilechat.proto
```

ProtoC took the proto file, output it to Python to create the formobilechat_pb2.py file. This file has almost 200 lines of code from a proto file with less than 30 lines of code.

Formobilechat_pb2.py

Even though it says pb2, this was made from a proto3 file. Notice the size compared to the .proto file itself.

```
# -*- coding: utf-8 -*-
# Generated by the protocol buffer compiler.  DO NOT EDIT!
# source: formobileAB.proto
"""Generated protocol buffer code."""
from google.protobuf import descriptor as _descriptor
from google.protobuf import message as _message
from google.protobuf import reflection as _reflection
from google.protobuf import symbol_database as _symbol_database
# @@protoc_insertion_point(imports)

_sym_db = _symbol_database.Default()

DESCRIPTOR = _descriptor.FileDescriptor(
  name='formobileAB.proto',
  package='',  syntax='proto3',
  serialized_options=None,
  create_key=_descriptor._internal_create_key,
  serialized_pb=b'\n\x11\x66ormobileAB.proto\"\xf7\x03\n\x0b\x41
  \x64\x64AressBook\x12\x11\n
  \tlast_name\x18\x01 \x01(\t\x12\x12\n\n
  first_name\x18\x02(\t\x12\x19\n
  \x11phone_number_cell\x18\x03 \x01(\x05\x12\r\n
  \x05\x65mail\x18\x04 \x01(\t\x12\x11\n
```

9.2.3 Creation of a Protobufs with Python

Now it is time to generate our first chat message using the Python files generated in the previous step. Therefore, a python script must be created, so this one will be named formobilechat.py.

First, the `formobilechat_pb2` has to be imported into the script and followed by any other imports or packages. Without the import, we would not be able to access the message types predefined. A variable is created, identifying the Fieldnames and entering data for those fields. Since *Reflection* is used, the developer must identify the fields used in the Protocol Buffer. In programming, reflection means that a programme knows its structure (introspection) and can modify it.

Program Code <formobilechat.py>

```python
import formobilechat_pb2 as formobilechat_pb2

FormobileChat = formobilechat_pb2.FormobileChat()

FormobileChat.chat_thread_id = 1
FormobileChat.chat_contact_id = "Karl Agathon"
FormobileChat.chat_text = "Patrick sorry you could not make it
    tonight to get your cut of the cash. We will use you for the
    next bank. Got something for you"
FormobileChat.chat_attachment = bytes([0xFF, 0XD8, 0XFF, 0x00,
    0x10, 0x4A, 0x46, 0x49, 0x46, 0x00, 0x01, 0x01, 0x01, 0xFF,
    0xD9])
FormobileChat.chat_latitude = 5.50559
FormobileChat.chat_longtitude = -0.08956
FormobileChat.chat_timestamp = 1616182435
FormobileChat.chat_direction = 1
FormobileChat.chat_status = 2
```

In our example, a chat message is generated with a Contact named *Karl Agathon*. In addition to the actual message text, a JPEG was also added as an attachment. The message is supplemented with position information (latitude and longitude) and a timestamp. Now that the sample message is complete, we can create a real ProtoBuf message from it in the next step.

Writing the Object to a Binary File

The message is now serialized using Protobuf and saved to a binary file. For this we create a new file named *FormobileChat.bin*. Then we write the content of the messages created with Python before into the file.

Program Code

```python
with open("FormobileChat.bin", "wb") as f:
    bytesAsString = FormobileChat.SerializeToString()
    f.write(bytesAsString)
```

The output file is then located in the same directory as the Python script used to create the binary.

Remember Size = Speed

Notice the size comparisons below. The first image shows the Python Script formobilechat.py and the FormobileChat.bin. This contains the complete chat_attachment jpg picture binary data.

Name	Size	Type
FormobileChat.bin	39 KB	BIN File
formobilechat.py	232 KB	Python File

Fig. 9.12: FormobileChat.bin in File Explorer

Notice the size comparison of the original proto file, the compiled pb2.py file, and the binary file. Note the FormobileChat.bin (has the full jpg picture chat_attachment binary data). The FormobileChatsmall.bin has a portion of the chat_attachment binary data as seen on the previous page.

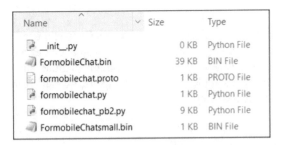

Name	Size	Type
init.py	0 KB	Python File
FormobileChat.bin	39 KB	BIN File
formobilechat.proto	1 KB	PROTO File
formobilechat.py	1 KB	Python File
formobilechat_pb2.py	9 KB	Python File
FormobileChatsmall.bin	1 KB	BIN File

Fig. 9.13: FormobileChat.bin in File Explorer

The Raw Binary Data

Opening the file in Hex-Editor does not really do this file justice. Well we can see the chat text and the file signature of a JPG, but that is it. So how do we handle this protocol buffer data?

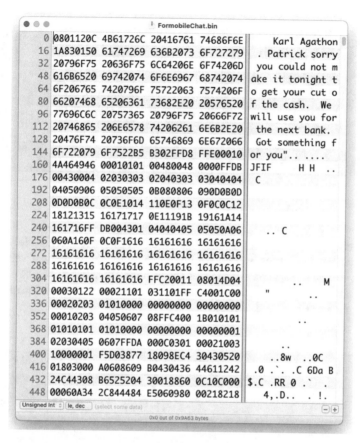

Fig. 9.14: FormobileChat.bin Hex

9.2.4 Reversing Proto Buffer Messages

In our example, we are in possession of the original *.proto* file as well as the generated binary. In practice, unfortunately, it is often the case that we do not have a schema file. But even without a interface description there is a way out.

The `protoc` compiler is not just for compiling data from a protocol buffer. But it can also be used in other ways. The `protoc` tool is very useful for showing the contents of protocol buffer data.

There is data here for us to find. We just need to know how to view it. That is where the `protoc -decode_raw` command comes in. We use the command line to decode the raw binary data from the `FormobileChatsmall.bin`. The command to use is `protoc --decode_raw < (File and Path)`. Our attempt to restore the data using the "decode raw" option was apparently only partially successful (see Fig. 9.15).

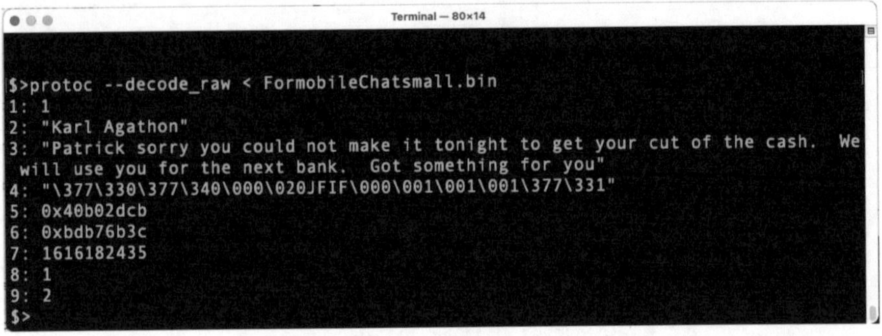

```
● ● ●                                Terminal — 80×14

$>protoc --decode_raw < FormobileChatsmall.bin
1: 1
2: "Karl Agathon"
3: "Patrick sorry you could not make it tonight to get your cut of the cash.  We
 will use you for the next bank.  Got something for you"
4: "\377\330\377\340\000\020JFIF\000\001\001\001\377\331"
5: 0x40b02dcb
6: 0xbdb76b3c
7: 1616182435
8: 1
9: 2
$>
```

Fig. 9.15: Decoded Protocol Buffer

Fortunately, there is a solution for this as well. Thus, there are a variety of pro-grams that provide a mostly accurate interpretation of the numerical values. The program *protobuf-inspector*[1] is one of those tools. It helps to reverse Protocol Buffers with unknown definition, i.e., missing .proto files. The command to use is main.py < (File and Path)

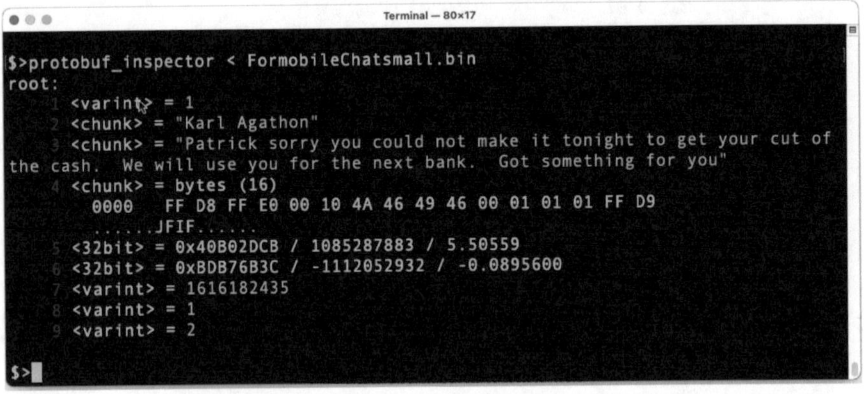

```
● ● ●                                Terminal — 80×17

$>protobuf_inspector < FormobileChatsmall.bin
root:
    1  <varint> = 1
    2  <chunk> = "Karl Agathon"
    3  <chunk> = "Patrick sorry you could not make it tonight to get your cut of
the cash.  We will use you for the next bank.  Got something for you"
    4  <chunk> = bytes (16)
          0000    FF D8 FF E0 00 10 4A 46 49 46 00 01 01 01 FF D9
          ......JFIF......
    5  <32bit> = 0x40B02DCB / 1085287883 / 5.50559
    6  <32bit> = 0xBDB76B3C / -1112052932 / -0.0895600
    7  <varint> = 1616182435
    8  <varint> = 1
    9  <varint> = 2
$>
```

Fig. 9.16: Close up of Protobuf-Inspector decode results

With both decodes, we see the data entered, and some of it is easily understood, and other parts are not. Take note above that the protobuf inspector does change the octal values to hexadecimal and also translated the Longitude and Latitude in the correct Decimal 5.50559 and −0.0895600. We can compare the encoded binary message with the original Python Script results (see Fig. 9.17).

---

[1] www.github.com/mildsunrise/protobuf-inspector

```
formobilechat ×
chat_thread_id: 1
chat_contact: "Karl Agathon"
chat_text: "Patrick sorry you could not make it tonight to get your cut (
chat_attachment: "\377\330\377\340\000\020JFIF\000\001\001\001\377\331"
chat_latitude: 5.50559
chat_longitude: -0.08956
chat_timestamp: 1616182435
chat_direction: OUTGOING
chat_status: READ
```

Fig. 9.17: The Original Entered Formobilechat Data (Python)

Data Conversion

While we may not know what the 1 and 2 flags mean, we can certainly look for data that we can do something about to start with. Location data in the case of 5.50559 and −0.08956 is shown in decimal, which is one way forensic tools represent it. However, what do we do when we are seeing something (maybe from a map application) that could be longitude and latitude and is in Hexadecimal: $0x40b02dcb$ $0xbdb76b3c$ If the Hex value starts with 8, 9, A, B, C, D, E, or F then it is a negative number. There are a few ways to do this, but the best we have been taught is HxD and a Python Script. We will show you how to use HxD's Data Inspector later in the chapter.

The Python Script requires 8 bytes, as seen below and do not name the script struct (as that is reserved). Also, be aware that you may input the data in the wrong spots mixing up the latitude and longitude. Test this with known data first to make sure it works in your part of the world.

Program Code

```
#convert Lat Long from hex to decimal
import struct

lat = struct.unpack('>d', b'\x40\x45\xF5\xE5\xF6\x6D\x59\x0F')[0]
long = struct.unpack('>d',b'\xc0\x51\xFA\xA3\xB1\xD3\x4B\x67')[0]

print("Latitude: ", (lat), "and the Longitude: ", (long))
```

Timestamp

In the above example, we see something that may be an epoch timestamp 1616182435. Unix time is based on the date 1970-01-01 00:00:00 (UTC), and Apple timestamps

(MAC Absolute time) use 2001-01-01 00:00:00 (UTC) as a start. Timestamps normally use seconds but may also use milliseconds, microseconds, nanoseconds etc.

The above example starts with 1 then it is probably a Unix time (when it comes to Android and Apple Devices). Apple Timestamps will most likely start with 3, 4, 5, or 6. We find epoch converter works well as an online converter or `Tempus.pyw` for an offline converter available at `http://github.com/eichbaumj/Python`.

Linux	CF or Mac Absolute	Apple HFS+
www.epochconverter.com	www.epochconverter.com/coredata	www.epochconverter.com/mac

Table 9.4: Epoch Timestamp Look Up Websites

Conversion of UNIX Epoch Time: **1616182435**

Date and Time:	**Friday, 2021-03-19 19:33:55 UTC**
UNIX Epoch Time:	**1616182435**
UNIX Epoch Time (Hex):	**6054FCA3**
CF Absolute Time:	**637875235**

Fig. 9.18: Epoch Timestamp Look Up

Pictures or other files represented by octal data

The easiest way is to look at the data in a Hex Viewer such as HxD or your forensic tool and copy out the file. In this case, the attachment is a JPG. The file signature for a JPG file is Hex FFD8FF, and the end of the file may have Hex FFD9. You can see the start of the file below. Highlight and copy the data and save it as a .jpg type file. Example files can be found here: `https://github.com/Xamnr/ProtocolBuffers`.

9.3 Practical Analysis of different Proto Buffers

Analyzing digital evidence when looking thoroughly at an application can be difficult enough. Within a normal investigation of a mobile phone, the investigator already has to evaluate many different file formats. Typical file formats, which are also found in this book, are Apple Property Lists (Plists), XML, SQLite databases. Of course, you can do keyword searches for `.proto` files, but as you saw earlier, that is probably

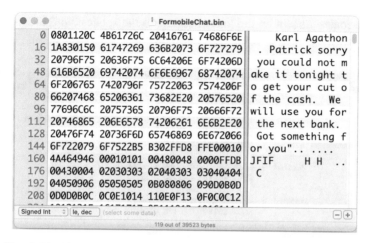

0	0801120C	4B61726C	20416761	74686F6E
16	1A830150	61747269	636B2073	6F727279
32	20796F75	20636F75	6C64206E	6F74206D
48	616B6520	69742074	6F6E6967	68742074
64	6F206765	7420796F	75722063	7574206F
80	66207468	65206361	73682E20	20576520
96	77696C6C	20757365	20796F75	20666F72
112	20746865	206E6578	74206261	6E6B2E20
128	20476F74	20736F6D	65746869	6E672066
144	6F722079	6F7522B5	B302FFD8	FFE00010
160	4A464946	00010101	00480048	0000FFDB
176	00430004	02030303	02040303	03040404
192	04050906	05050505	0B080806	090D0B0D
208	0D0D0B0C	0C0E1014	110E0F13	0F0C0C12

```
     Karl Agathon
. Patrick sorry
 you could not m
ake it tonight t
o get your cut o
f the cash.  We
will use you for
 the next bank.
 Got something f
or you".. ....
JFIF    H H  ..
 C
```

Fig. 9.19: ChatData - HexView, including file header of JPEG picture

not going to help you. To make even worser, proto buffers are often nested within other file formats rather than in their own files.

One of the issues is that these files already contain various types of data, such as Binary Large Object encoded Base 64. So, we need to be familiar with another XML or PList file within a BLOB, XML, Plist and/or Protocol Buffer Data within a BLOB. BLOBs are often also stored in a database table. In each case, we have to determine what content we are dealing with. Unfortunately, Protobuf does not have a real MagicNumber. We can only make a guess. Even more, Protocol Buffers can also be stored as GZip archive files. This adds another level of difficulty in finding these Protocol Buffers.

9.3.1 Mobile Device Artifact Examples

Some popular apps that use protocol buffers include Apple Maps, Google Maps, Badoo, Gmail, Google Allo, TamTam, Tango, WeChat, Wickr, Wire and many more. The Apple iCloud Backup system makes extensive use of protocol buffers. When dealing with application data, you are probably familiar with SQLite Databases, XML, and Apple Property List Files (.plist). You may not be aware that these files can contain data encoded Base64, such as a Binary Large Object (BLOB).

Example - Waze Navigation App

As a first example, we will use a typical app that uses Proto Buffers internally. *Waze* is a navigational guidance application for getting directions and showing the fastest

available routes. Shown on the following page is the application folder for Waze.
Selected is a file named `cache_data`, shown below.

> File Viewer	...
File Name	**cached_data**
File Size	**476 Bytes**
Path	**/private/var/mobile/Containers/Data/Application/com.waze.i phone/Documents/**
File Extension Mismatched	**No Extension**
Created	**2/11/2021 11:08:35 AM (Device)** **[2/11/2021 4:08:35 PM UTC]**
Modified	**2/15/2021 9:55:26 PM (Device)** **[2/16/2021 2:55:26 AM UTC]**
Status Changed	**2/15/2021 9:55:26 PM (Device)** **[2/16/2021 2:55:26 AM UTC]**
Hash (MD5)	**1303b0fff1558c5a465da38ad843b8c**
Hash (SHA1)	**40311eb40eb6f237aed38134a7d0896034b87b00**

Fig. 9.20: cached_data

Let us now take a closer look at the cache file. We use the forensic tool's hex viewer
to see what type of data the file contains, shown on the right. Well this is nice, we
can see some data immediately (see Fig.9.21). With a simple string search we can
already extract a number of artefacts. A couple things you should know about the
data (see Table 9.5).

Username: Millenium Falcon
Phone Number: +15166618197
Home Location: 375 Main Street, New London, NH 03257

Table 9.5: Some extracted data

In fact, this example is a protocol buffer. We save the file out as a binary file adding the
.bin file extension. Now to examine the file with both *protoc* and *protobuf inspector*.
In Fig. 9.22 Waze's cached_data decoded with ProtoC. Scrolling down through the
results, we come across the address and again some other data that we may or may
not determine. You may not figure out what the other data items are. Again, we do
not have the original code or legend. We can certainly see if data is a timestamp or
location.

Below in Fig.9.23 we take the same file into `Protobuf Inspector`. As we can
see, some characters on the screenshots are from escape sequences to make sure that
some chars (characters) are in bold, etc. This is an easy example, in my opinion, of a
protocol buffer. Using Protoc, Protobuf Inspector, or other Protocol Buffer decoding
tools can help break down and show the information. In this case, the data could

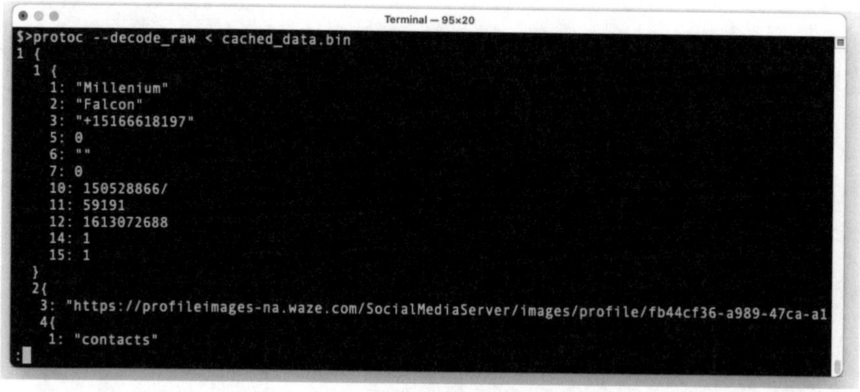

```
$>protoc --decode_raw < cached_data.bin
1 {
  1 {
    1: "Millenium"
    2: "Falcon"
    3: "+15166618197"
    5: 0
    6: ""
    7: 0
    10: 150528866/
    11: 59191
    12: 1613072688
    14: 1
    15: 1
  }
  2{
    3: "https://profileimages-na.waze.com/SocialMediaServer/images/profile/fb44cf36-a989-47ca-a1
    4{
      1: "contacts"
  }
```

Fig. 9.21: cached_data

be seen for the most part with the hex viewer. Other instances will contain Base64 Encoded data.

BASE64 Encoding

Some of you may remember reading about BASE64 and its use with Email Attachments. This encoding scheme is to take this raw data like a picture and make sure that none of the data will cause an issue. Looking at an ASCII chart, you will notice the first 33 decimal places (0-32) are reserved for functions like BackSpace, Space, and Carriage Return.

! Attention

Please remember that Apple Property Lists, XML Files, and Databases can contain pictures or web links to pictures, and of course, Protocol Buffers. Next, we will analyze some examples of Protocol Buffers found in each.

When we send raw data, we do not want these functions to be performed. So Base64 Encoding removes these from the equation. Binary Large Objects (like a picture or even an embedded XML or Plist file) are encoded with Base64. So, what are Protocol Buffers managing? Raw data. When it comes to plists, they are usually in binary form, only rarely in text format. A forensic tool like MSAB's XAMN will show such content in a readable (XML-like) format, making binary data appear as base64. The website used in the below example to convert the raw data to Base64: www.motobit.com/util/base64-decoder-encoder.asp.

```
ASCII

0  :   Millenium
  Falcon  +15166
618197( 2 8 P £
I x·I         p x
  ¿  ghttps://pro
fileimages-na.wa
ze.com/SocialMed
iaServer/images/
profile/fb44cf36
-a989-47ca-a1f0-
b9296fb80da6"P
contacts"@d9f117
0b6404cde3300963
ba61bd64e78febf8
fc5d7f40e28dd099
d2c5580a6a8 @ (
H              "     R
Q   NS
       "  .          !  0
↓:     ÞAO¥ÿÿÿÿÿ
   óâ0     375 Main
  St" Main Street
 * New London2 NH
 :  B  375J(googleP
laces.ChIJ_4k6xS
b44YkRjbQDEYOwBk
OP   ¨ü Z   Home
  " (£ üAï.    @ Hï
 ¬ð P#Z 1|global
|504040814`
```

Fig. 9.22: cached_data

```
● ● ●              Terminal — 48×9
$>protobuf_inspector < cached_data.bin
root:
        1 <chunk> = message:
                1 <chunk> = "Millenium"
                2 <chunk> = "Falcon"
                3 <chunk> = "157166618197"
                5 <varint> = 0
                6 <chunk> = empty chunk
:
```

Fig. 9.23: cached_data in Protobuf Inspector

Example: Apple Web Cache file

In Fig.9.24 you can see a Apple Web Cache file. The filename is *12.xml*. The BLOB is highlighted. But what is it about in this case? Is it a protocol buffer or something else?

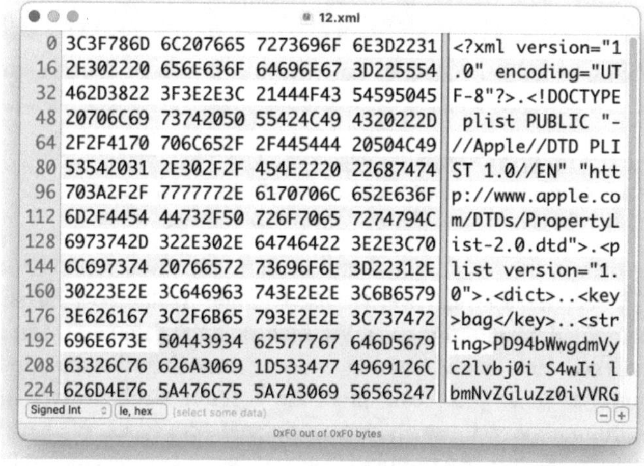

Fig. 9.24: 12.xml File Highlighting Encoded Data

We get the answer when we convert the raw data - probably BASE64 encoded - back into a normal UTF-8 string. The result is shown in Fig. 9.25. The BASE64 converted data, and we will notice that this is an XML file within an XML File. What can we learn from this? It does not always have to be a protobuf.

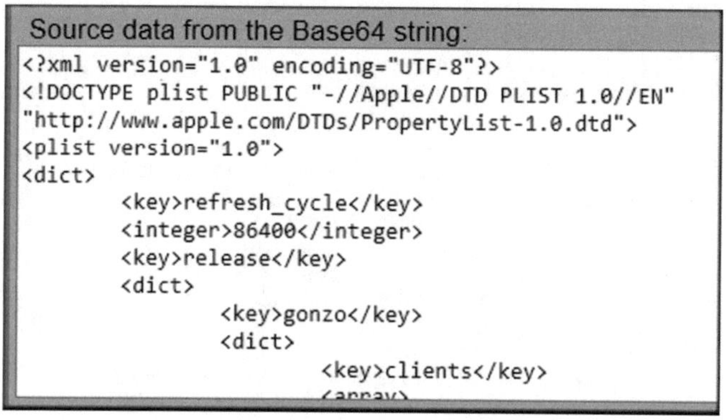

```
Source data from the Base64 string:
<?xml version="1.0" encoding="UTF-8"?>
<!DOCTYPE plist PUBLIC "-//Apple//DTD PLIST 1.0//EN"
"http://www.apple.com/DTDs/PropertyList-1.0.dtd">
<plist version="1.0">
<dict>
        <key>refresh_cycle</key>
        <integer>86400</integer>
        <key>release</key>
        <dict>
                <key>gonzo</key>
                <dict>
                        <key>clients</key>
                        <array>
```

Fig. 9.25: 12.xml File Base 64 Converted Data

Identifying Base64 Encoded Data

You know that Binary Large Objects (BLOBS) are usually, if not always, encoded with BASE64. Sometimes you do not know. As seen below, we look for the tell-tale equals sign "=" or two equal's signs "==" at the end of the data.

❗ Attention

Note the BASE64 encoded data does not always end with an equals sign.

CBYQACDA0QIoADAAYAKBfbWIbIcCwsJBKK5NOicKJQiL84igk82e1/
kBEhIJKzQQy2axRUARwjl2dDMFUsAYrk2QAwFA47ejkYoowAwB0gwk
OEVGRkMyRTAtQkQ1Qy00MTIGLTICQkMtMjRDRERBMzZBNDQw@WAA@=

This content data is then highlighted and copied. We saved it and decoded it using a base 64 decoder. In this case, we used James Eichbaum's Base64 Decoder (http://github.com/eichbaumj/Python). We then save the data as a .bin file and review it in the HxD Hex Editor (see Fig. 9.26). Protocol Buffer data does not have a file signature per se. If you recall, there are different Scalar values int32, int64, string, bytes, etc. . . . . Well these all have associated wire types. We have to look for hex values like 08, 09, 0A. In a protobuf, those values all correspond to key = 1 with different wire types:

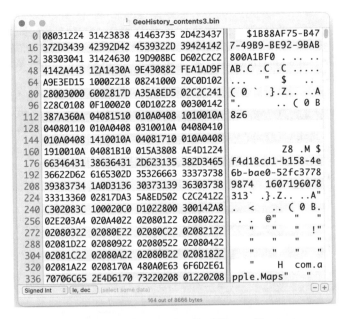

Fig. 9.26: Base64 Decode: GeoHistory Contents

08 varint (A variable length integer)
09 64 bit
0A length delimited

Table 9.6: Typical protobuf start values

A value like 08 is not a header byte. It is just a common value protobufs start with. If interpreted as key and type it translates to key = 1, type = varint. Another common byte at the beginning of protobufs is 0x0A which translates to key = 1, type = length delimited (i.e. nested message, string, byte array). Remember: We can only make an educated guess about the binary content since protobufs directly start with the serial data stream.

> **Important**

A file header for a GZIP File is Hex 1F8BC8 the file will then have to be saved and unzipped.

As we know now, a protocol buffer message is a series of key-value pairs. Therefore, the serialised message consists of a series of key-value pairs that are stored one after the other in the data stream. When a message is encoded, they are concatenated into a byte stream. The binary version of a protobuf message uses the field's number as the key. A concrete name and declared type for each field can only be determined on the decoding end by referencing the message type's definition (i.e. the `.proto` file). When the message is being decoded, the parser needs to skip fields that it does not recognise. This way, new fields can be added to a message without breaking old programs that do not know about them. To this end, the "key" for each pair in a wire-format message is two values – the field number from your `.proto` file, plus a wire type that provides just enough information to find the length of the following value. Mostly, this key is referred to as a tag [23].Fig. 9.7 demonstrates the wire types available.

Type	Meaning	Usage
0	Varint	int32, int64, uint32, uint64, sint32, sint64, bool, enum
1	64-bit	fixed64, sfixed64, double
2	Length-delimited	string, bytes, embedded messages, packed repeated fields
3	Start group	groups (deprecated)
4	End group	groups (deprecated)
5	32-bit	fixed32, sfixed32, float

Table 9.7: Available Wire Types

Just recall the *formobilechat* message from the earlier section. The protobuf binary (small one in this case) is shown in Fig. 9.27. The figure demonstrates the raw data; notice that it starts with 0x08.

The problem is we can figure out where it starts with these Hex values, possibly, but where does it end? Is it the end of the file, or only for a few bytes? Or is it 188 bytes like the aforementioned example. That is when the developers reply, "Welcome to our world."

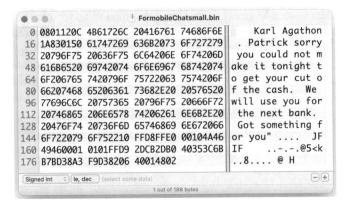

Fig. 9.27: Notice The Variable Integer 0x08 at the start

9.3.2 Yet another example: Apply Property List (PLIST) Files

Let's take a look at another example from our sample data. Fig. 9.28 shows data copied from the `GeoHistory.mapsdata.plist`. The value stored under the key "content" looks suspiciously like a BASE64 encoded value. And indeed, the data which appears to be BASE64 was copied and pasted into `www.motobit.com` decoder. The result was then copied and saved into notepad as GeoHistory_contents3.bin and opened into HxD.

Using the file `GeoHistory_contents3.bin` start with 08, but which one or ones? The file starts with 08. A search for Hex 08 results in 206 hits. See Fig. 9.29.

We manually look at each hit and the ASCII area for human-readable data that makes sense, which will not always be the case. In this first example, we take the results of the last hit, which starts at decimal offset 8579. Please copy the entire length to the end of the file and paste it into a new HxD file that we save and name with the offset (see Fig. 9.30).

Then the rest is decoding the data with Protoc and/or other tools. Moreover, try to figure out what we are looking at. Since the data belongs to a map application, we want to see if the hex values below are latitude and longitude. Maybe one of the other values is a date time stamp? See:

```
1: 0x4040cda6e5dc30e8
2: 0xc05c16c2f76aa800
```

Indeed, the values look like latitude and longitude in decimal. However, we do not want to assume that. This takes time and effort if we have to go through each search. Since the file started with hex 08, we can try `protoc` and our other tools against the entire `GeoHistory_contents3.bin` file. Keep in mind: Without the corresponding *.proto* file, we can only speculate about the meaning of the data.

```
<?xml version="1.0" encoding="UTF-8"?>
<!DOCTYPE plist PUBLIC "-//Apple//DTD PLIST 1.0//EN" "http://www.apple.com/DTDs/PropertyList-1.0.dtd">
<plist version="1.0">
<dict>
        <key>MSPHistory</key>
        <dict>
                <key>clientIdentifier</key>
                <string>0BB25E52-3840-48AE-90AF-DE804544E8E9</string>
                <key>records</key>
                <dict>
                        <key>09E098EF-EDEC-4129-B539-551AB39CB9F1</key>
                        <dict>
                                <key>contents</key>
                                <data>
                                CAESJDA5RTA5OEVGLVERUMtNDEyOS1CNTM5LTU1MUFC
                                MzlDQjlGMRlihjz7AsLCQTJHChZQaG9lbml4IGFyaXpv
                                bmEgYXJjYWRlIEgdBcml6h25hIiQpAADqMYWoQEAxAADY
                                82gYXMA5AAC4+yXZQEBBAAB2Mgj3W8BYAA==
                                </data>
                                <key>contentsTimestamp</key>
                                <data>
                                C7JeUjhASK6Qr96ARUTo6QAAAAE=
                                </data>
                                <key>modificationDate</key>
                                <date>2020-12-11T19:54:30Z</date>
                        </dict>
                        <key>17713B5A-4270-4CCE-BA34-398D761B5D1B</key>
                        <dict>
                                <key>modificationDate</key>
                                <date>2020-12-10T22:00:20Z</date>
                        </dict>
                        <key>1B88AF75-B477-49B9-BE92-9BAB800A1BF0</key>
                        <dict>
                                <key>contents</key>
                                <data>
                                CAMSJDFCODhBRjc1LUI0NzctNDlCOS1CRTkyLTlCQUI4
                                MDBBMUJGMBnZCLzWAsLCQUKKQxKhQwqeQwiC/qGtn6nj
                                7RUQACIYCCQQACDA0QIoADAAYAKBfaNajtUCwsJBIowB
                                CA8QACDA0QIoADABQjh6NgoECBUQAQoECBAQAQoECAEQ
                                AQoECAMQAQoECAQQAQoECBQQAQoECBcQAQoECBkQAQoE
                                CBsQAVo4CK5NEiRmNGQxOGNkMS1iMTU4LTRlNmItYmFl
                                MC01MmZjMzc3ODk4NzQaDTE2MDcxOTYwNzgzMTNgAoF9
                                o1qO1QLCwkEiwwIIPBAAIMDRAigAMAFCqALiA6QCCkAi
                                </data>
```

Fig. 9.28: GeoHistory.mapsdata.plist

9.3.3 Suggested Examination Process of a File

The idea is you create the process that works best for you. This may be completely working within your mobile forensic tool. The alternative is that you export out the file(s) of interest and review the data.

1. If unknown file type, then place the file into a Hex Viewer/Editor
2. Identify the File Signature (Research it if unknown to include possible file extensions). The data itself may be human readable as well.
3. Make sure the file has the right file extension
4. Open the file to view it natively i.e. as a database, xml, or plist file.
5. Look for Binary Large Objects (BLOB) or other raw data. Copy this raw data.
6. Decode this raw data with a Base64 Decoder and save. Devise a system to name the file and add a .bin file extension on it as a place holder.
7. Open this .bin file in a Hex Viewer/Editor
8. Identify the File Signature (as it could be an XML or Apple Property List file).
9. If this is an XML or PList File go back to Step 5. If not close the file and move on.

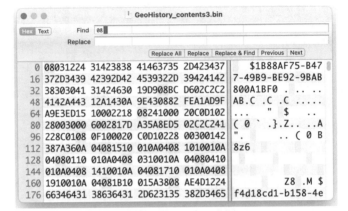

Fig. 9.29: Finding Protocol Buffer Data

Fig. 9.30: The extracted Protocol Buffer from offset 8579

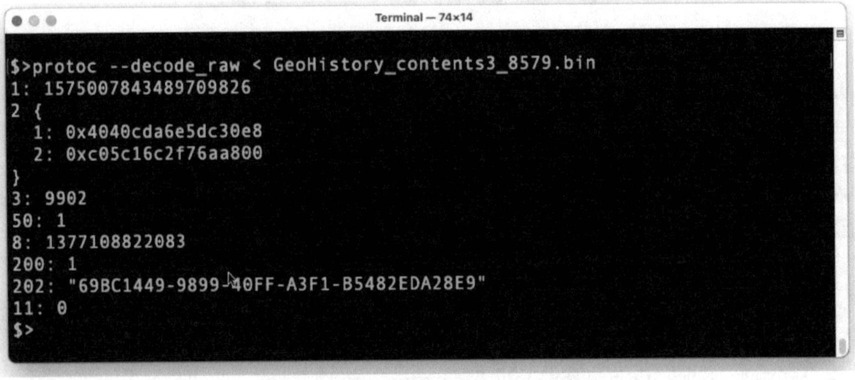

Fig. 9.31: Notice the Hex (0x) Values

10. Place the file in a folder with ProtoC executable.
11. Open a command prompt from this location
12. Type: `protoc --decode_raw < Filename.bin`
    Click enter.

```
● ● ●                          Terminal — 74×14
$>protobuf_inspector < GeoHistory_contents3_8579.bin
root:
    1 <varint> = 1575007843489709826
    2 <chunk> = message:
        1 <64bit> = 0x4040CDA6E5DC30E8 / 4629926533641548008 / 33.606656
        2 <64bit> = 0xC05C16C2F76AA800 / -4585765293939578880 / -112.35565
    3 <varint> = 9902
   50 <varint> = 1
    8 <varint> = 1377108822083
  200 <varint> = 1
  202 <chunk> = "69BC1449-9899-40FF-A3F1-B5482EDA28E9"
   11 <varint> = 0

$>
```

Fig. 9.32: Protobuf-Inspector converted Hex values. Lat and Long?

If you placed the file in the same directory as the *protoc* then to find the file automatically, without typing, after you type the "<" character click the space bar once and then hit tab to cycle through all of the files in the folder. Once you find the right file click enter.

13. See if you have Protocol Buffer data. If it Failed to parse the input, then that is not a protobuf (or you may need to review sections of the file for data).
14. To save the data. Highlight it and Left Click.
15. Paste into text editor.This allows you to use keywords as well.

! Attention

Now, remember the tools may obtain this data for you. However, it is nice to know where the data came from. Examining an unsupported application may have you uncovering protocol buffers for data as well.

9.3.4 Tools

We need to consider some of the tools in your toolbox for examining these artefacts. Some of these capabilities may be included with your mobile device forensic tools, such as MSAB's XRY and XAMN. If so, then these non-forensic tools will help validate your work. Most are free or have a freeware version. Some of these may cost money, so look for Freeware versions:

- Hex Viewer/Editor: HxD
- Sqlite database viewer: SQLite Expert
- XML file viewer: Notepad++
- PList file viewer: PList Editor for Windows

- Base64 Decoder: Motobit and James Eichbaum's Base64 Decoder.pyw
- Epoch Timestamp Converter: Epoch Converter Website and James Eichbaum's Tempus.pyw
- File Signature Analysis: Gary Kessler Website
- Windows Calculator in Programmer Mode
- Visual Studio
- Protocol Buffer Compiler: Proto C (protoc.exe) and Protobuf inspector

9.4 Conclusion

We have seen why Protocol Buffers are helpful. They take data make it small, and provide faster transmission speed. Coders themselves may not want to welcome the structure. As forensic examiners, we learned that understanding this structured serializing data is essential. Applications use Protocol Buffers to store data in Apple Property Lists (Plists), Binary Large Objects, and XML Files. We may find user data, time stamps, location data, and more. So, these applications alone show that protocol buffers are used and the importance of understanding them and how to analyze them.

The most important takeaway that we can provide is that now you will hopefully identify what you are looking at. Have a greater appreciation of Protocol Buffers how to make sense of this data and explain it if necessary. We learned what to look for, and now you do also.

Acknowledgements My thanks to my fellow MSAB colleagues Johan Persson, Sebastian Zankl, Oscar Choi, and Global Training Manager James Eichbaum for their time, contributions to this chapter and the forensic community.

References

1. Alendal, G., Dyrkolbotn, G. O., and Axelsson, S. (2018) Forensics acquisition — Analysis and Circumvention of Samsung Secure Boot Enforced Common Criteria Mode. Digital Investigation 24:60–67. https://doi.org/10.1016/j.diin.2018.01.008
2. Alzahrani, H. (2016) Evolution of Object-Oriented Database Systems. Global Journal of Computer Science and Technology 16(3). https://computerresearch.org/index.php/computer/article/view/1387
3. android.googlesource.com (n.d.) What is Flash-Friendly File System (F2FS). Git at Google. https://android.googlesource.com/kernel/common/+/22f837981514e157f8f9737b25ac6d7d90a14006/Documentation/filesystems/f2fs.txt. Accessed 28 May 2021
4. Apple (2020) Apple File System Reference. https://developer.apple.com/support/downloads/Apple-File-System-Reference.pdf. Accessed 28 May 2021
5. Balci, M. (2020) A Minimum Complete Tutorial of Linux ext4 File System. https://metebalci.com/blog/a-minimum-complete-tutorial-of-linux-ext4-file-system/. Accessed 28 May 2021
6. Blackberry (2015) 50 Million Vehicles and Counting: QNX Achieves New Milestone in Automotive Market. https://blackberry.qnx.com/cn/news/release/2015/6118. Accessed 28 May 2021
7. Blackberry (2010) QNX Software Systems Online Infocenter. http://www.qnx.com/developers/docs/6.5.0/index.jsp. Accessed 28 May 2021
8. Brown, N. (2012) An F2FS Teardown. Available via LWN.net. https://lwn.net/Articles/518988/. Accessed 28 May 2021
9. Caithness, A (2010) Property Lists in Digital Forensics. Available via CCL Forensics Limited. http://citeseerx.ist.psu.edu/viewdoc/summary?doi=10.1.1.190.762.Accessed28May2021
10. Carrier B (2005) File Systems Forensics Analysis. Addison-Wesley Professional
11. Dewald, A. and Seufert, S. (2017) AFEIC: Advanced Forensic Ext4 inode Carving. Digital Investigation 20:83–91. https://doi.org/10.1016/j.diin.2017.01.003
12. Echessa, J. (2017) Integrating Realm Database in an Android Application. Available via AUTH0. https://auth0.com/blog/integrating-realm-database-in-an-android-application/. Accessed 28 May 2021
13. Evans, D. (2014) Log-Structured File Systems. https://www.youtube.com/watch?v=KTCkW_6zz2k. Accessed 28 May 2021
14. Fairbanks, K. D. (2012) An analysis of Ext4 for digital forensics. Digital Investigation 9:118–130. https://doi.org/10.1016/j.diin.2012.05.010
15. FPL. (2020) FlatBuffers. https://google.github.io/flatbuffers/. Accessed 28 May 2021

© The Author(s) 2022
C. Hummert, D. Pawlaszczyk (eds.), *Mobile Forensics – The File Format Handbook*,
https://doi.org/10.1007/978-3-030-98467-0

16. Freeman, E., Robson, E., Bates, B., and Sierra, K. (2004) Head First Design Patterns. 2nd edn. O'Reilly.

17. Garg, S. and Baliyan, N. (2021) Comparative analysis of Android and iOS from security viewpoint. Computer Science Review, 40. `https://doi.org/10.1016/j.cosrev.2021.100372`. Accessed 21 June 2021

18. Göbel, T. and Baier, H. (2018) Anti-forensics in ext4: On secrecy and usability of timestamp-based data hiding. Digital Investigation 24:111–120. `https://doi.org/10.1016/j.diin.2018.01.014`

19. Google (2020) crc32c. `https://github.com/google/crc32c`. Accessed 28 May 2021

20. Google. (2008) google.protobuf.descriptor. `https://googleapis.dev/python/protobuf/latest/google/protobuf/descriptor.html`. Accessed 28 May 2021

21. Google Android Developers. (2021) Android Debug Bridge (adb). `https://developer.android.com/studio/command-line/adb`. Accessed 28 May 2021

22. Google Android Developers. (2021) Download Android Studio and SDK Tools. `https://developer.android.com/studio`. Accessed 28 May 2021

23. Google Developers. (2020) Encoding Protocol Buffers. `https://developers.google.com/protocol-buffers/docs/encoding`. Accessed 28 May 2021

24. Google Developers. (2020) Protocol Buffers. `https://developers.google.com/protocol-buffers`. Accessed 28 May 2021

25. Google Developers. (2020) Protocol Buffer Basics: C++ Protocol Buffers. `https://developers.google.com/protocol-buffers/docs/cpptutorial`. Accessed 28 May 2021

26. Google Developers. (2020) Protocol Buffers Language Guide. `https://developers.google.com/protocol-buffers/docs/overview`. Accessed 28 May 2021

27. Google Developers. (2020) Protocol Buffers Language Guide (proto3). `https://developers.google.com/protocol-buffers/docs/proto3`. Accessed 28 May 2021

28. Google Developers. (2020) Protocol Buffers Style Guide. `https://developers.google.com/protocol-buffers/docs/style`. Accessed 28 May 2021

29. gRPC Authors. (2020) About gRPC. `https://grpc.io/about/`. Accessed 28 May 2021

30. gRPC Authors. (2020) What is gRPC? `https://grpc.io/docs/what-is-grpc/faq/`. Accessed 28 May 2021

31. GSMArena (2017) Samsung Galaxy S8. `https://www.gsmarena.com/samsung_galaxy_s8-8161.php`. Accessed 28 May 2021

32. Haldar, S. (2015) SQLite Database System Design and Implementation. 2nd edn. `https://books.google.de/books?id=OEJ1CQAAQBAJ`. Accessed 28 May 2021

33. Hansen, K. H. and Toolan, F (2017) Decoding the APFS File System. Digital Investigation 22:107–132. `https://doi.org/10.1016/j.diin.2017.07.003`

34. Holzinger, P., Triller, S., Bartel, A., and Bodden, E. (2016) An In-Depth Study of More Than Ten Years of Java Exploitation. Proceedings of the 2016 ACM SIGSAC Conference on Computer and Communications Security (CCS '16). Association for Computing Machinery, New York. 10.1145/2976749.2978361 p 779–790

35. Horsman, G. (2018) Framework for Reliable Experimental Design (FRED): A Research Framework to ensure the dependable Interpretation of Digital Data for Digital Forensics. Computers & Security 73:294–306. `https://doi.org/10.1016/j.cose.2017.11.009`

36. Hörz, M. (2020) HxD - Freeware Hex Editor and Disk Editor. `https://mh-nexus.de/en/hxd/`. Accessed 28 May 2021

37. Huebner, E., Bem, D., and Wee, C. K. (2006) Data Hiding in the NTFS File System. Digital Investigation 3(4):211–226. `https://doi.org/10.1016/j.diin.2006.10.005`

38. IBM. (2019) Relational Databases. Relational Databases Explained. `https://www.ibm.com/cloud/learn/relational-databases`. Accessed 28 May 2021

39. ISO/IEC (2021) ISO/IEC 9075-1:2016. Information technology — Database languages — SQL — Part 1: Framework (SQL/Framework). `https://www.iso.org/cms/render/live/en/sites/isoorg/contents/data/standard/06/35/63555.html`. Accessed 28 May 2021

40. Karaiskos, C (2018) Understanding Apple's Binary Property List Format. `https://medium.com/@karaiskc/understanding-apples-binary-property-list-format-281e6da00dbd.` Accessed28May2021

41. Kernel.org (2020) Dynamic Structures. `https://www.kernel.org/doc/html/latest/filesystems/ext4/dynamic.html`. Accessed 28 May 2021

42. Kim, J. (2012) F2FS: Introduce Flash-Friendly File System. Available via LWN.net. `https://lwn.net/Articles/518718/`

43. Krebs,B. (2017) Beating JSON performance with Protobuf. Available via Auth0. `https://auth0.com/blog/beating-json-performance-with-protobuf/`. Accessed 28 May 2021

44. Leachi, P., Mealing, M. and Salz, R. (2005) A Universally Unique Identifier (UUID) Namespace. `https://www.ietf.org/rfc/rfc4122.txt`. Accessed 28 May 2021

45. Lee, C., Sim, D., Hwang, JY., and Cho, S. (2015) F2FS: A New File System for Flash Storage. 13th USENIX Conference on File and Storage Technologies, Feb. 2015. `https://www.usenix.org/system/files/conference/fast15/fast15-paper-lee.pdf`. Accessed 28 May 2021

46. Lee, C., Sim, D., Hwang, JY., and Cho, S. (2015). F2FS: A New File System for Flash Storage. USENIX FAST 2015, Santa Clara, CA, USA. https://www.usenix.org/sites/default/files/conference/protected-files/fast15_slides_lee.pdf. Accessed 28 May 2021

47. Levin, J (2013) Mac OS X and iOS Internals. John Wiley & Sons

48. MongoDB. (2021) Realm Files. `https://docs.mongodb.com/realm/sdk/node/fundamentals/realms/#realm-files`. Accessed 28 May 2021

49. MongoDB. (2021) Realm Object Types and Schemas. `https://docs.mongodb.com/realm/sdk/node/fundamentals/realms/#object-types---schemas`. Accessed 28 May 2021

50. Merkle, R. C. (1980) Protocols for Public Key Cryptosystems. 1980 IEEE Symposium on Security and Privacy. 122–122. doi: 10.1109/SP.1980.10006

51. Nikkel, B. J (2009) Forensic Analysis of GPT Disks and GUID Partition Tables. Digital Investigation 6(1):39–47. `https://doi.org/10.1016/j.diin.2009.07.001`

52. Nordvik, R., Porter, K., Toolan, F., Axelsson, S. and Franke, K. (2020) Generic Metadata Time Carving. Forensic Science International: Digital Investigation 33. `https://doi.org/10.1016/j.fsidi.2020.301005`

53. Olsen, J. (2017) Hard Drives: How Do They Work? Techbytes. April, 2017. `https://blogs.umass.edu/Techbytes/2017/04/04/hard-drives-how-do-they-work/`. Accessed 28 May 2021

54. Opyrchal, L. and Prakash, A. (1999) Efficient Object Serialization in Java. Proceedings of 19th IEEE International Conference on Distributed Computing Systems. Workshops on Electronic Commerce and Web-based Applications. Middleware. 10.1109/ECMDD.1999.776421 p 96–101

55. Oracle Corporation (2010) Character and Block Devices. `https://docs.oracle.com/cd/E19253-01/817-5789/fgoue/index.html`. Accessed 28 May 2021

56. Oracle Cooperation. (2021) Object Serialization Stream Protocol. `https://docs.oracle.com/javase/8/docs/platform/serialization/spec/protocol.html`. Accessed 28 May 2021

57. Oracle Cooperation. (2021) Serializable Objects - The Java Tutorials. `https://docs.oracle.com/javase/tutorial/jndi/objects/serial.html`. Accessed 28 May 2021

58. Panfilov, M. (2019) What the hell is protobuf? Available via MEDIUM. `https://blog.usejournal.com/what-the-hell-is-protobuf-4aff084c5db4`. Accessed 28 May 2021

59. Pawlaszczyk, D. and Hummert, C. (2021) Making the Invisible Visible – Techniques for Recovering Deleted SQLite Data Record. International Journal of Cyber Forensics and Advanced Threat Investigations 1(1–3):27–41. 10.46386/ijcfati.v1i1-3.17

60. Pawlaszczyk, D. and Hummert, C. (2019) "Alexa, tell me ..." - A forensic examination of the Amazon Echo Dot 3 rd Generation. International Journal of Computer Sciences and Engineering 7(11):20–29. https://doi.org/10.26438/ijcse/v7i11.2029

61. Pawlaszczyk, D. (2017) Digitaler Tatort - Sicherung und Verfolgung digitaler Spuren. In: Labudde D., Spranger M (eds) Forensik in der digitalen Welt. Springer Spektrum, Berlin, Heidelberg p 113–166

62. realm.io. (2021) realm/realm core: Core database component for the Realm Mobile Database SDKs. https://github.com/realm/realm-core. Accessed 28 May 2021

63. realm.io. (2021) realm-core/alloc_slab.cpp. Available via GITHUB. https://github.com/realm/realm-core/blob/master/src/realm/alloc_slab.cpp. Accessed 28 May 2021

64. realm.io. (2021) realm-core/alloc_slab.hpp. Available via GITHUB. https://github.com/realm/realm-core/blob/master/src/realm/alloc_slab.hpp. Accessed 28 May 2021

65. realm.io (2021) realm-core/alloc_slab.hpp. Available via GITHUB. https://github.com/realm/realm-core/blob/master/src/realm/alloc_slab.hpp. Accessed 28 May 2021

66. realm.io (2021) realm-core/array.hpp. Available via GITHUB. https://github.com/realm/realm-core/blob/master/src/realm/array.hpp. Accessed 28 May 2021

67. realm.io (2020) realm-core/node_header.hpp. Available via GITHUB. https://github.com/realm/realm-core/blob/2946c7a52449d3b8d038ff03d896b651615b8ad4/src/realm/node_header.hpp. Accessed 28 May 2021

68. realm.io (2020) realm-core/node_header.hpp. Available via GITHUB. https://github.com/realm/realm-core/blob/master/src/realm/node_header.hpp. Accessed 28 May 2021

69. realm.io. (2019) realm-core/realm_dump.c. Available via GITHUB. https://github.com/realm/realm-core/blob/master/src/realm/exec/realm_dump.c. Accessed 28 May 2021

70. realm.io. (2021) realm-core/test_allocations.cpp. Available via GITHUB. https://github.com/realm/realm-core/blob/master/test/test_transactions.cpp. Accessed 28 May 2021

71. Realm.io. (2021) Realm.io. www.realm.io/. Accessed 28 May 2021

72. Realm.io. (2021) Realm Demo File Download. https://static.realm.io/downloads/realm-studio/demo-v20.realm. Accessed 28 May 2021

73. Realm.io. (2021) Realm Groups. https://github.com/realm/realm-core. Accessed 28 May 2021

74. Realm.io. (2021) Realm Studio Download. https://docs.mongodb.com/realm-legacy/products/realm-studio.html. Accessed 28 May 2021

75. Rosenblum, M. and Ousterhout, J. K. (1992) The Design and Implementation of a Log-Structured File System. ACM Trans. Comput. Syst. 10(1):26–52. Association for Computing Machinery, New York.

76. Seacord, R. C. (2017) Java Deserialization Vulnerabilities and Mitigation. In: 2017 IEEE Cybersecurity Development (SecDev) 1:6–7. 10.1109/SecDev.2017.13

77. Science Direct. (2021) Data Definition Language. Data Definition Language - An Overview ScienceDirect Topics. https://www.sciencedirect.com/topics/computer-science/data-definition-language. Accessed 28 May 2021

78. SQLite Consortium. (2021) About SQLite. https://sqlite.org/about.html. Accessed 28 May 2021

79. SQLite Consortium (2021) Atomic Commit In SQLite - Draft. http://www.sqlite.org/draft/atomiccommit.html. Accessed 28 May 2021

80. SQLite Consortium (2021) Database File Format. https://www.sqlite.org/fileformat.html. Accessed 28 May 2021

81. SQLite Consortium (2021) Most Widely Deployed and Used Database Engine. https://www.sqlite.org/mostdeployed.html. Accessed 28 May 2021

82. SQLite Consortium. (2021) SQLite Database Header. `https://sqlite.org/fileformat2.html`. Accessed 28 May 2021
83. SQLite Consortium. (2021) SQLite Is Serverless. `https://sqlite.org/serverless.html`. Accessed 28 May 2021
84. SQLite Consortium (2021) Temporary Files Used By SQLite. `https://sqlite.org/tempfiles.html`. Accessed 28 May 2021
85. SQLite Consortium (2021) The Schema Table. `https://sqlite.org/schematab.html`. Accessed 28 May 2021
86. SQLite Consortium (2021) Write-Ahead Logging. `https://www.sqlite.org/wal.html`. Accessed 28 May 2021
87. Tanaka, K. and Saito, T. (2018) Python Deserialization Denial of Services Attacks and Their Mitigations. In: Lee, R. (ed) Computational Science/Intelligence & Applied Informatics, CSII 2018, Yonago, Japan, July 10-12, 2018. Studies in Computational Intelligence, 787:15–25. 10.1007/978-3-319-96806-3_2
88. TechTerms. (2019) NAND Definition. `https://techterms.com/definition/nand`. Accessed 28 May 2021
89. The Linux Kernel Organisation. (n.d.) What is Flash-Friendly File System (F2FS)? The Linux Kernel Archives. `https://www.kernel.org/doc/Documentation/filesystems/f2fs.txt`. Accessed 28 May 2021
90. The Sleuth Kit. (2019) HFS - SlethKit Wiki. `https://wiki.sleuthkit.org/index.php?title=HFS`. Accessed 17 June 2021
91. Vanura J. and Kriz P. (2018) Perfomance Evaluation of Java, JavaScript and PHP Serialization Libraries for XML, JSON and Binary Formats. In: Ferreira, J. and Spanoudakis, G. (eds) Services Computing – SCC 2018. SCC 2018. Lecture Notes in Computer Science, vol 10969. Springer, Cham p 413–61
92. Vickie, L. (2020) Exploiting PHP Deserialization - Intro to PHP Object Injection Vulnerabilities. Available via MEDIUM. https://medium.com/swlh/exploiting-php-deserialization-56d71f03282. Accessed 28 May 2021
93. Weyns D., Truyen E., and Verbaeten P. (2003) Serialization of Distributed Execution-State in Java. In: Aksit M., Mezini M., Unland R. (eds) Objects, Components, Architectures, Services, and Applications for a Networked World. NODe 2002. Lecture Notes in Computer Science, vol 2591. Springer Spektrum, Berlin, Heidelberg p 413–461
94. Azhar, M. A. H., Barton, T., and Islam, T. (2018). Drone Forensic Analysis Using Open Source Tools. The Journal of Digital Forensics, Security and Law. `https://doi.org/10.15394/jdfsl.2018.1513`
95. Mikhaylov, I. (2016). Forensic analysis of Flash-Friendly File System (F2FS). Digital Forensics Corp. https://www.digitalforensics.com/blog/forensic-analysis-of-flash-friendly-file-system-f2fs/
96. Zhai Yujia, Li Tao, and Hu Aiqun. (2020). Data forensics method of mobile terminal F2FS image file. Cyberspace Security, 11(8). `http://www.css.ccidgroup.com/EN/Y2020/V11/I8/11`. Accessed 28 May 2021
97. Larabel, M. (2020). ATGC Could Come In Linux 5.10 For F2FS, Much Faster Decompression Speeds Too—Phoronix. Phoronix. `https://www.phoronix.com/scan.php?page=news_item&px=F2FS-ATGC-Dev-Branch`. Accessed 28 May 2021
98. Yu, C. (2020). Support Age-Threshold based Garbage Collection for f2fs. LWN.Net. `https://lwn.net/Articles/828027/`. Accessed 28 May 2021

Index

© The Author(s) 2022
C. Hummert, D. Pawlaszczyk (eds.), *Mobile Forensics – The File Format Handbook*,
https://doi.org/10.1007/978-3-030-98467-0

Printed in the United States
by Baker & Taylor Publisher Services